Praise for

# MY FAIR JUNKIE

"Like Carrie Fisher's 1987 autobiographical novel, *Postcards From the Edge*, and Mary Karr's 2009 memoir, *Lit*, Amy Dresner's story of addiction and recovery, *My Fair Junkie: A Memoir of Getting Dirty and Stay Clean* (Hachette Books), is one for the ages."　　　　　*—Elle*

"Dresner, a former stand-up comic and current contributing editor for *The Fix*, writes about her recovery from drug and alcohol abuse with honesty and irreverent humor.... Readers meet Dresner at her worst, but she nevertheless charms throughout her healing."

*—Publishers Weekly*

"Darkly funny, the memoir reckons with demons—sex addiction, drugs, and the quest for sobriety—in brutally honest, entertaining prose."

*—Refinery29*

"[An] effortlessly candid and wryly written chronicle of a life hijacked by drugs, booze, and bad behavior. As a noted West Hollywood stand-up comedian and addiction journalist, she handles this complex tale with wit.... A hard-knocks addiction memoir buoyed with humor and insight."　　　　　*—Kirkus*

"In Dresner's unflinchingly honest, graphic, and darkly comedic account of her life as a junkie and the struggle to come clean, readers will find strength in the humanity of those at their lowest. Dresner brings humility, wit, and sensitivity to a topic many readers are unfamiliar with, and those [who] are will recognize her truths."　　　　　*—Booklist*

"Dresner's story of drugs, sex, and a handful of other addictions is wickedly funny and hauntingly honest."  —*FASHION* magazine

"Dresner's book is a sickening masterpiece. Hilarious and raw, she cuts to bony truth. I love her!"  —Margaret Cho

"Mortifying, hilarious, unsparing, and weirdly life-affirming, *My Fair Junkie* hits the ground screaming and never lets up. As with all great 'drug memoirs,' the subject of this raw squirm-fest of an autobiography is not drugs, but what made drugs necessary: the twisted history and relatably depraved torments of the author's own strung-out heart. For fans of *Beyond Shame*, low-bottom recollectors like Augusten Burroughs and Stephen Elliot, Amy Dresner has earned her spot on the shelf."  —Jerry Stahl, author of *Permanent Midnight*

"Funny, raw, real, and moving. Amy's memoir digs deep inside the world of addiction and takes you on a ride you'd pay to go on again. Amy, like addiction, is a complicated beast that needs to be unraveled and exposed to understand—and she does just that in *My Fair Junkie*, an incredible read."  —Amber Tozer, author of *Sober Stick Figure*

"I loved this book! Amy Dresner is the real deal; a fiercely funny writer whose insights into addiction and recovery—and life—are full of truth, free of self-pity, sometimes scathing, often poignant, irresistibly page-turning, and painfully hilarious."  —Stephen Guirgis, Pulitzer Prize–winning playwright

"The story she tells is hysterically funny at one moment and utterly harrowing the next—and often manages to be both those things at once."  —Lawrence Block, *New York Times* bestselling and award-winning crime novelist, journalist, and author of the short story collection *Enough Rope*

"Hypnotic, magical, mesmerizing. Truly great. Amy Dresner is the most startlingly alert, poetic, stunning writer I have come across in decades. She is a real talent such as one rarely encounters."

—Ben Stein, lawyer, economist, actor, and author of
*How to Ruin Your Financial Life*

"One of the funniest, most heart wrenching, real, raw, touching, revelatory, and beautiful memoirs I've ever read. It transcends just the addiction lit genre to become something far more universal—something profoundly human—and captivating. I found myself laughing out loud over and over again, while, at the same time, being deeply moved by Dresner's account of addiction to more than just substances, but the need for connection in this increasingly disparate and fractured world."

—Nic Sheff, author of *Tweak* and *We All Fall Down*

"Fascinating. Uncomfortable...This book is a confessional and an indictment. I've loved girls like Amy and they drug my heart through a human sewer of addiction. I've used girls like Amy, and I only feigned to care. Why do I find this so fucking attractive? Well written. Believable."

—Jack Grisham, author of *An American Demon*

"Amy Dresner breaks my heart into a million pieces—and then slowly helps me put myself back together again. This is a wonderful book, filled with a frenetic mixture of snappy dialogue and terrifying truth."

—Peter Scolari

# MY FAIR JUNKIE

## A MEMOIR OF GETTING DIRTY AND STAYING CLEAN

**AMY DRESNER**

## hachette
### BOOKS
NEW YORK   BOSTON

Hachette Books
Hachette Book Group
1290 Avenue of the Americas
New York, NY 10104
hachettebooks.com
twitter.com/hachettebooks

Originally published as a hardcover and ebook in 2017 by Hachette Books, Inc.

First trade paperback edition: September 2018

Hachette Books is a division of Hachette Book Group, Inc.
The Hachette Books name and logo are trademarks of Hachette Book Group, Inc.

The publisher is not responsible for websites (or their content) that are not owned by
the publisher.

The Hachette Speakers Bureau provides a wide range of authors for speaking events.
To find out more, go to www.hachettespeakersbureau.com or call (866) 376-6591.

LCCN: 2017016499
ISBN: 978-0-316-43093-7

Printed in the United States of America

LSC-C

10  9  8  7  6  5  4  3  2

*For anybody who thinks it's too late*

# AUTHOR'S NOTE

This is true to what I believe happened. I have changed names and some descriptions. And I have reconstructed dialogue to the best of my recollection and reordered or combined the sequence of some events. Others who were present might recall things differently. But this is my story.

The worst thing that happens to you may be the best thing for you if you don't let it get the best of you.

—*Will Rogers*

# CHAPTER ONE

It's maybe twelve thirty at night. I am high on OxyContin. My husband, Clay, and I are in our coldly decorated luxury condo, fighting viciously after a particularly tense and overpriced Christmas dinner with my mother at the Peninsula Hotel.

The marriage has been crumbling for a while. Clay has retreated into his work and I into my opiate addiction, but tonight, all of our hatred comes out of hiding to duke it out. I go out onto the balcony to smoke and try to calm down. Next thing I know, he's right there, and we're going at it mean and loud. I feel woozy, like I'm about to lose my balance. I can see the valet guys scuttling around below me, and I think, *This is what a Jew gets for celebrating Christmas.*

The fight moves back inside. More screaming. I shove him. We wrestle. He's a big guy. Almost three hundred pounds. And I'm maybe 115 with premenstrual bloat, holding a fifth of scotch. Then something inside me snaps. I don't have the best impulse control to begin with. The OxyContin took away what was left of it as well as making me unusually agitated. The marriage had become desolate and painful, and maybe on some level I just wanted to put it out of its fucking misery. I break away and stomp into the kitchen, grab a knife out of the knife block, and stomp back into the bedroom.

"I will gut you like a fish, you fat fuck," I hear myself say.

"I'm calling the police," he says. "You're done."

It was a game we'd played for a while now—me pushing him to extremes, him fighting back—and we were good at it. But tonight felt different. The ante was higher, the rage was deeper, and nobody was backing down.

"Yes, hello. My wife just pulled a knife on me," he says into the phone. "She's mentally ill and a drug addict."

I don't wait to hear any more. I snatch a bottle of Valium off the bedside table, grab my purse, and lock myself in the bathroom. I begin to panic. I pour out four pills and then shake out two more for good measure. If the police are coming for me, I need to be relaxed. Really fucking relaxed. I crush the pills with the handle of my electric toothbrush and cut thick lines with my credit card. I snort them quickly. My eyes water. Within minutes, that narcotic veil between me and reality will come down, and I'll feel safe. Safer, anyway. "Okay," I say. I run my finger under the running tap and stick it in my nostrils, wiping away any evidence. I catch my eyes in the mirror. They look glassy, feral, empty.

I bolt out of the bathroom, grab my car keys, and head for the elevator. Four cops come barreling around the corner of the hallway. I freeze.

The female officer among them approaches me and asks clinically for my version of the night's events.

"He kneed me in the ribs," I begin, trying to sound innocent, but my already deep voice is thick with anger and opioids, not the best quality for a wannabe damsel in distress. Also, I don't feel very high, and I'm pissed about it.

The officer isn't really listening, and it's soon obvious to me that it doesn't matter what I say; I am going to jail. I turn my head and see the other three officers down the hall talking with my husband. They are taking pictures of his neck and hands and writing things down. He holds up the knife I pulled. It is a large bread knife with a serrated blade and snubbed point. Whatever. It wouldn't have done the job anyway.

Moments later, I am handcuffed. The handcuffs are tight and cold around my wrists.

"You have the right to remain silent. Anything you say can and will be used against—"

"Yeah, yeah. *Law & Order* is my favorite show. I know the fucking drill," I say. The Valium is starting to kick in, and it's making me mouthy.

I am put in the back of a cop car. The seat is hard plastic. They make them like that for easy cleanup in case arrestees puke, bleed, or shit themselves. I have never been in the back of a cop car. My bony ass is chafing on the rigid seat. My hands are cuffed so tightly that I can't lean back so I am pitched forward. I stare into the glass divider. And then I start crying hysterically.

"This is bullshit!" I scream to the cops, tears streaming.

"Tell my partner," the cop in the front says mechanically. I go silent and then decide to change my approach.

"Perhaps I was just jousting?" I say, trying to break him with humor. I am a professional comedian, after all. Maybe if I can get a laugh out of this guy, we can all forget about this and go home.

"Hello?" I tap on the glass with my forehead. He ignores me.

I switch tactics yet again.

"Fucking shit! I can't believe this is happening. I am a nice Jewish girl from Beverly Hills. I graduated magna cum laude..." I shake my head violently. "I'm not a bad wife, I swear! I'm not crazy. I'm not a fucking criminal. I..." And then my words are just swallowed up by sobbing.

They take me to jail. It's all a bit fuzzy because of the Oxy and Valium. It is surprisingly quiet in the West Hollywood police station that night. It's Christmas, and it looks like only assholes like me get arrested on Christmas.

They take away my purse and shoes and give me some dirty tube socks with orange stripes to put on. My mug shot is taken, and I am fingerprinted. Maybe it's shock; maybe it's the drugs; but it all feels surreal. Like I'm just watching, anesthetized, as it all happens to somebody else.

I am given a wool blanket and thrown in a holding cell. I pace around the small, cold cell in my jail socks. Numb. There is a pay phone on the wall. It mocks me. Inside that pay phone is the answer to the ominous question: *Who are your real friends?* I am about to find out.

I take a deep breath and call a woman I know from AA, Trina. In fact, I had been Trina's sponsor years ago. Back then, I'd been her guide, and she had been the newbie in the program. I'd been like her Sherpa, her priest, and her therapist all rolled up into one. I had just tried to offer her laughter, stability, unconditional love, things she'd been hard pressed to find in her own upbringing. And even though we'd kept in touch, casually, it felt like a lifetime ago.

Trina was fiercely independent, sensitive, loyal. She was also a bail bondswoman. And I needed both her empathy and her expertise right about now.

"Hi, Amy. Merry Christmas!" she answers cheerily. "How are you?"

"I'm in jail."

Trina gets in touch with my mother and organizes my bail (10 percent of $50,000, which is a hefty $5,000) and springs me from the clink herself. Trina is a pretty, busty, forty-something ex–hard-core drug addict gangster girl who's remade herself into a respectable businesswoman. She holds her cards close to her chest but her big, brown, doelike eyes reveal a lifetime of sadness and disappointment.

She takes me to the posh hotel in Beverly Hills where my mother is staying. My mom is visiting from Santa Fe, in town for the holiday festivities. I don't think having her only child arrested for felony domestic assault with a deadly weapon was exactly what she wanted from Santa. Despite my mother's feeble protests, I raid the mini bar, get shithoused on tiny bottles of vodka and sneak out to smoke cigarettes. Then I pass out for the next two days.

# CHAPTER TWO

O nce I've sobered up, I go home to my husband. There is a quiet and palpable tension. I think we both know the marriage is over but just haven't admitted it to ourselves yet. I offer to sleep in the den. I collage him a card, with a big red "X" over a knife, trying to make light of a potential homicide. I don't know what's worse: the fact that I pulled a knife on him or the fact that I thought a cutesy card would make everything okay. I apologize profusely, with pleading eyes, wrapping my legs around him.

"Amy, don't."

"Oh, God, you hate me," I mutter and start crying.

"Don't fucking cry. This is always what you do. You do something shitty and crazy, and then you cry and make it about you."

He's absolutely right. I start fidgeting with the long shag rug, ashamed.

"You're abusive. You really need help," he says.

"I was high."

"You were abusive before you got on that shit."

"You gaslight me, Clay! You provoke me, and then, when I react, you tell me I'm crazy. You've been doing it for years."

"'Gaslight'? Where'd you learn that term from, *Cosmo*?" he snorts.

"It always my fault, right?" I rage. "*All* my fault. You're fucking allergic to apologizing. You can never take any bit of responsibility."

"Responsibility?" he says. "You lie in bed all day while I go to work. And sure, maybe you go and tell some dick jokes at night...for how much money? Oh yeah...none. So don't tell me about responsibility, princess." Contempt drips from his every word.

"Clay, I can't do this right now. I'm three days into an Oxy withdrawal."

"Of course. It's alwaaaaays something."

Another day of bickering like this and he decides that it would be best if I go stay with my best friend, Linda, "temporarily."

Linda is a bipolar bisexual from Nebraska. She's one of those haute hippies who only wears cashmere and the highest-grade designer leather, loves animals almost violently, and has a house stocked full of crystals and "natural" cleaning products. She wears $300 perfume and $2,000 boots, but won't shower for days. She is an aspiring singer, but, in the meantime, makes great money as a personal assistant to the demanding rich and famous of Hollywood. When I first met her, she was medicating her bipolarity with marijuana. Eventually, I urged her onto a hefty dose of psychiatric meds and away from all of that "hippie bullshit," as I called it.

Linda and I are both depressive Scorpios, obsessed with true crime shows and threadbare vintage tees. We bond over the world's darkness and the absurdity of everyone. Other people's lives seem like *Portlandia* to us, and nothing is sacred. She is brutally witty and, despite a background of trauma and some serious mental illness, she is super high functional. She keeps her shit together, something I can't manage to do. I admire that.

Linda lives in Eagle Rock, a relatively new hipster enclave of a primarily Mexican neighborhood of Los Angeles, where overpriced coffee shops are perched next to shitty stores selling piñatas. It's only a thirty-five-minute drive from where I had been living, but it feels like a completely different world. I can just be a tourist in this magical boho land. Not a chance I'll run into anybody I know. This is good. It will make it easy to compartmentalize the wreckage of my life and pretend everything is okay.

We go to her favorite coffee joint, frequented by young, tattooed moms, famous alt comedians, and successful underground actors. On the walls hang overpriced amateur artworks, which we both make fun of relentlessly.

"What do you want, dipshit?" she asks.

"Two iced agave soy lattes. With three extra shots. Each."

She gives me a look like "it's your life."

"Don't judge me, fag," I say while I put her in a headlock.

We get our coffees and go soak up the sun in the nearby park.

"Are those the new shoes I just bought you?" she asks, referring to my cream-colored suede boots, which are already grayish.

"Guilty as charged."

"You shouldn't be allowed nice things. You're dirty."

"When's the last time you washed your hair?"

"I can't remember."

"Okay, so shut your mouth."

Yeah, that's the nature of our friendship. Deeply sardonic with a love and loyalty that rivals sisterhood. I was never sure exactly how Linda and I became best friends, always wondered why a seemingly together, successful woman like Linda would be inexorably drawn to me. That was, until she told me about her dad. Linda's dad lived in that space where genius and insanity meet for a beer. He was indestructible, despite his chronic penchant for self-destruction. He was an alcoholic who lived for twenty years with a brain tumor that doctors claimed would kill him in six months. After a slew of seizures had paralyzed him, he'd just roll himself to the front door in his wheelchair and then army crawl on the pavement to the car because, goddammit, he could do it himself! He was so stubborn he even kept smoking years after cancer took one of his lungs. Suffice it to say, she was used to, dare I say magnetized by, chaos and people on the edge, those circling the drain. In Linda's mind, the "Danger" sign that most people saw hanging above my head was soothingly familiar and probably read "Welcome."

One day Linda takes me shopping at Loehmann's in Beverly Hills. I am extremely agitated. My Oxy withdrawal is surprisingly painless, aside from some pronounced irritability and mild but terrifying bouts of mania.

I'm on the phone with my mother, who's "very concerned." She's in her managerial "fix-it" mom mode and it's annoying me.

"Honey, are you taking your vitamins? Last time you sounded this agitated, you had stopped taking your B$_{12}$ and weren't meditating. Can you find a way to start doing those two things again?"

"Mom, I'm coming off drugs. Hello!...What the fuck?!" I say loudly as I push violently past a wide-hipped woman. "They need to make these aisles bigger or the shoppers smaller."

Linda shoots the woman an apologetic smile and frowns at me.

"Baby, you sound very upset, very angry," my mom says flatly, stating the obvious.

"Yeah, Mom. I am angry. My life is fucking over. It's shit."

"Now, honey, that's not true...The universe will take ca—"

"It is fucking true, Mom! Please don't tell me some New Age bullshit right now. I might go to fucking jail..."

My mom is still talking, but I just hand the phone to Linda. "I can't deal with this right now...Here!" I say, and I walk away to look at some cheap purses.

"Hi, Mrs. Dresner..." I hear her start. Linda ends the phone call with my mom and quickly escorts me out of the store.

And as we exit the elevator to the parking structure, two perfectly coiffed, flamboyant gay men cut in front of us and out of my mouth pops a rude "Yes, of course! Ladies first!"

"Amy!" Linda clamps her hand over my mouth and pulls me toward the car.

Linda works a lot. When she's home, I kind of keep it together. We watch *Intervention* and eat cheap tacos, and she drives me to AA meetings. But when I'm alone in her little house, I quickly come unglued. My head starts talking to me, and it's not good. That's when I drink.

I am really trying to embrace sobriety again, but the grief around the loss of my marriage and my life as I knew it is so exquisitely overwhelming that I turn to booze for a much needed but fatal reprieve.

My new favorite poison is Four Loko. You can buy it at most gas stations and 7-Elevens. It's malt liquor laced with caffeine. It has the highest alcohol content of any stuff they sell. It comes in different horrible fruity flavors, which makes it a little more palatable when it comes back up—which, I promise you, it will.

One day, I drink a few of these bad boys and decide to go by my old place. I'm still drawn there like a sad homing pigeon. Clay is there. I have my engagement ring cleaned before I go by, a pitiful symbolic gesture.

"Look how sparkly my ring is," I say, smiling awkwardly.

"Have you been drinking?" he asks me.

"No," I lie.

"Amy, I can smell it."

I have the brazen coldness I get when I drink. I don't give a fuck, and it's such a relief. I'm normally so sensitive. Everything hurts: what you say, what you think, what I think you think. So, it's an emotional oasis for me to not care, even temporarily. Other people, however, don't enjoy it as much.

I am sitting cross-legged on the floor, back against the wall, buzzed.

"I just wanted you to love me the way I loved you, and you never could," he says.

I say nothing.

Then he begins to weep. The weeping morphs into heavy sobbing. He is lying on his belly on the bed. I get up and begin to rub his back, a lame attempt to soothe him. But I feel numb, empty. Maybe it's the booze. Maybe I'm dead inside. Neither of us says a word. The silence says everything.

Eventually, he flips onto his back, wiping away his tears, embarrassed.

"I'm gonna go," I say.

"Yeah, I think you should."

I leave. I *need* to get *drunk*. Really drunk. It is not a good idea, but it's all I got. I really shouldn't be drinking and driving Linda's car anymore, so I get the ingenious idea to buy a bunch of Four Lokos and then drive to her work at Mr. Bigshot producer's house.

I park outside her boss's ten-million-dollar mansion and just sit in her car and drink until six o'clock, when I am supposed to pick her up. I get out of the car to pee. There I am smoking, squatting, and crying on the dark, quiet, ritzy sidewalks of the Hollywood Hills.

At 6:05, she walks out the big electronic gate. I am standing by her car, wobbly, a can of booze in my hand.

"Oh, my God," Linda says when she sees me.

"YO!" I salute her. "You should probably drive."

"Uh, yeah." She is irritated but concerned.

"I had...a rough day," I say. "I saw Clay. Wasn't good." I shake my head like a child. "Not good."

"Have you been driving my car...loaded?" she asks me.

"Of course not. I parked and *then* I got loaded. Don't worry. I was very..." I can't think of the word.

"Responsible?" she offers sarcastically.

"Yes. Responsible!" I am very pleased with myself.

Linda helps me into the car and begins driving us home.

"Hey, can I ask you a question?" (Here comes the booze-induced honesty.)

"Sure."

"Are you in love with me?"

"No, Amy. Just because I'm bisexual doesn't mean I'm in love with you."

"I mean it's okay if you are. I've just never had a friend be this... devoted."

"I see you as the sister I never had."

"But you can be in love with your sister," I slur.

"No, Amy, I'm not in love with you."

"Well, that's good." I look out the window at the speeding cars. Everything is blurry. I am really fucked up.

"I'm gonna be sick," I say.

She thrusts a plastic grocery bag at me, and I immediately begin to vomit into it. Violently.

"Not good," I gasp. "Four Loko...so...sweet." I vomit some more. There is a hole in the bag, and the vomit leaks out onto my pants.

"It's on me," I say, a little confused. "How is it on me?"

"Oh, fuck," Linda says. "Let me pull over." She stops in front of a church. People are outside smoking. It is dark, but I can still make out the oversize glasses, asymmetrical haircuts, and cardigan sweaters.

"Is that an AA meeting?" I ask, puzzled. "Hi!" I yell and wave. The sober hipsters look at me with disdain.

"I need to take my pants off," I announce.

"No, Amy. Don't."

"Yes! They are wet! Need to take pants off now." I struggle with my wet, puke-covered corduroy pants.

"Goddammit," Linda says as she helps me yank them off.

"Thank youuuuu," I say. I put my boots back on, bracing myself on the hood of the car. I am now in transparent red net underwear and suede moccasin boots.

"Get in the fucking car."

"Look! I don't have any pants on!" I dance around like a puppet.

"Come on, let's get you home."

I comply, getting back in the car, half naked, wet, and drunk.

"I think I drank too much," I mumble.

"Ya think?"

I manage to stay sober for a month or so. Linda and I go to AA meetings on the East Side. She thinks they're interesting and hilarious. I dread each and every one. Also, Clay and I are trying to reconcile. I promise to be a better wife: I'll cook, I'll clean, I'll bring in money. We both pretend to believe me.

It's odd that even when you know a relationship isn't right, it's still hard to let go. I don't want to admit that I failed at my first attempt at domesticity, and I'm sure he doesn't want to admit that his third marriage has crashed and burned. And what the fuck would he do about that embarrassingly huge tattoo of me on his arm? Every time he gets out of the shower, his shoulder screams: "HI! REMEMBER THIS BITCH?!"

Clay is returning from a business trip, and we arrange that I'll grab him at the airport and we'll spend a few hours together—you know, feel it out. However, as soon as I see him walk out of the arrivals gate with that dour expression on his face, I know I'm making a huge mistake.

We drive home, making small talk, but it is awkward. He feels like a stranger. I can only imagine what I feel like to him.

As I follow him into our condo, I can't help but notice that it doesn't feel welcoming. In fact, it doesn't even feel familiar. Granted, none of my stuff is there anymore. Clay had put all my clothes and jewelry into garbage bags for Linda to pick up weeks earlier. I open the closet where my vintage hippie tops used to hang, and it's packed tight with his button-down shirts and expensive jackets.

"You didn't waste any time, huh?" I mean to say it as a joke, but it comes off bitter. Looking into the seemingly sterile and corporate closet, I feel sadder than I expected.

Clay flops down dramatically onto the bed.

"Lie with me," he urges.

I crawl onto the bed and lay my head on his chest, but I quickly feel a deep anxiety building. I look at my hands. They're trembling.

"I feel...really weird," I say.

"Maybe you don't love me anymore," he says flatly.

"Maybe you're right," I answer.

I get off the bed and go out to the patio to smoke. I feel confused. I think I still love him. I *want* to still love him. I feel self-hatred rising in my throat like bitter bile. Here is the only man aside from my father who has ever truly loved me or taken a chance on me, and I am about to throw it all away.

I go back inside, quiet, somber.

"It's over, isn't it?" he asks.

"Yes, I think so," I mumble, almost to myself.

"I'll walk you down."

As we wait for the valet to bring around Linda's car, I hug him. His arms hang limply by his sides.

"We can still be friends, right?" I offer lamely.

He is mute. The only sounds are the rushing of traffic down La Cienega and the soft Spanish chattering of the valet guys.

As I'm speeding back to Eagle Rock, chain-smoking, my phone rings. It's Clay.

My heart jumps in my throat, and I answer it with something vaguely resembling hope.

"You just wanted to see if you could get me back, you sick bitch! You never really wanted to reconcile."

His anger is sudden and palpable.

"Oh, my God, that is so not true."

"Yes it is. You're so fucking manipulative."

"I swear that's not true. I really wanted it to work, but when I saw you, I..."

"What? You forgot what I looked like? You changed your mind?"

"There's just too much water under the bridge, now...it's broken. I'm broken. We broke it...I don't know."

"You fucking broke it! You just got what you needed, and once you were done with me, you threw me away. You're a fucking user. You're a piece of shit—"

I hang up and throw the phone on the passenger seat. My entire body is trembling. He calls back, but I don't pick up. He calls again and again. The phone rattles plaintively on the vinyl seat like a fish gasping for air, for anything.

I'm in court, waiting to be sentenced. My chest is tight. I can't breathe. I feel like I'm on bad coke. The judge is an older woman, maybe late fifties, brunette, stern face, black robe. *She'll be on my side,* I think. She's a woman. She must have dated or married an asshole once in her judicial life. Besides, this was my first arrest ever. I'm sure I'll just get probation or something...

I have my blond hair in a messy bun, and I'm wearing a vintage India gauze blouse. I don't have on a stitch of makeup. My intent is to look young, innocent, peace-loving—not like a psychotic, mentally ill drug addict who would try to stab her husband.

"Amy Dresner, you are hereby sentenced to two hundred forty hours of community labor and one year of domestic violence and anger

management class for a plea of 'no contest' to the charge of 'misdemeanor assault and battery with a deadly weapon,'" the judge says.

"I can't believe this shit," I say under my breath.

"This sentence is to be completed in no more than fourteen months
from this date. Understood?" she asks.

"Yes," I say robotically. She raises an eyebrow at me. "Your Honor," I
add quickly.

I look over at my lawyer in disbelief. He's an old looking forty-
something, thinning hair, nerd glasses. Granted, my soon-to-be ex-
husband had hired him, paying half of his retainer back when we were
still considering a reconciliation. I'd never really felt he was on my side.
And he had not prepared me for this outcome.

I just look at him, speechless.

"Will I have a record? Am I on probation? I don't—" I start.

"Listen," he cuts me off. "I've done way more than you paid me for. This
is it. You are on your own now," he says. And with that, he hands me a
bunch of papers covered in scary legalese, grabs his briefcase, and is gone.

It occurs to me that lawyers are just like prostitutes. They pretend to
care, take your money, and then fuck you.

# CHAPTER THREE

Thanks to my little knife-pulling incident, the City of West Hollywood automatically slaps a restraining order on me. However, that doesn't keep me and Clay from contacting each other occasionally, which, unsurprisingly, usually ends badly. Here's an example of one memorable conversation I recall standing in Linda's bathroom. I'm sure he remembers others.

"You are a fucking sociopath and a pathetic piece of shit," he yells through the receiver.

"I need to get off the phone because I need to get drunk," I say quietly.

He keeps berating me. I start to cry.

"I'm sorry. I really can't listen to this anymore. You're making me want to kill myself."

"Oh, don't pull that borderline shit on me, Amy."

I hang up on him.

*Don't drink*, I think to myself. But then, suddenly, I am watching myself walking down to the liquor store, hippie moccasins scuffing along, leading me to the Promised Land of booze and cigarettes. At no time do I feel I can turn back. In fact, it feels like the right thing—the only thing—to do. My heart races as I get closer to the store. It's that eager excitement you get right before you score—hands shaking, mouth watering, heart pounding. I can't get back to Linda's house fast enough and get the poison—the elixir—in me.

I crack a can and chug greedily. I feel that sense of numbness and relief I craved. Ahhh. All too soon, though, that feeling is followed by desperation, entrapment, and remorse. I put on the song "Where Is Everybody," by Nine Inch Nails, and play it over and over again. Trent Reznor's words and music make me feel validated—vindicated, even— in my pursuit of total self-destruction. I drink and think and I drink and think some more, basking in my self-pity. As the booze rises to my demented brain, I begin the all too familiar and regrettable round of phone calls. The people I call are angry, perplexed, saddened, impotent. I walk into the kitchen and pick up a large chopping knife and plop back down onto the black sheets of Linda's bed. I take another long swig from the can and began to cut: perfect, symmetrical, straight lines across my wrists. Blood oozes. *I'll show them*, I think. *I'll prove to them how much pain I'm in and how unbearable it is to be me.* In my drunken idiocy, I text photos of my slashed wrists to my friends and Clay. *I can't make it on this planet. Don't any of you fucking get it?*

Not twenty minutes later, I hear sirens in the distance, and I know they are coming for me. Déjà bloody vu. And then there is that ominous knock. I open the door to two cops. I've put on a long-sleeved sweat-shirt to cover the fresh wounds on my wrists, and I attempt to compose myself and keep from slurring. *I'll talk my way out of this*, I think. *I might be lacking in many life skills, but I certainly have the gift of the gab*. Within minutes, they handcuff me "for (my) own protection," and, in the process, they see the gashes on my wrists. *Shit. I'm fucked.*

I am taken to the hospital against my will: 5150ed. (For those of you who don't have a hobby of suicide attempts, a 5150 is a seventy-two-hour involuntary commitment to a psychiatric ward when a person is considered a threat to themselves or others.) This is my fourth 5150 in eight years. I am beginning to be a pro.

After I put in a few drunken, sobbing hours in the Glendale Adventist ER, I am escorted into the lockdown psychiatric wing of the hospital. It is decorated in early institutional: putty-beige walls and cold linoleum floors. People in green gowns pace the hallways. Others are methodically doing puzzles. One old woman weeps softly as she rolls slowly along in her wheelchair.

I plop down on the hard plastic mattress in my room, dazed. The air is cold and empty, except when it's interrupted by low moans, bedeviled murmurings, and the buzz of the nurse's intercom. I curl up in the fetal position, puzzled by that haunting question, "How did I get here again?"

For the first two days, I don't eat or shower. I don't leave my bed. It occurs to me how odd it is that they send depressed people to the psych ward when the psych ward is, if nothing else, incredibly depressing.

On the third day, I pull myself together and join the rest of the constituents. As I'm heading off to chow, I am almost run over by Rick, a man with a bandaged arm who never speaks but is constantly, furiously pacing the hallway.

"Whoa, dude. Watch it," I say crankily.

"Rick, we need to change your dressing," an orderly says to him.

"Okay, how about Thousand Island?" he responds. It is the only time I ever hear Rick speak—gallows humor at its best.

The psych ward used to be all about coffee and cigarettes, but the days of psych patients chain-smoking and mumbling in the yard are over...at least at this facility. If you tick off the smoker's box on the intake form, they slap a nicotine patch on you. Caffeine is also in short supply. We get a tiny Styrofoam cup of atrocious coffee at seven in the morning. In the afternoon, I see some regular patients ("returnees," I call them) make instant coffee with tap water. I pass. I dream about Starbucks, cigarettes, and freedom.

A short Greek man with extraordinarily long nose hairs is battling a depression so severe he is undergoing electroconvulsive therapy (AKA electric shock therapy...yeah, they still do that). I never see him change his clothes. He wears the same navy blue food-smeared hoodie every day.

"I can't believe there's no Internet here," he grumbles. "I'm really into porn."

A four-hundred-pound biker chick with tattoos and missing teeth pushes her walker over to us. She bends down, her cleavage sagging with sadness.

"Corn?" she says. "They have corn here. It's very good...I used to be in your room," she continues, addressing me.

"Yes, you broke the bed in nicely," I counter. My comment is lost on her. I take my small plastic dining knife and pretend to slit my wrists. The orderlies try not to laugh, unsuccessfully.

"I've been here so many times, I know the pay phone number by heart," she says. She recites the number and then adds, "That's how many times I've been here. That I know the pay phone number. So if you ever want the number, I know it. By heart."

Kind of her, but I didn't want or need her help. The number is written in chalk on a board directly over the pay phone. Also, I am not in the psych ward to make friends. I am in here to do my time and get the fuck out.

There is one slim brunette girl, maybe mid twenties, who has the scariest blank stare. She has large, dark-brown eyes that look like something out of an anime, but with a much more confused but also somewhat sinister look. Occasionally, she puts her fingers in her ears to drown out other patients' conversations and rocks back and forth.

One time, I am on the phone with my mother, bawling, when the brunette girl comes up to me and says casually, "Get off the fucking phone."

With a quiet rage that surprises even me, out of my mouth comes, "Are you threatening me? I will take you fucking down, bitch."

She looks at me blankly and walks off to tell a nurse.

I have thoughts every night of how I might hang myself from the curtains, but I'm not that ingenious. So I just lie in my bed and hope to die. And then I begin to pray. I get on my knees and say the simple prayer so common to every desperate soul, every drug addict and alcoholic: "God fucking help me." As they say, nobody is an atheist on their deathbed, and I might not actually be dying, but it sure feels like it.

I go to the therapy groups, but only because I want to get discharged. I can kill myself on the outside. Mental institutions are designed to keep you from offing yourself. I'll have a much better chance at home. Plus, I can get a drink.

I avoid grooming group (I know how to brush my own fucking hair, thank you) as well as occupational therapy, but I go to the substance abuse meetings and "talk therapy." I sit there—sullen, shoeless—in a ripped-up .38 Special T-shirt and worn-in black cords. Next to me is a young woman in a hospital gown with a creepy smile on her face and a faraway look in her eyes. *These people are crazy,* I think. But I am in here, too. So I must also be crazy. But is it crazy to want to kill yourself? To want to free yourself from a life rife with despair? Honestly, it seems the only sane recourse.

With four rehabs and three previous psych ward stays under my belt, I am convinced that Darla, the substance abuse counselor, won't possibly have anything new or insightful to share. But I go to her group anyway. With her long gray ponytail, brown cargo shorts, and black trouser socks, she looks more like a psych patient in Portland than a therapist in L.A. She hands out the usual shit—flyers that explain that "HALT" stands for Hungry, Angry, Lonely, and Tired—and a couple of pages explaining neurotransmitters. I try not to look bored.

I call Clay from the pay phone. "I'm so sorry," I sob. "Please forgive me."

That same slim crazy brunette comes up to me and says, "Can you get off the phone soon?"

"Yes, as soon as I wrap up this conversation," I answer as politely as I can muster, tears streaming down my face.

"Why are you lying to me?!" she demands. Puzzled, I turn back to the phone.

"Hi. Sorry. Are you there?" I sniffle. It is silent.

"Hello?" I say again.

There is a deep sigh and then this: "I can't do this anymore, Amy. Get yourself out of there and get a job." And with a click, my husband hangs up on me.

"Hello? Hello?"

Silence.

"You said till death do we part, you fuck!" I scream. And then I start crying. The sound echoes off the barren hallways of the psych ward and what I hear back is piercing, disturbing, like a wounded animal caught in a steel-jaw trap.

# CHAPTER FOUR

---

$M$y mom makes some calls and pulls a magic trick, getting me scholarshipped into a rehab—my fifth. A tech from a very posh Hollywood Hills treatment center comes to collect me from Glendale Adventist psych ward. I am in a green gown and slippers. I haven't showered for four days. My hair is greasy and flat. My face is puffy from sleep and sadness.

"Do you have a cigarette, by any chance?" I ask, squinting at the unfamiliar sun.

"Of course." He is tall and gangly, with glasses and a timid demeanor.

We smoke in silence, standing by the black SUV that will take me to the next chapter of my nightmare.

"Good look, huh?" I joke, glancing down at my psych ward attire.

He smiles. "Whatever it takes, right?" he says as he exhales smoke.

We pull up the long, winding driveway to the gated treatment center, nestled high in the hills. The owner of the treatment center is a charismatic guy in his fifties who liberally uses the words "motherfucker" and "bro." Whether he's trying to be hip or is just stuck in the seventies is anyone's guess. He has hypnotic blue eyes and a commanding demeanor. I knew him well through my soon-to-be ex-husband. He'd always liked me. Back in the day, he'd joke around, saying things like, "What are you doing with him? Call me later." When my mom blindly called the rehab and mentioned my name, they took me in immediately, no questions asked. Whether it was out of pity, altruism, or to possibly avenge my ex, I will never know and don't really care. I needed help.

When I show up at the rehab, the owner smiles and says, "Welcome to the family. I own you now." And then he starts laughing—a laugh that sounds like a donkey choking.

This rehab where I will spend my next seven months is beautiful: three separate houses and two pools, all nestled in the woody hills of L.A. Rumor has it that it used to be Rock Hudson's estate. What really stands out to me is the grittiness of addiction set against this posh background. Drugs do not discriminate. So, although some client might be a millionaire lounging by the pool in an expensive monogrammed terry robe, lift a sleeve and you will see the track marks and abscesses of any skid-row junkie. Addiction is a brutal and unforgiving mistress.

I'm led to my room after signing pages and pages of documents. For the first time in my life, I am not high off my face while checking into treatment. I am tired and depressed and sad, but not high.

My room is clean, hip, and modern. I smile weakly at my new roommate and climb into the soft bed. Ahh, a real bed. Not like that government-issued, plastic-encased crap at the psych ward. I fall deeply asleep.

The next few days are a blur, but I must have been pretty hysterical because I am immediately put on a hefty dose of Valium. My blood pressure is a limp eighty over forty for the first four days, so tattooed techs periodically drag me out of bed to walk laps in the parking lot. We walk in circles, and I yammer on about how I used to have years of sobriety and a great marriage. They pretend to listen and be impressed.

My roommate, Amanda, is a twenty-four-year-old artist, a high-end escort, and a sex addict. She is beautiful, with big blue eyes, long red hair, and an amazing ass. She is also shy and terminally depressed. When she says she likes the "throwback music" I play, I realize for the first time that I'm getting old.

"I could actually be your mother. How scary is that?" I say one evening, lying on the carpet, peering into my computer screen.

"I don't even think about how old you are because I fuck guys old enough to be my grandfather," she answers casually while putting on makeup in the bathroom.

"Nice. Do you really hook?" I ask her.

"Yeah. Been doing it since I was sixteen."

"Wow...interesting. What's that like?"

"It's easy money, and I like sex."

"What if they're gross?"

"I've been doing it so long, I can kind of disassociate. I mean doing it sober...might be a whole other deal."

I nod my head, fascinated.

"Like one of my clients flew in from San Francisco to fuck me in the ass and paid me three thousand dollars. That was the other day, and I haven't even thought about it once since."

"Just another day at the office," I joke.

I am disgusted but also intrigued by her complete emotional detachment from sex. Little did I know that state would soon be all too familiar to me.

The days are pretty full: yoga, groups in spiritual solutions, relapse prevention, gardening, emotional recovery. But I can still find time to feel sorry for myself and ponder, in astonishment, the wreckage I have created: a criminal trial, shattered marriage, lost friendships, no home. I have managed to burn my life down to the ground. Again. It seems to be the only thing I can do consistently.

My counselor, Liz, is a short blond woman with steely blue eyes and a terrifyingly direct demeanor. She is as tenacious and perceptive as a sniffer dog, and, in time, it becomes obvious that she gets assigned the relapsers and the "very problematic" clients. I am scared of her, but not too scared to be a smart-ass and talk back. Plenty of arguments ensue.

"I don't understand," Liz says. "Why are your car *and* your phone in Linda's name?"

"Because I have the credit score of a crack whore."

"So you basically went from your husband paying for everything to your best friend paying for everything?" Liz harangues.

"She doesn't pay for my car or my phone!"

Liz gives me a withering look.

"Okay...my dad does," I say. I start laughing hysterically.

"You think this is all a game, Amy? You've been enabled your whole life. It's all part of your *disease*. You need to take this seriously."

"I *am* taking it seriously. But if I don't laugh, I'll cry. And I'll probably never stop."

Liz is jotting something down in her notes about me. "I think you should cut contact with Linda," she says.

"Oh, yeah...I'm sure she'll appreciate that: 'Hey, Linda, thanks for being my loyal friend, but I don't need you anymore. So see ya!'"

Liz is not impressed. "Do you want to get better or not?!" she snaps.

Yes, of course I want to get better! But I can't deal with all of this change all at once. Change is fucking terrifying to an alcoholic. We are fear-based people who have a difficult time tolerating ambiguity, and change is nothing if not "Hmm, well, let's see!" Also, everything she's suggesting feels horrible and wrong and completely against my nature.

Then again, look where my "nature" has gotten me so far. Liz *is* the one they send the hard cases to—and she has a track record of helping assholes like me, so she must know something. Ugh. I really don't trust her—but I want to. And I need to. I need her to walk me through this difficult period as I transition into my new, sparkly life as a single, sober, and (most important) independent woman—something no shrink or parent has ever been able to do. (Good goddamn luck, lady.)

"The universe has a plan for you," Liz keeps saying. Yeah...but in my mind that's always been drinking, anonymous sex, and suicide.

One day, I confess that I recently fucked a guy in a bathroom at an AA meeting. I say it casually in the hope that it will be received casually, seen as just a stupid stunt and not as the beginning of a new burgeoning problem.

"You can't possibly feel good about that," she says to me.

"Well, the speaker sucked," I answer.

"I'm serious, Amy."

"Well, I don't feel bad about it, either, if that makes any sense."

Shame and I parted ways a long time ago. We had to. We had an unhealthy relationship. Shame always made me feel like shit. I felt remorseful for things I couldn't keep myself from doing, and if I couldn't stop myself, then why feel remorseful? I decided to embrace my vices.

Fuck shame.

About two months in, my treatment team wants to take me off the Valium. I do not want this. I don't give a shit if, in AA thinking, it doesn't make me classically or technically sober. It does something more important than that. It makes everything bearable, smoothing out the rough edges, allowing me to glide through a razor-sharp life. But when you aren't the one controlling your meds, you don't have a choice. I'd heard that benzo withdrawal was one of the worst, and I get to experience it for myself. They aren't kidding. Kicking coke and meth was a breeze in comparison. Despite the doctor slowly tapering me off, the withdrawal is brutal: months of anxiety, trembling, and sweating. I feel like I am falling all the time . . . but on the inside. The ugly mug of reality slowly comes back into crisp focus, and I cannot, will not, look at it. I begin searching for some goddamn thing to grab onto, but there is nobody and nothing left. And that's when I discover my newest nemesis and coping mechanism: sex addiction.

Sex addiction feels a lot like drug addiction and can get you almost as high. No wonder they call it "two-legged dope." I can't get high anymore, so I check out with sex. Granted, it's a little tricky when you're in residential treatment, but thanks to sexting, FaceTime, and the occasional clandestine rendezvous, I manage. What should be about intimacy and connection is just another drug to me now. I want from sex what I wanted from booze and pills: numbness, obliteration. All my addictions have the same formula: I put something in my body, and I change my feelings. It doesn't matter if it's a donut or a Xanax or a cock.

By the time you're on your fifth stint in rehab, you learn some things—like about "rehab goggles." They're the treatment version of "beer goggles." They basically make you attracted to fellow inpatient clients that you'd otherwise never have anything to do with. It's a small, limited population, and you pick among what's available. A decade earlier at another rehab, I fucked a very talented, extremely notorious movie star. I would just sneak into his room and push him onto his bed.

"Amy, we can't," he'd say. "If I get kicked out of here, I go to prison."

"Shut up and fuck me." And with that, my mouth smashed onto his, and I yanked his pants off.

This time around, the pickings aren't half as good. I finally set my sights on a pretty twenty-two-year-old kid who sings and plays guitar. He's kind of boring and quiet, but once I hear him sing, I see him as this beautiful little songbird, and I have to have him. We have a few heated make-out sessions, and then the kid tattles on me. He says I bum-rushed him in his room. What an asshole.

The owner of the rehab grabs me by the back of my hoodie and drags me outside for a "chat."

"Uh, are you a fucking predator?" he asks. "What the fuck?"

"I'm a cougar," I say and smile smugly. I lose my phone privileges for a week.

However, it isn't long before I'm on the prowl again. Sam, a twenty-four-year-old husky rich kid, is my next victim. He's a recovering junkie in day treatment who looks like he just stepped off an Ivy League campus. Incredibly, we are granted a pass to go to a day meeting and end up fucking in his Hancock Park apartment instead.


We are a motley crew of clients. There is a man with borderline personality disorder from Jersey who is addicted to steroids and food and occasionally takes a fork to his muscular forearms and mutilates himself. The techs call him "juice box." There is a young Southern belle with Tammy Faye–style makeup and sweaty, bountiful cleavage who falls asleep in every group as she detoxes off Suboxone. There is a junkie who is a straight throwback to the seventies, complete with cartoonish print shirts open to the navel to reveal an overabundance of chest hair. I'm shocked to find out he is a criminal lawyer who has been going to court high on heroin for ten-plus years. There is a whiny, blond, anorexic mom who, despite being from the moneyed enclave of Brentwood, knows all the words to every rap song I've never heard of. She denies she's an addict; she'll only admit to suffering from "anxiety." There's a terrifyingly smart (if pretentious) heir to a famous brand, who can paint like Picasso but is crippled with Lyme disease. We periodically find him convulsing on the bathroom floor, but he's always cheerful and claims to be "super wonderful." When his seizures get really plentiful or violent, "shadow nurses" are called in to follow his every move 24/7. I don't know what's creepier, getting paid to watch someone sleep or paying someone to watch you sleep.

There is a male model who's so vain he has more products than your local Sephora. We share a bathroom for a hot minute.

"Wait, is that blood on the floor?" I ask him.

"No, it's bronzer," he says.

"God, I don't know what's worse," I quip and walk away.


The rehab regularly takes us all to "outside meetings." Every night we get packed into a van with loud music and vape smoke and driven down the winding roads of Laurel Canyon to AA meetings in the city. It is humbling to come tumbling out of the "druggy buggy" with all these guys at some of my old regular AA spots. Yep, it's me. And I'm in treatment. Again.

Inpatient treatment is communal living at its finest. We are stuck together all day in multiple groups, eating meals together, smoking on the patio together, and going to evening meetings together. It feels a bit cultlike—as if we're in some weird quasi-spiritual compound—but here, everybody's religion is addiction.

Day by grueling day, I push forward, resisting my impulse to get loaded or take myself out. This is the same rehab dance I've been doing for more than two decades, and I am tired and out of hope. So is my father.

"You've drained me financially and emotionally for years. I'm over it. I'm over the roller coaster. Call me when you have good news, or don't call me."

Ouch. These are the most devastating words a daughter can hear from her father. But I understand. Everybody is sick of my shit . . . myself included. This wasn't supposed to be the way it turned out.

I was born into a Richard Neutra house in Bel Air. My mother was a model and then a fashion designer; my father, a novelist and screenwriter. When I see pictures of myself back then, I just look like a happy, chubby baby with a big blond Jewfro. And maybe at some point I was.

My parents were well matched in that they both loved to drink and fight. My father came from a long line of Jewish depressives, and my mother had a family tree rife with schizophrenia and addiction. Their dynamic wasn't so much pouring gasoline on a fire as much as it was putting an IED into the fireplace. They were divorced acrimoniously by the time I was two. From then on I was swatted like a badminton birdie between New York and Los Angeles, Los Angeles and Mexico, and then, just Los Angeles and Los Angeles: spending half the week at my father's house in the posh Hollywood Hills and the other half at my mother's in the hippie stomping grounds of Laurel Canyon.

My parents are a study in opposites. My father is a drinker, garrulous and social, charming and witty. He couldn't give a shit about clothes. My mother, who got sober at thirty-nine, is quiet. She is an artist, a loner, a listener. Back then, she wore all Armani, in earth tones, with ethnic silver jewelry, and sported a perfect blond bob.

In the seventies and eighties, my dad was making good money writing movies and schlocky sitcoms. That meant I went to the best schools, had lavish birthday parties, nannies, and an ample clothing allowance. Working as a writer, he had the time to take me to school, pack my lunch, write me "secret notes" (where all the words in the message were anagrams and the note was signed with a slapdash cartoon of his bearded and bespectacled face). My mother, on the other hand, was downtown every weekday, all day, feverishly trying to carve out a career for herself as a sportswear designer in a sexist and ageist profession. She'd come home at seven p.m., and I would run to the door and try to tackle her or cling desperately to her leg.

"Amy, please let me get changed first," she'd always say. "You'll get my pants all wrinkled." Her pants could wait. I couldn't.

On the weekends, my mother would sit out in the backyard and sunbathe, sketching. I can remember feeling bored and lonely, playing with my dollhouse in my beautiful room—a room that I refused to sleep in. I actually slept in my mother's bed with her till I was twelve. She'd been beaten as a child and didn't really like to be touched, so it was the only time I could be close to her.

On the weekends with my dad, he'd take me to the toy store or to the basketball court, or do some activity with me, like teaching me how to ride my sparkly royal-blue Schwinn. In retrospect, maybe he wanted a son. As a consolation prize, I do have a voice lower than Tommy Lee Jones's after a bender.

I remember one Saturday, my dad and I were driving around, and we saw a dog in the backseat of a car. I must have been eight or nine at the time. My dad said, "Ames, see that dog. That dog is so rich, it pays that man to drive him around." I believed that was true until about high school. That's how much sway he had over me.

When I was thirteen, my mom, broke and on the verge of a nervous breakdown, told me she was going down to Mexico "to visit." She didn't come back to the States for ten years.

The next year I got into a very prestigious all-girls private high school—the kind where all the students wear uniforms—and my father bought a house a stone's throw away. With my emotionally unavailable mother even more unavailable after she took off to live in another country, my papa and I grew very close—probably too close, as he was forced to be both father and mother. I, in turn, became his emotional companion, his surrogate wife. But I knew that if my father saw me as a woman, he'd push me away. I'd no longer be able to climb into his bed at two in the morning when I had a nightmare. So I didn't date, and I was a straight-A student and a teetotaler, eschewing any display of my own burgeoning sexuality. When I got my period at fourteen, I threw a note on his desk and then ran and hid in my closet, hysterically crying. The note said, "I got my period. Please don't think I'm a grown-up now." Staying an asexual child was a small price to pay to keep your only parent.

My divorce is in process, and it is nasty. I have some cheap C-level Van Nuys lawyer that my mother is paying for. Clay has some expensive shark of an attorney from Beverly Hills. He is also threatening a "spousal abuse" defense if I try to get any alimony or any of his assets.

"I think he'll win," my shitty lawyer says.

"I just wanna walk away," I tell her. "Financially, my family can't afford to fight, and emotionally, I can't handle facing him in court. He can keep his blood money. I just need this to be over."

I begin to seriously unravel. Ideas of suicide and even vague plans become more prevalent and appealing. I begin cutting myself. I crush the head of a plastic razor and extract one of the blades. I inhale long and slow and draw the blade across my arm. Red blood erupts in a thin line. I cut again. And again. And again. In neat, parallel lines. The endorphins flood my system, and I feel high. It's more of a numb buzz than I'd like, but I'll take it. I can't bear to feel my feelings. I can't bear to feel how lost I am or how my husband loathes me or how much I loathe myself. I don't want to feel the regret for the things I've said and all the things I didn't. I want out.

Amanda, my escort roommate, knows what I'm doing. (I don't have black trouser socks tied tightly around my wrists as a fashion statement.) Plus, there's blood peeking out.

"Please don't tell anybody," I say.

"Lemme see," she says.

I show her.

"I used to do it. My old therapist said cutting is about rage and the little 'slices' are mouths screaming."

"That's fucking creepy," I say.

"Oh, you made a grid," she notices, smiling. "We could play tic tac toe on your wrist now."

I'm going to have scars on my wrists now. Everyone will know that there were moments in my life so painful that the only way I could cope was to cut myself and watch myself bleed. It's embarrassing. I'm weak.

# CHAPTER FIVE

In addition to the cutting, my newest addiction, sex, is really getting out of control. Amanda and I are a terrible influence on each other. Each of us will just report back to the other the details of our latest scandalous rendezvous, feeling safe that there will be no judgment or shaming. I wouldn't say we encourage each other, but we certainly don't discourage each other.

It seems weird that I'd come to this. I was never particularly slutty. You could blame it on "divorce backlash" or some unhealthy enmeshment with daddy. But if I've learned anything: you don't need to know *why* you do what you do. You just have to want to stop.

Well, I want to want to stop. But I don't want to stop. Not yet.

It's eleven p.m. and my phone rings. It's him. My newest limerent object. We met a month ago on Facebook, both part of the stand-up community. Phone calls and naked pics ensued. He's finally in the States from the U.K., but we have yet to meet in person. It isn't going to last. How do I know? Because it never does. And he seems too good to be true, which is always a bad fucking sign.

"I've got to see you," he says in his clipped English accent.

"I can't. I'm in rehab."

"I'll take a cab up there. You sneak down. We'll have a kiss and a cuddle, and then I'll leave."

"Uh…"

"Come on. I can't wait to kiss you."

I'm silent.

"Please, Amy."

I have a niggling feeling I'm being none too smart, but who could turn down the chance to suck face with a hot Brit?

As I creep down the dark driveway of the rehab, I am blinded by headlights. It's a tech in a van—an uptight pretty boy who takes his job way too seriously. He rolls down his window.

"And where are you going, lady?" he asks.

"Just going for a walk," I say, trying to sound casual and failing miserably. I am the world's worst liar.

"Okay," he says suspiciously.

I smile tightly and continue on my mission.

As I near the gate of the property, another tech—a beautiful blond ex-tweaker—pulls up beside me in her car.

"Where do you think you're going, miss Amy?" She smiles.

"Uh . . ."

"Going to meet somebody?" she asks bluntly.

"Please don't report me," I beg.

"Just don't get loaded, for God's sakes," she says and drives off.

I jump the fence of the rehab, surprised at my skill, as I'm an out-of-shape Jew. But, hey, the possibility of a stranger's tongue in your hungry mouth puts a little spring in a girl's step.

A yellow cab pulls up, and he steps out. He's shorter and less good-looking than his pictures. However, he seems thrilled at the sight of me.

We sit on the curb and chat and kiss excitedly, like teenagers. Suddenly, he pulls away.

"So, you're, like, paying to be locked up like a prisoner?" he asks me.

"Yeah—it's called rehab."

"I don't understand. You're an adult. If you want to leave, can't you leave?"

"Yes, but . . ."

"You're crazy, aren't you?"

"You're the one who took a cab to rehab to make out with a girl he's never met."

"True." He kisses me again.

I taste booze on him and the bitterness of cocaine.

"I'm so fucking paranoid...I've got to put this somewhere," he says, pulling an eight ball of blow out of his jacket pocket.

My heart pounds. I can feel my veins swell expectantly. But I pretend I'm not bothered.

He puts the coke down his pants.

"Just in case they catch us," he says, wiping away the white crust around his nostrils with the classic thumb and forefinger move.

"So why *are* you here exactly?" he asks between kisses.

"I'm a drug addict," I say bluntly.

"Aren't we all?"

"And I'm a sex addict," I add.

"But aren't we all?"

"I don't think you understand addiction."

"Well, I'm British," he concedes.

Just then, a flashlight shines in my eyes. I'm busted. Two techs have swung by on the rehab's golf cart. They order me onto the back of the cart, and one tells the Brit to "get the fuck out of here before I call the cops."

I lose my phone and computer privileges for a week.

Awesome first date.


My counselor, Liz, calls addicts the "puddle people" because we have no emotional skeleton, nothing internal to hold us up. At four months sober, that is exactly how I feel—empty and collapsing into myself.

"What would make you feel safe?" she asks.

"Get a large pad and pen," I joke. "Sit down. This is gonna take a while."

But the truth is, I don't know. I have never felt safe, because I don't trust myself. I, more than anyone, make myself feel unsafe. For a long time, I'd thought safety was having a man. And now, with an ugly divorce pending, I am at a loss. Does work make you feel safe? Beauty? Youth? I'd had all of those, and I still felt as if I'd been treading water my whole life. Drugs worked for a while, insulating me against my feelings and the world, but it was a temporary and certainly artificial safety.

Like all alcoholics and addicts, I hate structure, but I completely fall apart without it. As I graduate through the ranks at rehab, I'm moved from full residential care to "partial day" treatment. That means I only have to go to half of the tedious groups during the day, but I'm housed now in their nearby sober living. I begin to spend more and more time in my room alone, falling into a deep depression.

"Usually pain moves people into willingness," Liz tells me. "What's so interesting about you is that it doesn't. You just stay in the pain."

Oh, I know. Pain doesn't motivate me to take action. It just paralyzes me until I hit my breaking point and act out in any way to get numb. Numb and dumb. That's what I'm looking for.

She urges me to start my domestic violence class. It's every Sunday morning for twelve months (and I only have thirteen months left before court). She says she'll give me car privileges and issue me a weekly day pass. I comply.


It's early, not even eight a.m. I'm speeding down the empty streets of Los Angeles in my newly leased car (thanks, Dad), chain-smoking Newports and chugging Mountain Dew. Treatment has transformed me from a Jewish American Princess into an Appalachian hillbilly.

I park in front of the tiny counseling center off La Cienega where I've been ordered to go for my "domestic violence and anger management" classes. Every Sunday, a bunch of women and I "process" our week and learn about boundaries, self-love, substance abuse, and breathing. It is an odd and sundry group of ladies, a mixture of abused women (attending voluntarily) and abusers (court-ordered to be there).

Purse slung over my shoulder, soda in hand, I plop down in a chair with a deep sigh. I smell of sleep and cigarettes. It's only eight thirty, and I can already feel the tears coming.

The therapist is a petite woman with glasses and a light South American accent. She is lovingly confrontational, with a good sense of humor. I am, alarmingly, one of the star students—if only because I can spout off concepts from cognitive behavioral therapy and AA. I sound great. My actions, on the other hand, are another story.

The "check-ins" begin on my left; the basic how you're feeling, how your week was, what's going on. First up is a dumpy Brazilian woman who always wears skin-tight Lycra dresses and sunglasses. The bold print of her stretchy dress reveals her big stomach and drooping breasts. She is there for walking on her boyfriend's Ferrari. She's a huge stoner and comes to group high pretty frequently. She isn't the brightest cookie to begin with, so you can imagine my delight when she is baked and offering ridiculous, unsolicited advice.

Next to speak is a working-class bleached blonde with pointy teeth that make her look vaguely vampiric. She has that raspy smoker's voice and working-class hands. She'd gotten a DUI, and after the accident, in her drunken rage, she grabbed the other driver's eyeglasses and ground them into the pavement with her heel. She still hasn't confronted her drinking problem. Even now, months later, with a Breathalyzer installed in her car, her idea of "a couple" of beers is six. But I like her.

I kind of tune out as an Indian woman whose husband ignores her for days at a time checks in. She doesn't talk much, and what she does say is always about cooking or her children. Her stories are boring and her English is poor, but I do envy her domesticity—the kind I thought magically came with marriage.

There are not one but two Orthodox Jewish women. One is a tiny, slender brunette (well, that is the color of her wig) and the other is heftier and—surprisingly—black. (Imagine the dual fun of anti-Semitism *and* racial prejudice!) Both are always clad in long skirts and other modest attire. Both were abused by their husbands and are there, to my astonishment, by choice. I feel a kinship with the slender Jewish woman.

We periodically shoot each other looks when the Brazilian stoner goes off on a tirade. She doesn't seem offended by my brazen talk of fucking or my foul mouth. The thick black Hasidic woman, however, is prone to giving long, self-righteous sermons on self-esteem. I just smile and nod.

My least favorite one of the lot is a hotheaded fifty-year-old chain-smoker who pulled a knife on her daughter and threatened to kill her while the 911 operator was on the line. (Nicely done!) She is constantly playing the victim, crying, "I've turned the other cheek my whole life. I won't be stepped on anymore!" And then, not two minutes later, she's recounting a heated episode with a stranger in the produce aisle. She uses the word "cunt" a lot. She also claims to be a "casual" (read: daily) pot smoker, despite having been a raging crackhead for years.

The therapist confronts her on her drug use. Pointing at me, Ms. Hothead tells the therapist, "I mean, she takes all those prescription medications for her moods. I smoke pot. It's my medicine. What's the difference?"

"Let's stay on topic here. There is a big difference between marijuana use and psychiatric medications," the therapist says.

"Yeah...nobody ever killed somebody on pot," she says.

I flash her a death stare. "Don't even fucking get me started on this," I warn her. I cross and uncross my legs. This is a touchy subject for me.

Her denial that she has a problem is thick, but so is every addict's.

What really strikes me about the group is that what landed most of us here was just one wild impulse, one irate moment, one too many drinks. Isn't everyone capable of that? This isn't a roomful of murderers or monsters. This is a roomful of people who lost control, who threatened somebody and were called out. And I will tell you, the remorse and the shame hang heavy in the room. A box of tissues is diligently passed around. Many tears are shed for the deeds we can't undo and the horrible, resounding repercussions of those deeds.

We are all very different, yet all so similar. We are all in shock that we ended up here and initially in denial that we had done anything wrong except for getting caught. Anger bounces around the room: anger at the cops; anger at our victim for calling the cops; anger at ourselves for drinking, smoking, doping too much and losing control. Eventually, that veneer of denial falls away and sadness surfaces as each of us struggles to take responsibility.

I pretend that I'm better than these women. But the reality is that I'm worse. I am more violent, more mentally ill, with a worse drug problem and a shorter and more dysfunctional marriage. I came from a privileged upbringing with loving parents and a crippling amount of money. I don't have more excuses. I have less.

Tonight, instead of our usual evening AA meeting, they take us to a recovery book launch party at the 12-Step Store. A 12-Step Store is basically a store that sells AA shit: books, chips (sorry…"recovery medallions"), gold necklaces with the AA emblem, key chains, coffee mugs emblazoned with recovery slogans, and stupid T-shirts that say "Sober Princess" or "Survivor" or whatever. So much for the anonymous part of Alcoholics Anonymous. I find stores like this completely unbearable, but going to anything anywhere is a welcome change from another fucking meeting.

I'm making fun of some refrigerator magnet that reads "Steps, Hugs, and Rock 'n' Roll (some things never change!)" when I hear an astonished, "Oh, my God—Amy!" I turn around and see the insane movie star that I fucked three rehabs ago (at my second rehab). Holy shit. It's probably been eight years since we've last seen each other. He claims that he's sober, but he's really skinny and pouring sweat. Sweating like only cokeheads do.

"I want to eat your pussy right now," he whispers in my ear, leaving a snail trail of perspiration on my face.

"Jesus Christ… Well, you haven't changed a bit."

"You fucking love it. Gimme your number."

"It's still the same."

"I'm gonna call you. We are gonna fuck!"

It sounds like a threat as much as a promise. I flash back to the last time I saw him, years before.

We'd both relapsed after getting out of that rehab. He'd invited me to come "hang out" at his house, which I knew really meant "get high and bone." I drove up the swervy roads of Mulholland Drive, nervous and gakked out of my mind. He still had a big, gated house deep in the hills. He hadn't lost all of his money to his drug habit and his army of lawyers . . . yet.

His "assistant," a hot, dark-haired woman, greeted me. Even high as fuck, my instinct told me she was his quasi-girlfriend, but he insisted that she was his "assistant."

We sat on his bed and talked. He didn't look well. He pulled out a glass pipe and started smoking meth. I'd brought coke with me.

"Have some of this GHB," he said, pouring me a capful. "It will make you horny."

"I'm already horny," I protested, but he insisted.

Twenty minutes later I was throwing up mercilessly. His assistant/fuck friend cooked me a frozen burrito, which, within minutes, also made its way back up. She rubbed my back and held my hair for me as I hurled into one of the many toilets in the house.

The rest of the visit is a bit of a blur. I do remember fucking him at one point when, without knocking, his lawyer came striding right into the bedroom and started talking to him about some legal issue. They both acted like it was no big deal, which made me suspect this must have been common house protocol.

Later, after Mr. Movie Star showered and asked me to scrub his back, he turned on the TV and started watching old videos of himself getting awards.

"I had it all," he sobbed—between hits off the pipe.

The whole scene was kind of nightmarish.

Not even three days after the book launch at the 12-Step Store, he makes good on his promise to contact me for a fuck rendezvous. I drive down to his loft in downtown L.A. A very young black girl opens the door. He loves black girls. She doesn't seem that surprised to see me— or maybe she's too fucked up to be surprised.

"Your friend is here," she calls into the bedroom.

"Bring her into the bedroom," I hear him say.

I walk in, but I'm already anxious to leave. He's on the bed in his underwear and there's an empty bottle of Jameson on the bedroom floor.

"That's not mine," he clarifies.

"I don't give a shit. I'm not your sponsor. I'm here to fuck you, not work the steps with you."

I notice there is an impressive collection of unmarked prescription pill bottles on the bedside table. He sees me take in the stockpile of orange bottles and, with one move, sweeps them into a drawer. I don't ask.

"Lakeesha, baby. Come in here," he calls to the young black woman. He pats the bed where the two of us are.

I'm not a fan of threesomes. Somebody always gets left out. Plus, I'm not into chicks. Sure, a little kissing when you're drunk is nice. And I might dress like a homeless lesbian, but the idea of eating pussy is possibly the most revolting thing I can think of.

Yes, I am as straight as straight comes. I realized this at twenty-four, when I was shit-faced and making out with a girl. I put my hand down her pants, and it felt like sticking your finger into a jellyfish. I was repulsed, and never did it again.

But of course, I'm also a people pleaser. And this guy is a loose cannon. He has an infamously bad temper, which I have yet to witness, and I'd like to keep it that way. I end up fucking him and his black girl *du jour*.

He moans my name as she is blowing him, and she slaps him and says, "It's me, motherfucker."

This is going well.

I make it back just in time for curfew.

I want you to know I wasn't always a soulless fucking machine or a drug addict, for that matter. In high school and college, I had been obsessed with "purity." No sex, no drugs, no drinking, no smoking. I didn't even kiss a boy until I was eighteen, and when I finally did, I broke out into hives for six weeks. Hello, repression!!! I was afraid of sex but dressed that up in the guise of "waiting for Mr. Right." Then, as the years passed and I stayed a virgin, what was once this "gift" became this albatross of immaturity and prudishness. Being a teetotaling virgin in college wasn't cool, it was freakish. So I duly got rid of that unsexy status, getting drunk one night and losing my virginity a few weeks later.

And let's be real: nobody wants to fuck a nineteen-year-old virgin. We don't know what we're doing; we bleed; and then we fall in love with you. Who wants that?

So, yes, I was nineteen, and I was drunk. It was 1990, and I was a junior at Emerson College in Boston. It was cold there. I was too smart for the school, and they were too dumb to notice.

I was madly in love with one of the school playboys, and he knew all too well but pretended he didn't. He also knew I was a virgin. Because I told him.

The playboy and I were in his cramped dorm room. I was loaded, wobbling gently on my high heels. I was also terrified, but too drunk to show it. As the room began to spin, I sat on the edge of the bed.

"No clothes on the bed. That's the rule," he said.

"What?"

"I'm serious. If you're going to be on the bed, you have to take your clothes off."

I undressed mechanically. This was not the romantic night I'd envisioned for my deflowering. But I'd decided that this was the night I'd shed my prepubescent take on the world—and cut that cord that kept me "daddy's little girl."

The next thing I knew, he was on top of me naked. We were not kissing. He was pressing his cock against me, but I was so tight and he was so big that he couldn't enter me. Instead, his dick kept nearly nudging me off the top of the bed. He grabbed me by my forearms and pulled me back down to try again. Finally, after two or three attempts, he pinned my arms down and gave a strong thrust with his pelvis. The pain was sharp. I yelped. He put his hand over my mouth to muffle my whimpering.

More thrusting, more pain, some blood, and it was over. Welcome to the world of sex, Amy.

One night, I'm sitting in a circle of chairs in a church. I'm in an AA meeting in the San Fernando Valley. And I'm pissed. This is typical. I've been crying, and my eyes are puffy from tears. I've got on a black fox-fur jacket and big dark sunglasses. People think I'm high or blind. I don't give a fuck. I hate AA at this moment.

I am digging around in my purse, trying to look busy so nobody will talk to me. No such luck. There's a hand on my shoulder. A high-pitched voice.

"I'm Anna. I just wanted to say hi and welcome," some woman says to me. "I heard your 'share' last week. It was so funny. You're so bitter and angry. It's hilarious."

"Oh, thanks…I guess." I have no idea who this woman is, and I don't care. She's just like every other Big Book thumper in the rooms, reaching out to the newcomer. A Big Book thumper is the AA equivalent of a Bible thumper, preaching the joys and salvation of a life in sobriety. I go back to prospecting for imaginary items in my purse, hoping she'll go away.

"Well, I'm glad you're here," she chirps. "Enjoy the meeting!"

"Yep." I don't look back up.

This meeting is a grueling hour-and-a-half Big Book study where we read passages from the Alchoholics Anonymous book and then people share their experience on the reading. There is no official break during that time. You're allowed to get up and get coffee or go outside and smoke. I go outside to vape and text pictures of my naked ass to shallow, lecherous men.

I'm at this meeting because I have a new sponsor, a woman, and she is part of a creepy "lineage," if you will, of sober women who are very old-school and traditional. This means that if you're a part of their "thing," whenever you speak at a meeting or take a cake to celebrate another year of sobriety, you have to wear a skirt or dress to show respect.

I'm the most disrespectful person I know. Plus, I never wear dresses. I don't like the attention. When I wear a dress, I feel like I'm being served up on a platter to men: open, vulnerable, ready to be eaten. So I just wear jeans, short boots, and holey rock tees so I can fly a little below the radar. But men like dresses. They like femininity. And I like men. So maybe I should wear more dresses. I don't fucking know.

I cut myself some slack because I was wrangled through puberty by my dad, a six-foot, four-inch, bearded, Jewish Papa Hemingway type. So, how do you turn out when you're raised by a hard-drinking writer? Well, you can mix a mean drink, play poker, and bowl. You cannot cook, put on makeup, or pick out a bra that fits.

Though I grew up idolizing my father and imitating his wit and sarcasm, when I got out into the world, I quickly found out that it isn't what men want. At all. They want soft-spoken, nurturing women in tight skirts and tighter sweaters, with gleaming, manicured hands and formidable high heels.

When I was twenty-four, a guy once explained my man problem to me this way: "You're too analytical, too intellectual . . . too much like me."

"A man with a pussy. What more could you want?" I said.

Anyway, so I'm in this goddamn meeting. I don't open my book to read along or highlight like a good alcoholic student should. I just stare at the clock and gulp Diet Coke.

The woman next to me—a total stranger—leans over and chirps, "Closed book equals closed mind," and then smiles.

I chortle, but I really want to punch her in the throat. I do not open my book. My eyes are fixed on the clock. Only seventy more minutes to go.

Five minutes later, she leans over and whispers, "Don't you follow along and highlight your book? I mean, it *is* a book study."

My patience has hit its breaking point, and I turn to her and say, "Listen, it's a miracle I'm still here. I usually bolt about ten minutes into this hellish meeting and go blow some guy. So just give it a rest, okay?"

Her mouth gapes, her eyes go big. She gives me a superior snort and turns away. I go outside and think to myself: *Fuck it, let's drink.*

I do have to say, when you're an alcoholic or a drug addict on the verge of a relapse, nothing "makes" you get loaded. You've already decided days before. You have your reason. You're just looking for an excuse.

I have been thinking about drinking for a few weeks. I need a respite from my head and a recess from my life, and sleep and sex just aren't cutting it. The emptiness inside is too big and too deep for either. As my whirlpool of despair grows darker and picks up speed, I am just waiting for that one small thing, that flippant remark to tip me into self-destruction. Today is that day.

I can't drink. I know this. It's the odd occasion that I don't black out and get sick immediately, and this time is no different. I don't know if I had some delusional notion that this drinking binge would be different from all the other über grisly ones, or if I just didn't care. For alcoholics and addicts of my variety, drinking and using is like a temporary suicide. We just don't leave a note.

Back in the rehab's sober living facility, I do a little cutting. I mean if I'm going to self-destruct, why not pull out all the stops? I reslash where I'd been cutting, and as blood pours down my wrist, over the faded "x's" and "o's" that Amanda had drawn, I feel relief. I feel like I'm saying "fuck you" to everybody. Fuck you. Fuck him. Fuck me. Especially fuck me.

There is a bottle of expensive vodka in my trunk, a birthday present for a friend. I'd had it in my car for a few days, which was fucking stupid. What was I thinking? Playing chicken with myself? Being arrogant in my sobriety? As I walk down the stairs to fetch it, a thought comes into my head: *Don't do this. Call your sponsor.*

"Fuck that bitch," I say aloud to no one and continue down the stairs. I pop the trunk and pull the elegant bottle from its iridescent gift bag. I stomp back up the stairs and return to my bedroom in the sober living. *Here we go again,* I think. Fucking *Groundhog Day.*

When I open the bottle and drink, it goes down smooth. It's fancy stuff. I wait for that "ahhh" feeling—for that moment when ease or numbness or pleasure clicks in. Nothing. I take another swig. I wait. Again, nothing. I don't remember the progression, but the next thing I know, I am shit-faced—I mean, really, really drunk. Then I begin the phone calls. All those things I need to tell all those people—things they really need to hear. Right now. I have no idea what I say, but I'm sure it is dramatic—confessions of secret love or venomous spewings of hidden hatred. Nothing good. Nothing I shouldn't keep to myself.

I call Brendan, one of the boys in my "stable." This one is a comedian. He is ten years my junior, and blond, with prancing blue eyes and a sharp, pointy nose. He has a nice body, and he's a decent fuck and loves to eat pussy. I've come to realize that comics, for the most part, are the darkest, most self-loathing and damaged people on the planet. I can say this with some certainty, as I was one myself for five years. Comics typically are either in recovery or they are full-blown addicts and/or alcoholics. The social drinker or occasional drug user comic is about as common as a rainbow-maned unicorn.

"I'm drinking," I warn him via text as he's on his way over.

"So am I!" he shoots back. He'd also been in rehab with me. Obviously this place is doing wonders.

Twenty minutes later, he arrives to pick me up.

"You're drunk," he says, annoyed.

"No, I'm not. I'm shit-faced," I correct him. As we drive to his house, I roll down the window and begin to throw up. A lot. It goes all down the side of his car.

"Are you sure you're okay?" he asks.

"I'm fine!" I say with some irritation.

I vaguely remember being in his dark bedroom, taking off my clothes and laying myself out on the bed in what I perceived to be a provocative, "come hither" pose.

"Did you fucking cut yourself?"

"Shut up. Let's do this," I bossily slur. He fucks me briefly, and I complain that he doesn't eat my pussy first. I get up to go to the bathroom, and I stumble and fall backward—flat on my back, naked.

He looks alarmed. "You all right?"

I burst out laughing. "Of course!" But I am far from all right. I am an alcoholic who is drunk as fuck, cutting myself with a razor, having unprotected sex that I'll barely remember, and weighing the pros and cons of suicide. No. I am not all right.

As he drives me back to the sober living, I vomit relentlessly. Yet, instead of thinking, *I should not have drank,* I think, *I should have just done coke.* Welcome to the mind of an alcoholic addict.

# CHAPTER SIX

No surprise, they kick me out of the rehab's cushy sober living. I hear I am considered "resistant." I prefer to think of it more as "invulnerable," but whatever. Gone are the marble floors, flat-screen TVs, and gourmet chef. I'm shipped off to an independent halfway house in Tarzana. "Halfway houses" can be pretty shabby and poorly run, more about making money off addicts' desperation than helping people find sobriety. They are notoriously overpriced and overcrowded.

I drive, chain-smoking, over the curvy roads of the Hollywood Hills to that remote shithole part of the San Fernando Valley. My little car is packed with my few belongings. I don't cry.

I finally arrive at the large, gray, imposing house.

*This isn't bad*, I think. I knock on the door, and an old biker chick with long purple hair opens it. She has only one whole arm. Her other arm ends abruptly at the elbow.

"Welcome. You must be Amy."

"That's me."

"I'm Violet, the house manager."

I smile bleakly. Do I shake her other hand? I don't know what to do.

"I'm so happy to have another girl in the house," she continues. "There are five guys here right now. Finally I have someone to help me get dressed."

Five guys? They sent a female sex addict to what's essentially an all-male sober living house? Genius.

I try not to look at her arm. Did she lose it shooting dope? Was she born that way? I don't ask. We go to the back patio to smoke as she reads me the litany of rules. I nod and say "no problem," but I'm not listening. All I'm thinking is "How do I get the fuck out of here?" I feel panic building in my chest. I want to leave, but I have nowhere to go. I've been displaced from my marital abode. I'm not allowed back at Linda's because her brother who owns the place has banned me—thanks to my little wrist-slitting incident. Both my parents live out of state. I mean, sure, I have a handful of close comic friends who check in with me occasionally, but most aren't sure how to help or are too poor to. So this is home now, like it or not.

She shows me to the tiny room that will be mine. Two single beds with ugly bedspreads and a broken TV. That night I dream that I call my ex-husband and ask him to rescue me. I sleep twelve hours but still wake up tired and dazed.

I pad down to the kitchen. I grab a coffee cup out of the dish drainer. It's supposed to be clean, but there's something crusty on the lip. There's a sign by the sink that reads "Do not leave dishes in the sink. Your mama doesn't live here." Funny. Welcome to living with five men.

I grab a spoon out of the drawer. It's bent. Heroin or magic trick?

"Time for morning meditation!" Violet, the house manager, yells. She is in her bathrobe, holding a pack of Pall Malls in the crook of her stumpy arm.

You can hear the groans of cranky, newly sober young men.

"Wake up, princess. Time for morning meditation," she calls into a dark, musty room.

Three young guys file into the den. Two are wearing black hoodies with the hoods up. One resident is missing. He didn't come home last night. Another, an older alcoholic who does art department on movies, is already at work. He had eight years of sobriety—twice—and is also a chemical dependency counselor, but relapsed during his recent divorce. I get it. He picked up smoking in the last six months, but he just takes two drags off a cigarette and then puts it out. The ashtray is always full of long, white, bent cigarettes.

I'm sitting on the couch, holding my knees tightly to my chest. I hate this. I hate change. I wonder how long till I really lose my shit again. I can only imagine how this sober living with mostly men and a no-nonsense den mother will react to my crying and cutting and borderline bullshit.

In a house full of men, there's no drama. And, having been raised by my father, I'm comfortable around guys. Being the only girl in the place, aside from the house manager, is oddly soothing to me. But most of these fellas are loners—not very social—so it feels quiet...too quiet...and I interpret the silence as loneliness and depression. They also do not like to talk in the morning, so the "morning meditation" is brief, consisting mostly of Violet making some poor fuck read from the Big Book and then ordering everybody to do their daily chores.

None of the guys eat breakfast. Few even drink coffee. I just hear the popping of Coke cans and grumbling. After we read from the Big Book, everybody retreats to their rooms to go back to sleep. Soon, the smell of homemade chili wafts throughout the house. I tell myself that this peaceful atmosphere is good for me. I can write. I can meditate. I can get my shit together. But I feel scared that the quiet despair I fight daily will rise to the surface and overwhelm me.

The only real sound in the house is the regular maniacal laugh of Tony, a twenty-four-year-old ex-tweaker who makes sandwiches at a deli during the day and goes to school to be a pastor at night. He's young, in good shape, and makes a lot of goofy sexual innuendos—like greeting me with "You've come just in time. Which is more than I can say about my last two girlfriends."

After a few of these orgasm double entendres, I call him out.

"I thought you wanted to be a priest or some shit."

"Sin now; pray later." He smiles, winking like a used-car salesman.

He's actually a sweet guy, and very spiritual despite his obvious prurience. We have long talks by the fireplace about the God that I don't believe in. I envy his faith and the solace it gives him. I try not to freak him out with my atheism, and I try to downplay my sordid past. I don't want to lose a friend, and I definitely don't like the idea of him pulling his pud at X-rated images of me.

One of the guys in the house is a thirty-year-old website developer.

He's an opiate and gambling addict. He is also going through a divorce. That makes three of us. The guy lives on pizza and Pepsi. His big belly sags below the bottom of his T-shirt. He looks terminally sad. I want to give him a hug, probably because I need one. We both have that heavy stench of grief and loss.

There's a bald ex-tweaker who lives off the laundry room. He has a sign on his door that says "Welcome to the Pleasure Zone." He tells me how he liked to take crystal meth and Cialis, and how he had a hard-on like a hood ornament. I laugh. I'm already one of the guys. I'm relieved. The first two days, they all said "sorry" anytime they mentioned the word "pussy." For the first time in my life, I don't want to feel special. I just want to belong.

Once a week, there is a "speaker meeting" at the house where somebody from the program comes and shares their story with us. Dinner at seven; meeting at eight. Violet, the house manager, has been in and out of the program for twenty years, so we know a lot of the same people— either people I hate or people I have slept with, or both. (Let's be honest... they're not mutually exclusive.) This week, the guest speaker is somebody who has watched me come in and out of the program for seventeen years. I feel anger toward him, but I realize even then that it's really shame in disguise.

"Amy, can you help me with something?" Violet asks. She wants me to chop onions for her chili. My eyes tear as I cut them up. She's a good cook. I have two arms and I can't make an egg. I have mad respect for her. She is devoid of self-pity. I want that.

What I am starting to realize is that I'm never happy. I never understand what I have till I've lost it, be it a comfortable marriage or a posh sober living situation. I complained constantly at the other facility: there was too much structure; they were AA robots; none of my young housemates understood the trials of a divorce. Now I'm in a very relaxed sober living facility with people closer to my age—a few of whom are also going through a divorce—and I still complain: there's not enough structure; nobody is really serious about their recovery; I'm the only girl.

There's a saying in the program: "If you don't like something, change it. And if you can't change it, change your attitude." It's not original. It's actually a bastardized form of a quote by Maya Angelou. But whatever its origin, I come to see that it's spot on: How we choose to look at any situation will determine our happiness. There are beautiful millionaires who want to blow their brains out, and there are eight-year-old kids with cancer who are happy as fuck. My shitty situation is temporary, and it is a direct result of my own actions. I decide to do something I had only heard about before. I try to be "positive."

Luckily, for me, being positive involves arts and crafts, something I mastered during my days as a tweaker.

First, I make a vision board, cutting out things I want from magazines and pasting them onto poster board. It's mostly women I'll never be and things I'll never have, but I guess that's the point.

I start making lists of things I'm grateful for in my present life. Sometimes my list only has a few things on it: health, sobriety, my hair. (My hair is pretty much the first thing on the list every day. I got lucky in the hair department.)

I also make a commitment to get in the habit of looking for the good in people. I tend to be very critical and judgmental, so this looking for the good thing doesn't come easily. I mostly don't do it, but sometimes I catch myself thinking shitty thoughts about other people and stop. Does that count?

One of the guys helps me see how negative I am by punching me in the leg anytime I complain. It is an aggressive form of behavior modification—or the beginning of a BDSM relationship. The bruises trailing up my leg soon become mottled time stamps showing how often I bitch about things. Despite my less than ideal living situation (isolated, with addicted strangers, in a run-down mansion), I *do* feel calm. I'm not cutting. I'm not acting out sexually. And I'm not crying. Well, not every day. I have no strict rules to rally against here. No Liz to bust my ass. No drug testing. It's all on me.

This is classic addiction. You think you've got the monster in the box. You're hopeful, relieved, maybe even arrogant that you have a handle on it, and then *bam!* You eat dirt. Alcoholism is a sneaky bitch. She waits for the one moment when you trust her and let your guard down. You have to be ever vigilant against her, and I am anything but.

I've been in my tiny, dank room for days, just writing and trolling Facebook. I climb out onto my narrow balcony and smoke while staring blankly at the bleak cul de sac and then stuff the butts into a Diet Coke can. I'm not going to many meetings because I'm not a fan of San Fernando Valley AA. That Big Book study where I was admonished for not following along was in the Valley. The one where I left and relapsed after. But now, rationally or not, all of Valley AA is forever seared into my brain as horrible and fundamentalist and righteous. However, the upside of the Valley is that nobody knows me. And the downside is that nobody knows me.

I remember that I have one friend who lives in nearby Sherman Oaks. He'd been sober for over a decade, but now he drinks pretty moderately. As he collected years in recovery, he began to see more and more of the hypocrisy, absolutism, and sexually predatory behavior that goes on in the rooms of AA. It eventually drove him out of the program, but he still respects and uses a lot of the tools. I should go see him. He's smart and funny and hot. And I can get out of this dilapidated castle of recovery for a few hours.

There's a sign-out book by the door. It's very casual. Old one-arm isn't going to check whether you're really having coffee with your sponsor or getting finger-blasted by some loser. It's just for the façade of "control" and "accountability" and all those other unappealing adultish words.

I'm at my friend's house, and I see him sipping cheap vodka and having fun. He can pace himself. He can stop. It looks divine, that little respite from reality.

"You can have *one* swig," he says.

That's exactly what we alcoholics want to believe, that we can have just one sip. It's the experiment we do over and over in hope of finding an answer that's different from the usual "no, you really fucking can't." I feel deeply unhappy. My life is in shambles, and I have no idea how to fix it. I need escape, and I'll take it temporarily from a bottle. I use his comment as permission to try once again to show myself that I can control my drinking.

I take one swig, and that's all it takes. Every trip to the bathroom, I sneak another sip from the bottle that's on the hallway table. Soon the bottle is almost empty. He's barely buzzed, and I'm pretty loaded, making aggressive advances on him and dancing badly to cheesy eighties songs. Fuck.

It's getting late. He wants to go to sleep, so I leave. I tell him not to worry; I'm going directly home; but of course I don't. I go straight to the liquor store.

Before I know it, I've been drinking for three days straight. Each morning, I say to myself, "Not today! Today it stops." But, within hours, I'm buying more booze. There are maybe five huge Foster's cans crushed up under my bed and half a dozen more in the dirty clothes hamper. My bedroom smells like a brewery, but nobody seems to notice. Everybody here sleeps all day. And I mean all day. I can't be the only one using.

The next morning, I vow not to drink, but I wake up trembling, and within a few hours, I've caved and have a beer in my hand. This vicious cycle continues on for four more days, and I know it is only a matter of time before I am discovered and kicked out. But despite this, I can't stop. I remember how they defined addiction in treatment: "use despite negative consequences." Yep. That's pretty much it.

One night I find myself drunk at a marathon AA meeting. People are always shocked when you're loaded at a meeting, but meetings aren't only for once you've gotten sober. Despite knowing that, I feel extremely self-conscious, and running into the wife of the guy who owns the rehab I just got kicked out of doesn't help.

She gives me a bony hug. "How are you?"

"Fucking fabulous," I say with boozy breath, grabbing for bravado to cover my discomfort. She pretends not to notice I'm loaded, and I pretend not to be.

As the speaker, a voluptuous Texan girl with six years sober, tells her story, I drift in and out, alternately feeling moved and hopeful and then buzzed and bored. Applause jolts me awake and then there's hand-holding and a prayer. I sway unsteadily.

After the meeting, I see Sam, the wholesome looking junkie I banged at rehab. He spots me and comes over. I'm smoking and trying to look sober.

"Beer or vodka?" he asks.

"Shit. Is it that obvious?"

"How long have you been drinking?" he asks.

I shake my head. It's all a blur. "No fucking idea...a few days? A week?"

"Should I call Liz?"

Yeah, I'm sure Liz would be thrilled to hear from her most "resistant" recalcitrant client again.

"I don't have money or insurance, and they're not going to take me back. They kicked me out."

But before I know it, he's got Liz on the line, and I am telling her everything, my voice full of angst, my mouth full of tears.

"I'm so fucking lost," I sob. "I don't know how to build a life for myself. And I keep getting loaded over Clay and the grief and the loss. I know it's not an excuse. I need help. I don't know how to do this." And then I begin to cry even *harder*—the cry of the hopeless and the helpless and the lost and the damned.

"Come up to the unit. Now," she says.

The rehab agrees to detox me. For one week. They will not take me back long-term. It takes me two and half days to stop shaking from the booze. From *beer*. And that's when I know: I am a real alcoholic. The finality of it, the total conviction, is an odd relief. There is no more wiggle room. There are no more "maybes" or "could I's" as in "maybe I can drink moderately" or "could I have just one?" I'm not just a drug addict. I am a crying, blackout, fall-down drunk, just like my mother.

# CHAPTER SEVEN

A fter detox, I move into another sober living. It's a small, quaint house in West Hollywood and the personal home of the house manager. Sober livings are independently owned halfway houses for addicts reintegrating back into society. It's not rehab, but it's not normal independent life, either. It's like life with training wheels. And if this is her personal home where she still lives? Well, you know it's gotta be nice.

"Sound desperate and willing or the owner will never take you," the rehab program director warns me.

The owner is Mariana, a beautiful blond Brit with ten years of recovery. She is too gorgeous—an ex-model with long, slender legs and even longer platinum blond hair. But she is so nice, so loving, that you can't hate her. You can only wonder what it would be like to be her—to bring men to their knees, speechless, with your mere presence.

This sober living is an all-woman house. I've never particularly liked women, especially in groups. Like other loner druggies, I abhor sororities, teams, and social clubs. I find gaggles of women annoying, with their high-pitched voices and incessant chatting about nothing. They also make me feel a bit masculine with my low voice that many people—including my own mother—sometimes mistake for a man's on the phone.

I move into a shared room with two twin beds and two desks. My roommate, oddly enough, turns out to be the blond anorexic Brentwood mom from my last treatment center.

"Oh, wow, it's you," I say when I walk in.

"Yep. It's me," she says with mock enthusiasm.

There's an awkward silence.

"You were never nice to me in rehab," she continues.

"I'm sorry," I say. "I was in a bad place, and I can be an asshole on the best of days. I'll be nice to you now."

"Yeah?"

"Your bed is six feet from mine. What choice do I have?" I smile.

She laughs.

Living in a small confined space with somebody who starts off as a stranger can be ... challenging. You quickly learn "boundaries," "tolerance," and "consideration"—all things I sorely lacked before. Also, there is no semblance of privacy, so forget masturbation ... except when they're asleep, which I admit is pretty creepy. You can also throw modesty out the window, unless you're willing to trot off to the bathroom or duck into the closet to change every time.

I come to learn that Terry—that's her name—is a nurse with three kids she lost custody of following an "accidental overdose." She denies it was a suicide attempt.

Terry is a total caretaker, and thank God, because I need her. She is the only person to ever put up with my unnaturally loud snoring. She also reminds me every week to wash my sheets. Lots of times she'll even do my laundry for me.

"I'm doing a load," she'll chirp. "Wanna throw anything in?"

And nothing beats living with a nurse. She has something in her well-stocked cabinet for every cold, cough, or infection you could ever dream up. And drug addicts, believe it or not, are total hypochondriacs once we get clean. It's so odd, since we used to shoot stuff into our veins that some Mexican guy in a hoodie spit out of his mouth on a dark corner.

Terry's also in great shape. Despite those three kids, she has washboard abs and the ass of a twenty-four-year-old stripper. She takes kickboxing, Zumba, and all those other types of group torture classes. Because she has discipline and I need some, we start going to the gym together. She wears a white lululemon sports bra and matching yoga pants and impeccably clean running shoes. I wear a ripped T-shirt, droopy sweatpants, and dusty old sneakers. We are the odd couple of sobriety.

I'm waiting impatiently by our bedroom door, ready to get my gym on.

"Are you putting on lip liner?" I ask, watching her crouched in front of the full-length mirror.

"Yes."

"We're going to the fucking gym. Who puts on lip liner before they go to the gym?"

"This insecure bitch."

"Let's goooooo . . ." I groan.

"Okay, okay! But please don't make those weird grunting noises when we're there, and don't sing aloud to your headphones."

"Boner killer."


I drive to the Volunteer Center in West L.A. to sign up for my community service. My court date is looming, and I haven't even started to chip away at the 240 hours of community service I need to complete to have my domestic violence charge dismissed. My other quasi-criminal friends tell me that you have to at least start your sentence to have any hope of getting an extension from the judge. They also tell me that there are plenty of work options to choose from. If you're lucky, you can score a stint at a local thrift store, sitting on your ass and getting all the good stuff before it hits the floor. So I am hopeful.

I walk into the tiny, barren office. I'm surprised that there is no line. I sort of imagined it as a DMV for lawbreakers. I hand the woman behind the counter my court paperwork, and she pulls out a sheet with potential venues I can volunteer at.

"Ooh, yeah. That thrift store in Echo Park would be perfect," I coo.

"No," the thirty-something compassionless Hispanic woman says. "This one is for you." And with that, she and her two-inch glittery nail point to "HBT" (which I learn is short for "Hollywood Beautification Team").

"What is that?" I ask.

"Graffiti removal," she says.

"Um…yeah. I'm not great at that kind of, uh…manual labor in the hot sun kind of thing. What else you got?"

"Nothing else for you. Because of your offense, you have to do hard labor. Only this."

"My offense? Excuse me?"

"NEXT!" And with that, she hands me a sign-in paper with endless lines to be filled with dates and signatures. On the back are instructions for the Hollywood Beautification Team: "Bring your ID. Arrive at seven a.m. Don't be late. Wear work clothes. Bring a sack lunch."

I go home. Terry is FaceTiming with her kids.

"Please don't swear," she whispers.

I roll my eyes. I flop onto my bed and look at my phone. I have a new Facebook message from a New York comic-slash-actor named Bradley.

"Facebook says I should poke you," he writes.

"Well, I think poking is stupid, and I wouldn't recommend taking life advice from Facebook," I write back.

Then I log onto Tinder. It's become evident that none of the guys on Tinder actually read your "profile," they just look at the pictures. I get it. Male sexuality is primarily visual. And Tinder isn't exactly land of the soulmate seekers. So I delete my witty blurb about being a writer and a comic and replace it with: "If rehab, jail, and mental hospitals turn you on, I might be the girl of your dreams…" I then add "I'm also handy with knives," but I delete that. I'm already a magnet for psychos.

No sooner do I post my new profile than I match with some new guy. He sends me a message: "You're hot and you know it and it kinda bugs." Charming intro. I block him.

# CHAPTER EIGHT

I am walking down Hollywood Boulevard. It is 6:45 a.m. and it is my very first day of community service. The air is full of morning fog and the stench of stale urine. I am pale and sleepy, wearing old sweatpants. I'm carrying my "sack lunch" of girly nibbling food: grapes, nuts, Pirate's Booty, and three cans of Diet Coke. I pass a nudie club: "Deja Vu Showgirls—1,000s of beautiful girls and 3 ugly ones!" There are a few homeless dudes shuffling down the sidewalk and some annoying perky girls jogging. I see a solemn bald man look longingly into the window of a men's wig shop.

I turn onto Cherokee. A bunch of Mexican men in hoodies are sitting on the curb. I walk up and sit down. I smile awkwardly. Nobody says a word to me.

Right at seven a.m., the doors open. We all file in. I am one of only three girls and the only white chick.

"If you are only working four hours or have paperwork, get in the blue line. Everybody else, green line," barks a thick, mean-looking Native American woman with hair down to her ass.

I stand frozen in the green line, not sure where to go.

A rocker dude with a ponytail, tattoos, and a nose piercing nudges me. "You're new, right? You wanna be in the blue line."

"Oh, okay, thanks."

I make my way to the front of the blue line where I'm given the lowdown. They copy my ID, take my paperwork, and send me off.

"I'm going to be cleaning graffiti, right?" I ask an older male Mexican crew boss.

"No. Today you are sweeping the streets," he says. He has a bushy mustache and a shitty faded tattoo on his forearm.

"Oh."

"You've swept before, right?" he asks me.

"Well, I've swept privately ... I've never swept *publicly*. I'm more of a private sweeper ... like the Tina Turner song." I laugh. He doesn't.

"Okay, here." He hands me a disgusting broom and a huge, crusty dustpan. "You want gloves?"

"Uhh ... yeah. And a hazmat suit if you have one." Again ... crickets.

I am doing what is officially called "volunteer" community service, but I'm not sure exactly what I'm "volunteering" for. *Not* to go to jail? In a similar vein, I believe the Chinese Army was referred to as the People's "Volunteer" Army. Anyway, according to the courts, I have "volunteered" for thirty long days of "community labor," which is "community service" but with a heavy dose of grunt work.

I spend the next eight hours sweeping up dirty diapers, syringes, whip-it canisters, and cigarette butts off Santa Monica Boulevard. We have a ten-minute break in the morning, thirty minutes for lunch, and another ten-minute break in the afternoon. If you are caught on your cell phone at any time other than break time, you get sent home. If you don't wear your seat belt while in the truck, you get sent home. If you cop an attitude or slack off, you get sent home. You get the picture.

"So how much time you got?" the rocker guy asks me. He's one of the very few jailbirds who speak English at all.

"Thirty days," I answer.

"Jesus Christ! What'd you do? Rob a bank?"

I quickly learn that most people are here for DUIs, garnering them about ten to fifteen days. One other girl is also here for domestic violence. She's some semi-infamous girl from a TV show who beat the shit out of her boyfriend, but unlike me, she only got fifteen days because she didn't use a "weapon" (although I'd hardly call a dull bread knife wielded by a skinny desert Jew on a three-hundred-pound dude a "weapon"). After hearing her drone on about her outfit for the Playboy party and her appearance on Playboy radio, I couldn't resist Googling her. She is famous, but only for her fake tits, fake nose, fake lips, and bitchy personality. I also stumble upon what appears to be her tweet for that day: "Just finished hiking for 8 hours with underprivileged kids." Really? Is that what you'd call it?

At lunch at Jack in the Box, I eat my hippie rabbit food and drink endless Diet Coke. One of the girls on my chain gang asks me, "What's that tattooed on your finger?" referring to my ex-husband's name branding my ring finger.

"This? Just stupidity and optimism, my friend. Stupidity and optimism…"

After the brief lunch break, we are back on the broom.

"Just pick up the trash; don't worry about the leaves," the Native American crew leader tells me.

"Okay," I call to her.

Fifteen minutes later: "Don't just pick up the trash; get the leaves!"

"Oh, okay."

Fifteen minutes later: "Listen…you are the only one I am having to correct. If I have to speak to you again, you are going home."

"I am trying my best here. Really I am." It is evident she hates me, and I can do nothing right.

At three thirty, we are released. I have never been so tired in my life. My back has seized up. I'm sunburned. There are leaves in my hair. My feet are throbbing. I am limping.

Four things I learn from my first day of community labor:

1. My back hates me and hates sweeping even more.
2. I need to learn Spanish immediately.
3. There are lots of condoms east of La Brea and south of Santa Monica Boulevard.
4. I look terrible in a tan Dickie's shirt that says "Clean Team" on the back.

I get home to the sober living house, hobble into the kitchen, and wolf down anything I can find. I hobble into the bathroom to hose down. I take off my shoes and socks, and my feet are black from street soot. I can hear myself moaning. After eight hours of sweeping up Hollywood, I smell like an underground New York nightclub: all sweat and latex. I watch as the street dirt washes off my body and circles the drain. I hobble into my room and collapse onto the bed. I fall immediately into a deep sleep.

I'm in bed for two days. I'm so fucking exhausted and sore that I can't move. Linda comes to pick me up. She takes me to a cheap Thai spa at a local mini mall. I listen to the soothing sounds of a CD of bamboo pipes and stare at a bad wall mural of the Huangshan Mountains while a stocky Asian guy who speaks no English vigorously rubs me down. Cheap massage and Tylenol…a Beverly Hills princess-turned-felon's best friends.

It's always amusing to me to see Linda try to tell some guy who doesn't speak a lick of English about her hip. Thanks to bad genetics and a lifetime of long-distance running, Linda had a hip replacement at thirty-seven. I remember going with her to her first doctor's appointment. I thought the waiting room would be filled with athletes, sports stars, and marathoners, but there were only eighty-year-olds shuffling around on walkers.

Linda shot me a look as she took in the scene, and I ran out of the office and collapsed onto the hallway floor laughing. Finally I walked back in, wiping my eyes.

"Keep it together," she whispered out of the corner of her mouth, pinching my arm.

Of course, when she met with the orthopedic surgeon, the first thing out of his mouth was "You're way too young to have a hip replacement." But then he took a look at her X-rays and immediately scheduled her for surgery. As he rattled off all the drugs he'd give her for pain during and after the surgery, I gave Linda an excited thumbs-up on the heavy narcotics and a disappointed thumbs-down on the Tylenol-based and non-opiate meds. The night she had the operation, I slept in a chair in her hospital room, even though she was too sedated to need me or remember. It was a rare chance to try to repay just a tiny bit of her angelic devotion to me. For months after the surgery, she walked with a limp, and she had a handicapped parking permit for the next half year. God, that premium parking was divine.

So this Asian guy is standing there about to start his aggressive rub-down, and she says, "No good. Hurt. Operation," pointing to her left hip.

"Ahh," the masseur says, not understanding a fucking word.

"She used to be a man," I pipe in, lying on the table next to her.

"You're still a man," she shoots back.


I pull into my now-usual parking lot for community labor. It's run by an old Iranian guy who's always in his minivan listening to Christian radio. Today he's asleep. I tap softly on the glass. He wakes up, takes my money, tears off my orange ticket, and tells me to "Have a good day." The first day I parked there, I asked him how much it would be. "Seven dollars," he said. "Today."

"What do you mean, 'today'?"

"Tomorrow might not be seven dollars. Might be more."

"Great. But it will never be less, right?"

"No."

"Uh-huh." Yeah, praise the lord, Achmed.

I'm on the street-sweeping crew again, this time with Geraldo, a lanky Hispanic guy, maybe sixty, with a handlebar mustache and eyes that lin-ger too long. The day's route is down Vermont—from Hollywood Boule-vard to the 101 and back. It's easily four miles, and all in the blazing sun. The good part about Geraldo is that he's a lazy fuck, so we get a lengthy lunch break—an hour—and then if we finish early, we get to sleep in the truck until it's time to head back to the center. The bad part of Geraldo is that he's a lecherous fuck. "You so *flaca* (Spanish for 'skinny') and flex-ible. Why your husband get rid of you?" he keeps asking me, followed by unwanted shoulder massages. This type of shit keeps happening until I ask him casually what "sexual harassment lawsuit" is in *español*.

I notice that most people don't talk to any of us on the crew. In the mornings, the homeless—already drunk—will bid us "good morning," but everybody else ignores us. Once in a while, some dumbass will thank us for our "environmentalism" or "volunteer work." But most people, even the hobos, know who we are. One ratty black homeless guy yells, "Keep doing what you are doing. I know it sucks, but it beats the pen!" We all laugh.

You learn a lot sweeping the streets. For instance, did you know that Sunday August first is the Annual Festival of El Salvador's Independence? And more importantly, did you know it is also "Latin Labor Day" at Club Papi?

I come home absolutely fried. Terry is in our room, slogging away on paperwork to get custody of her kids.

She is amped. "Oh, my God, my ex is such a dick. And look how dark my spray tan is. I look like an Oompa Loompa. And that shmuck I went out with last week blocked me on Facebook. What the eff?"

"Terry, you have to shut up. I just swept poo in the sun for eight hours. I wish my problems were an orange spray tan or some douche on Facebook."

I am a working man now. When I come home, I want a sandwich, a blow job, and silence. I pull off my T-shirt, and Terry notices I'm emaciated. The stress and exertion from community labor are taking a toll on my naturally slim frame.

"You're too skinny," Terry says.

"I don't care. I just don't want to go to jail." I yawn, picking a twig out of my hair. "I'm rocking the Auschwitz winter casuals look," I joke.

"Seriously, Amy, you're not eating enough. You're walking all day. When you're doing that, you can eat frosting and lard and still lose weight."

Terry then switches into mommy gear. Every three hours for the next few weeks she comes into my room with mac and cheese or an apple and peanut butter. And despite her soft voice and sweet demeanor, she can be a mean food Nazi, hovering over my bed and refusing to go away till I eat everything. Thank God for her, because within a month, I'm still thin but I no longer look terminally ill.

Terry is always hounding me. "Get off your phone and eat, Amy."

"Okay, okay."

"What are you doing?" she asks.

"I'm on Tinder."

"What's Tinder?"

"It's like eBay for cock."

"Ewww!"

"I'm serious. It's too easy to get laid on here. 'Crazy' and 'criminal charges' seem to fly if you're hot enough."

"I thought you wanted a boyfriend?" she asks.

"I do want a boyfriend. I want to get married again. But I'm not going to stay celibate till I find the next Mr. Dresner."

"Are you telling these guys you're sober?"

"Yeah—and that's not going over so well. It's what I'd guess having herpes must be like. They're into you, and then you tell them and it's like 'sayonara, bitch'!"

"Are there cute boys on there?"

"Yeah, but most of the hot ones can't spell. And if you can't spell, I can't deal. Keep it moving, honey."

"We have totally different taste, though," Terry says.

"Right...you like old Jews. Yeah, I can't fuck my own tribe. They're all yours."

*Bing!* I look at my phone. I have a new match. He's twenty-five. Jesus Christ...

He instantly sends a message: "u seem fun. But can u keep up w/a wild child like moi?"

I chuckle and message back, "Honey, u have no idea who ur talking to..."

# CHAPTER NINE

There's a new kid on my crew. I guess—accurately—that he's twenty-seven. I smell money. We spoiled kids can sniff each other out. He's also newly sober. I smell that, too.

"What'd you get busted for?" I ask as we take our morning break outside McDonald's.

"DUI and possession of Xanax," he says, glancing over stupid-looking oversize yellow Ray-Bans.

"Party on!" I say sarcastically.

"So dumb. I was totally done with my last community labor, even finished the DUI class. I was going in that morning to see the judge and have everything dismissed."

"And?"

"I put on this jacket that I hadn't worn in a while..."

"I already know where this is going."

"...and I set off the metal detector in the court building. They searched me and found some foil with heroin trails. Bam! Not just violating probation, but a whole new charge of felony possession."

"Ouch."

"Yep." He takes a drag off his cigarette. "So...what...we just sweep all day? Doesn't seem bad."

I laugh. "You're obviously new."

I lay down the rules for him: Don't look at your phone while sweeping. Don't talk to strangers. Don't smoke while sweeping. Make sure you get the gutters and all the cigarette butts. Don't take off your community labor shirt.

"God, you could work here. You know everything."

"Dude, after a week of this shit, so will you."

We are slowly making our way down Vermont. The new kid is lazy and slow and misses all the fucking cigarette butts. He doesn't realize it's a *team* effort and that what he doesn't pick up, doesn't *not* get picked up. It gets picked up by the rest of us. Working on the street sweeping crew, I've come to realize that it's just as easy to do a job well as it is to do it poorly. But try telling that to a twenty-seven-year-old junkie... or even to me a few weeks ago.

Then it hits me: I finally have a work ethic. Holy shit, miracles do happen! I'd heard a saying tossed around the rooms for years: "How you do anything is how you do everything." I had just scoffed. I did some research, and it's not classic AA scripture but a quote from T. Harv Eker. Think about it: how you do anything is how you do everything. I'd been half-assing my whole life. I'd figure out the least work I needed to do, and I'd do only that. Not a fucking smidge more. But how had that been working out for me? Not very well. What if I started to give my all to everything I did? And not because I was being yelled at by my father or a sponsor or a Hispanic crew boss?

"Hey..." the kid asks me, "ever find money or drugs out here?"

"Dude, it's community labor, not a fucking treasure hunt."

He chuckles. He's easygoing. Later, I try to make him smell my disgusting sweaty hands, fingertips all pruny from hours in rubber gloves. I mean if I can't haze the new guy, where's the fun in being the old hand on the chain gang?

I occasionally snap a picture of these guys (from the back, of course, to preserve their anonymity). I show Linda, and she tells me she wants one of the uniforms—a holey, paint-splattered T-shirt, or one of the grimy ones that say "Business Improvement District," or maybe a tan button-down with "Clean Team" on the back.

Her request does not come as a surprise. She collects all the clothes from my bad decisions and wears them as pajamas. So far she has jail socks, psych ward pants and gown—and soon—a community labor T-shirt. Needless to say, she has an obsession with the dark side of life—while somehow avoiding all of the legal and psychiatric pitfalls herself. It's nice to have a friend who sees the humor and, dare I say, the souvenir opportunities, in my epic life fails.

We are on Vermont, up by Hollywood Boulevard, sweeping the gutters. A slim young girl with erratically chopped hair, smeared black eye makeup, and rotting, chipped front teeth is manically gesticulating and walking up the street. She is obviously a speed freak. She is wearing a T-shirt that barely covers her ass with ratty underwear underneath. No pants. She has on stained fringed boots and something tied around her head. I feel a weird fear come up inside me, but then I remember my newest motto: "See everybody for their humanity—the way you want to be seen for yours."

She walks up and smiles and does a twirl.

"Where are your pants, girl?" I ask.

"Some Armenian bitch burnt them!"

"Oh, shit."

"Are you Argentinian?" she asks.

"No, I'm from here. Why?" I smile.

"Because with your hair up like that . . . you look Argentinian."

"Thanks." She is referring to my messy bun that keeps my long blond locks off my sweaty face and away from the street filth.

She starts to ramble on about how she can feel people "meditate." I just smile and laugh and pretend to understand. Then she gently touches my arm and prances off. My heart breaks a little.

I remember the first time I did speed. I was twenty-four and had moved from L.A. to San Francisco on a whim, looking for answers. San Francisco—the city with the highest population of lost souls, transients, and fuck-ups. I don't know why I thought salvation was being doled out on every corner there like some flyer for a free show, but I did. And I couldn't have been more wrong.

Driving up the I-5 from Los Angeles in my '67 navy-blue Thunderbird with the Red Hot Chili Peppers blasting (fuck you, it was 1993—they were very cool then), I was trying desperately to convince myself that I was on the precipice of a life epiphany. This was a great—no, *the* great—new chapter in my life where that missing piece would be revealed, and everything would finally fall into place. On my drive, I got food poisoning from a tofu burger that had sat in my car for too long, and then I spent the night puking in a Motel 6. I tried not to let that spook me as a bad omen. I had decided this would be a vision quest. In retrospect, it was really just an alcoholic pulling a geographic.

When I was fifteen or sixteen, my father, in an attempt to bring up his kid in Beverly Hills with "a sense of values," had made a bet with me: if I didn't smoke, drink, or do drugs before age eighteen, he'd give me $1,000. Yes, that's how Jews raise their kids. Bribery.

Drugs scared me. I'd always maintained they were a cop-out, a cheap escape from your own feelings, from real life. In college, I was disgusted when I came back to my dorm room one day to find my roommate and her bouncy sorority sisters snorting lines of coke off my laptop.

By this point, my parents had already endured my eating disorders, clinical depression, and chronic unemployability punctuated with radically unrealistic career choices: actor, model, filmmaker. Since I hadn't shown a predisposition toward drugs by twenty-four, I think they felt it a safe bet that they wouldn't be one of my adventures in self-destruction.

As I drove up north, I had this overwhelming feeling that I didn't really know myself (as if we ever do). Had I been avoiding sex, drugs, and performing just because I was afraid? Or was I really not interested in these things? Fear and aversion can feel pretty similar.

I *had* to find out who I was. But how do you do that? I decided I'd figure out who I was by figuring out who I wasn't. It would be a process of elimination. I made a vow to myself. I would say yes to every experience that presented itself, no matter how much fear or aversion I had. I would embrace whatever came my way with gusto.

I didn't know a soul when I moved up north, nor did I have a job. But within a week, I had both. Cool. This new "throw yourself into it" thing was working for me.

Excited, I called my father.

"I got a job," I said.

"Oh yeah? Doing what, Ames?"

"I'm working at a restaurant."

"Are you a hostess?"

"No."

"Are you a waitress?"

"Nope."

"I give up."

"I'm a dishwasher."

"Do they know you've washed about ten dishes in your whole fucking life?"

Honestly, dishwashing turned out to be a pretty sweet gig. The place I worked was a tiny Italian bistro in the Upper Haight owned by a couple of queens, walking distance from my new pad. I would wash dishes in the back and watch TV while the owner's boyfriend, Larry, cooked these fabulous pasta dishes. It was low stress except for this aggro lesbian who, for some mysterious reason, sneered at me and hated me from the moment I arrived.

San Francisco in the early nineties was the opposite of Los Angeles. L.A. was all cookie-cutter beauty, fancy cars, and bling. S.F. was creative expression, drugs, and anti-capitalism. There, panhandling was cool. It's the pride of the underdog. I'm pretty sure half the scruffy kids with lip rings begging for change on the Haight had college degrees and middle-class parents. But—hey, man—they were bucking the system, choosing freedom over corporate America. And they did seem free, and I envied them for it.

A month or two in, it was obvious I needed a second job. There were lots of opportunities if you could cocktail or waitress, but I'd never done either. I am incredibly clumsy and have never been able to do the standard restaurant thing—balance three plates on an arm or even one tray topped with fancy drinks. But one day strolling down the Haight, I saw an Ethiopian restaurant. I noticed that African food is served on a single manhole-size plate, and a single plate I *could* carry! I filled out an application and, miraculously, was hired. I quickly became the highest-tipped waitress there, though I have to be honest, only because I was funny. Even with just one plate to balance, agile I was not.

One evening, exhausted from my afternoon dishwashing shift, I was worrying how I'd get through my waitressing shift. My neighbor offered me a line of some pinkish powder, saying it would give me energy. Without much thought, I snorted it. It burned like fire. I went to work, and soon I was shaking, overly energized and not a little bit irritable. I vowed never to do the stuff again.

Fast forward a few months. I was deep in the local spoken-word scene, where the poets had nicknames like "Stinky," "Mike Prophet," and "Dick Ranger," and most were junkies, tweakers, and/or alcoholics. I was drinking. A lot. I was primarily living off a small trust fund that my grandfather had left me. But nobody around me had money, so I pretended I didn't have any, either. I wore long skirts, ratty T-shirts, and sandals. I sported toe rings, greasy hair, and wooden beads.

One night at this dive bar where we all read bad poetry, I was again offered a line of speed, and for some reason, I took it. But this time, it made me feel different. Years of self-hatred and anxiety instantly vanished. I felt like it was okay—good, even—to be me. This is what I had been chasing with decades of therapy and psychiatric meds. And here it was: Prozac...with wings! Synthetic self-esteem and bliss. From that moment, I was hooked. Who wouldn't be?

I began to snort speed daily, and within seven short months, I was completely strung out. I never saw it coming.

It's like bingeing on food. You don't gain weight overnight. You wake up months later and you're like: holy shit, I'm fat. It's the same with drugs. You don't become a drug addict overnight. Months go by, and you wake up one day and you're like: holy shit, I'm a tweaker.

Substance abuse was unknown territory for me. I hadn't even ever been *around* drug addicts. I thought I was just a tourist in druggyland, visiting, experimenting…even if that experimenting was all day every day. I was lying to myself, but I didn't realize it till years later. Or maybe I knew, but I wanted to believe the lies. Same difference.

I had been living in Cole Valley at the time, renting a room from a husky redhead who fancied herself a musician but tended bar to pay the bills. She was adamantly against hard drugs but drank like a sailor and smoked pot like a hippie. The apartment always stank like my Nag Champa incense and her shitty cheap perfume.

One day, she frowned at me from across the living room, and then asked, "Are you high?"

I was busted, and instead of being cool, I got rabidly defensive.

"You first. Are *you* fucking high?" I fired back.

"You're on speed," she said. "I'm just stoned."

"Ooh, the devil's lettuce," I mocked, the speed spurring me on. "Yes, pot is just an herb! In fact, it's God's medicine!"

She just stared at me, speechless.

I glared back at her and then continued, "Oh, give me a fucking break! We're both on drugs, okay?" I was high and angry, and the words came out like bursts from a machine gun.

"You need to move out," she announced calmly.

"My fucking pleasure!" And with that, I stomped into my bedroom and slammed the door.

In my room, I laid out some thick lines and snorted them. I counseled myself, "Stay high. Stay numb. Don't freak out." Then I heard one of her many boyfriends come in. Some whispering. Then fucking. She let out little yelps as her stupid red head banged against the wall.

"Fucking whore," I said aloud.

Within a week, I moved to Lower Haight, across from the projects, into a three-bedroom place with skinheads and gutter punks. We all paid rent, but it felt more like a flophouse.

My drug habit quickly escalated in this new habitat, and it became increasingly apparent that I needed to start buying my own stash instead of mooching off my junkie roommates. I remember the first time I copped. There was this Venice gangster named Blade, a massive white dude with long, thick dreadlocks. He spoke slowly, like an old-school cowboy, using words sparingly, as if each one cost him money. He sold guns and weed but was known to be able to get anything.

"I want speed," I said, trying to sound casual.

"I don't deal that shit. It'll kill you," he said flatly.

"Oh," I said, dejected.

"I know somebody. They'll call."

As I started to thank him, he hung up. Evidently I was too polite for the drug trade.

A few hours later, somebody was at my place handing me a quarter bag of crystal meth. He was in a dark hoodie, and he looked pissed off.

"Hold on," I said. I left him standing in the empty living room as I took the small plastic bag of grimy powder around the apartment, showing it to my roommates. *Does this look like good quality stuff? Is this a fat quarter?* I was clueless.

The guy looked irritated but said nothing. He took my money and left.

The phone rang. It was Blade. "Listen, you're a little green. I'm gonna hook you up with this girl who slings crystal. Name's Belinda. I think she'll be a better fit." Later, I found out that the guy wanted to beat the fuck out of me, but Blade stepped in. Apparently, there was also some talk of kidnapping me and selling me into the sex trade. Honestly, I was kind of flattered.

Belinda was a bosomy Goth girl with translucent skin and jet black hair. She had a very relaxed demeanor for a speed freak, but her house reeked of "tweaker"—clutter everywhere: shit she'd found, was collecting, refinishing, fixing. The land of broken toys.

I'd call her regularly from a pay phone, with the usual coded question to see if she was holding: "Are you on the program?"

Every now and then, she and her boyfriend would clean up, and I'd be forced to find another source.

"Oh, no. I don't do that anymore. Speed is evil. It's bad for your heart. You should quit."

"Whateverrrrr." I'd hang up, annoyed. Luckily, she never stayed clean for long. Within weeks, she'd be dealing again.

The shithole where I lived got creepier and more crowded as it became the hangout/shelter for the local homeless druggies. There was an alcoholic marine who got so shit-faced, he fell through our glass coffee table. There was a speed freak named Bicycle Bob, who had Graves' disease and always rode a bicycle. He had a long, narrow face and bulging eyes. One day he got hit by a truck and split his head open. Hospital stapled it back together. Next thing I know he was "recuperating" on our couch for a week, like a bug-eyed druggy Frankenstein.

My least favorite person was this guy known as Dancin' Dick Dorsey. His skin had that green hue not uncommon to chronic drug addicts. He spoke quickly, with conviction, like a TV minister, and always wore a long black trench coat. We hated each other. I knew he was an evil sociopath, and he knew I was a fraud—some trustafarian masquerading as a tough girl junkie.

My favorite housemate was Stinky, a self-loathing geek with short, bleached-blond hair, oversize Buddy Holly glasses, and a big bone through his septum. We had the same birthday, though he was a year younger, and I felt a deep kinship with him. Like Stinky, I felt broken, ugly, and unwanted. I just didn't wear those sentiments on the outside. Stinky, however, tried to look as hideous as possible. His body was a billboard for all his negative feelings about himself, with ridiculous tattoos, cut marks, and repulsive piercings. His life revolved around comic books, fucking fat girls, and speed. He was always broke—but ever innovative. There was a bar near our place that had a "ladies' night" when girls drank for free. Stinky would dress up in drag, handcuff himself to the bar, and get his drink on. He didn't care. In fact, I think he enjoyed being humiliated.

One night, I was at a house party in Upper Haight. All the poets and spoken word people were there, including a buff UPS worker who liked to play guitar in a tutu and went by the stage name "Captain Magliano." I thought he was an idiot, but we had hooked up a few times. I'd been high, and it was hard to say no to a body like his, even if he had a personality like a windy tunnel. Making matters worse, he was Catholic, extremely chauvinistic, and really angry that he was attracted to a mouthy Jew like me.

On this particular night, I was very drunk. I turned toward the door just as Stinky walked in, wearing a scoop-neck black Freddie Mercury–like leotard, miniskirt, heels, and long white gloves. He was covered in silver glitter. His eyes and chest sparkled like broken glass in the low light. He looked completely androgynous, and he was, for the first time, astonishingly beautiful. And he knew it.

"Can I talk to you for a second?" I asked him innocently.

"Sure."

I lured him into the bathroom and immediately locked the door behind us and shoved him against the wall.

"You look so fucking hot," I said. And with that, our mouths met, and we began furiously kissing and violently grappling at each other. Five minutes later, we walked out of the bathroom like nothing happened. We never spoke of it.

One night, Dancin' Dick took Stinky out to a strip club to see some titties and let him shoot speed for the first time. Of course, like the novice he was, Stinky shot the whole quarter out of the gate and immediately went into amphetamine psychosis. Convinced that the stripper's flower was miked, he jumped onto the stage to try to dismantle it. He and Dancin' Dick were quickly kicked out of the club, at which point Dancin' Dick just parked Stinky outside our door and took off. Yep, Stinky was our problem now: paranoid, hyper, talking a mile a minute about nothing.

I stripped him down to his boxers. As I pulled off his T-shirt, I saw "bed-wetter" crudely tattooed on his back.

"When did you get that?!" I asked in horror.

"I can hear the cops. Don't you hear the helicopters? They are *coming!*" His speech was pressured, like he couldn't get the words out of his mouth fast enough. And his eyes—they were huge and shiny and black like marbles.

I tucked him into my bed.

I tried to sound stern and convincing. "I'm going to the store. Don't fucking move."

"Watch out for the pigs. They've bugged everything." His hands were flying around him like little birds.

"I'll do that, Stinky."

Returning from the store, as I approached the apartment, I noticed that "HELTER SKELTER" had been freshly painted in red on the front window... from the inside.

Fuck.

I walked in the door, and the smell to which I'd grown immune suddenly hit me: moldy carpets, stale dishes, dirty laundry, and the slow decay that accompanies addiction.

"Stinky?" I called to him.

I turned the corner into the living room to see Stinky standing there. He was clad only in black patent leather high heels, fishnet stockings, and women's red lace underwear. He was clutching an unplugged electric carving knife.

"Come get me, you fucking pigs! I'm ready for you!" he yelled.

"Nobody is fucking coming," I said, irritated. "Jesus. Please get in bed." I gently took the carving knife from his hand and led him back into my bedroom.

His psychosis lasted for weeks. I was worried he wasn't going to come out of it. There was a guy on the scene who had done acid once and had a psychotic break. He had become really fucking weird ever since— still sweet, but kind of permanently out to lunch. After a few days, I let Stinky go back to work at the underground bookstore, the local poet hangout. Every night for weeks he'd come home and report on all the unmarked cars that had followed him throughout the day.

You'd think watching somebody lose their mind right in front of you might be enough to put you off drugs forever. It wasn't. In my defense, and I'm no geneticist, but I think there was a biological element to my immediate and unmitigated adoration of speed. I eventually discovered that my mother had been addicted to amphetamines for fifteen years, starting when she was a young model. They were given to her to help keep her weight down. And then there was my uncle, her schizophrenic brother, who had been a meth freak for the majority of his life. I'm not pawning it all off on biology. There was definitely a psychological hook as well. I can only describe the sensation of being high on speed for me as "coming home," a feeling of sweet relief, like I'd been psychically drowning for years and had just stumbled across a pharmaceutical life raft. Granted, that life raft was pinkish white powder that came in small zip-locked bags, but it still felt like salvation to me. And I wasn't giving it up without a fight.

# CHAPTER TEN

I'm driving home, exhausted, sweaty, and covered in paint from another day of community labor. Only twenty-three more days of this shit to go. Holy fuck, am I going to make it? My phone bings. A text from my ex. Ugh. This should be fun.

"Well, it's official. We're divorced. Best of luck to you."

*Best of luck?* The formality alone should make me laugh. That's what you'd say to an applicant you interviewed who didn't get the job, not somebody you were married to for almost four years. But it doesn't make me laugh, it makes me sad. Really sad. I'm struck by the complete lack of sentimentality, like he was casually flicking a bug off his sleeve.

I walk into my room at the sober living, and Terry is there.

"Hey!" she pipes up.

"Hey," I say dejectedly.

"How'd it go today?"

"Exhausting, as usual."

"Your eye is red."

"I've been crying."

"No...like it's really, really red."

I look in the mirror, and my right eye is pomegranate red and the corner is swollen. "Fucking great. What is that?"

Terry inspects it with nursely precision. "Conjunctivitis. You've got pinkeye."

"Perfect. More treasures from the street."

I take my eye into the shower, do my usual *Silkwood*-style scrubdown, and then lie down on the bed. I'm just dozing off when Terry yelps, "Oh, my God!"

"Wha...?"

"You know Brendan? From our rehab?"

"Yeah, I used to fuck him. Why? He hitting on you?"

"He's dead."

Brendan, at thirty-three years old, died of a heart attack in his sleep. He was having a pretty severe relapse. We hadn't spoken for a while because, after my drunken debacle at his place, he deemed me "crazy" and cut all ties. But when I'd last seen him, he'd been on his newest kick to "moderate" his drinking, "The Sinclair Method." The Sinclair Method involves taking naltrexone, an opioid antagonist they typically give to people with compulsivity problems (sex, gambling, etc.). You take this drug *before* you drink, and it's supposed to quell that insatiable urge that makes alcoholics keep drinking well after the party is over. Well, Brendan's "moderate" drinking on naltrexone included putting away fifteen beers in a few hours while gambling on the latest game and having sex with me, so I was none too impressed. And now he was dead. Ultimately, of alcoholism. So that Sinclair shit obviously didn't work.

"His funeral is next Sunday," Terry told me. "You wanna go?"

"Yeah. For sure...You mind if I turn the lights down? I'm so tired."

I hit the switch and lie down in my bed, staring at the ceiling, tears streaming down my face in the dark. I can't believe Brendan died. Jesus Christ. I wish I had been able to say good-bye or sorry or even just have a laugh about that vomit-splattered drunken rendezvous.

"What were you crying about earlier?" Terry asks in the dark.

"My divorce is official," I say.

I'm now a forty-two-year-old divorcée. A fucking cliché, clinging to my youth through meaningless sex with young dudes, one of whom is now dead. God, I'm pathetic.

"That's great. Congratulations. He was an asshole."

"Yeah, but so was I. I don't know. I feel fucked up about it, like I'm still in mourning. Not so much for what we had, but for what we could have had. I swear, divorce is kind of like grieving a death, except the person is still alive, hates you, and doesn't want to give you any money. Does that make any sense?"

"Totally."

"I'm single again, and that's cool, but now I'm a divorcée... somebody good enough to marry but too damaged to stay married to."

There's a long silence, and then I add, "But hey, I'm still alive. I still have a chance to fuck up another relationship. Brendan doesn't even have that."

When I'm not chipping away at my community labor, I'm either having empty sex with people who don't love me (mostly comics) or attending Sex and Love Addicts Anonymous meetings to try to stop doing it. I did stand-up professionally for almost five years and was married the majority of that time. Back then, all the fellow comedians who wanted to fuck me were grudgingly respectful of my vows. However, once they heard I was going through a divorce, I was inundated. Didn't matter if they were married or living with their girlfriends, they were on my jock. Finding comics who want to fuck is like finding a vegan who wants to talk about being a vegan. Beyond easy.

Just like with drugs, I keep thinking I have a handle on my sex addiction. I get a few weeks or even months under my belt without "acting out," and I tell myself, *Oh, I got this.* And then I relapse. What I've come to realize is that the beast of sex addiction takes lengthy naps. During those naps, I am convinced I am cured. But then it is on me again, like a spirit possession. I notice that the urge to check out with sex is often triggered by a call from my ex and all the feelings of rejection and trauma that he provokes in me. Whatever the cause, the urge gets stronger and stronger until it cannot be denied, and I cave. There's even an anticipatory trembling on the way to meet a date, oddly reminiscent of the rush to meet the dealer. But afterward, I almost always feel empty—filled only with shame. That's when I make those meaningless promises to myself: *That was the last time... never again.* Until the next time, of course.

What is becoming increasingly clear to me is that I am lying to myself. What I really want is love and companionship and tenderness. Sex is a cheap second prize but the only thing I think I deserve or can find. Also, it's weird how I can have great sex with people I don't feel connected to, but I can't have even decent sex with somebody I care about. This is concerning. Intimacy disorder, anyone? It feels like sex and love are in two different boxes for me, and the idea of combining them requires a level of intimacy and vulnerability that is nothing short of terrifying.

In the meantime, I get busy rationalizing my promiscuity as being "free" and "liberated." *I can fuck like a guy,* I say to myself. *I'm not a slut. I'm a female stud.* It's total bullshit, and deep down, I know it. I bond to each of these losers I fuck, and then I need to fuck somebody else to break the attachment, and then somebody else to break *that* attachment. It's a horrible cycle.

I've been sleeping with this one comic, Ethan, for months, but I have known him for years. He's also sober and lives out of town but travels for his day job for some consulting firm. He's in town every few weeks, staying at some shitty Travelodge, and I go there and we have aggressive sex, and I leave.

One time, he doesn't kiss me. I shouldn't be upset, because he's a terrible kisser, but the reality of what I am to him, what this is to him, becomes brutally evident. I glare at him and blurt out, "I get that we're 'sport fucking,' but for God's sake, if you're going to treat me like a whore, leave some money on the table next time. Honestly, I've had more intimate encounters with the fucking barista at Starbucks."

Ethan always hands me a hot wet towel after we have sex so I can wipe myself down, like I'm a customer at a sushi restaurant or sitting in one of the better seats on an airline. It is all so clinical and impersonal. But Ethan can be funny and he's a good fuck, so I keep coming back for more. However, each time, I feel more emotionally stripped—sometimes even sobbing as I drive home—so I hope that I'm starting to hit my bottom.

Around that time, I stumble upon a quote from John Barrymore: "Sex: the thing that takes up the least amount of time and causes the most amount of trouble." It seems almost biblical in its revelation...Too bad I don't believe in the Bible.

When I first start going to Sex and Love Addicts Anonymous (SLAA) meetings, I absolutely despise them. Ironically, the people in SLAA are the most unattractive crew I've ever seen gathered in one place. It's astonishing to me that these people are getting laid, let alone complaining about it. It's also kind of hard for me to take the "disease" of love and sex addiction seriously—as this "fatal illness"—when I've had needles in my neck. Personally, I'm on the fence about whether it is a disease. Sex and love addiction certainly feel compulsive at times, but the disease mentality pushes it for me. I think it's more about getting a hit of dopamine and acting out unresolved childhood issues. But if there is one thing that really bothers me about twelve-step programs, it is their need to pathologize everything.

In case you're not familiar with SLAA meetings, when you speak (which is called your "share"), you are not supposed to indulge in "graphic descriptions" of your "acting out" behavior. If you do, some other member might raise their hand while you're speaking to stop you because they feel they are being "triggered." How mortifying, right? Needless to say, I live in terror of this happening to me. Every time I share at a meeting and am not immediately shut down by somebody, I feel a weird sense of relief and elation, like I just riverdanced through a field of IEDs and still have both my legs.

I had a SLAA sponsor for a while. When I first met her, she told me that I wasn't allowed to even talk to men for thirty days. That felt very unrealistic. When I told her how out of control I was sexually, she adjusted, making her only requirements that I use a condom and not fuck a certain specific sweaty, promiscuous movie star. Well, okay. That seemed doable.

Despite her more than generous guidelines, I began acting out sporadically and stopped calling her. Then, of course, I ran into her in an AA meeting. SLAA considers itself the graduate program of AA. They feel that it's only after you get sober that you realize your *real* problem is relationships. Nothing like the one-upmanship of twelve-step programs.

"How are you, mama?" she asks and gives me a tight hug.

"I'm okay. I haven't been acting out," I say quickly. It had been almost a week, which was a lifetime for me then.

"That's good," she says. "Call me."

"The idea of acting out is kind of grossing me out."

"For now," she adds.

"But what's the deal when you stop acting out? Like now, suddenly, all these dudes are on my dick..." As soon as I say it, I realize how crass I sound. But I plow on. "Like yesterday, I was crying and on my period and two guys texted me, trying to have sex with me..."

She smiles. "That's the way it works," she says. "You set a boundary, and it gets tested."

Let me explain the lingo here for a second. Boundaries, or "bottom lines," as they're known in SLAA, are behaviors you will not engage in or people you will not engage with. So not breaking your "bottom lines" is what determines your sexual "sobriety." This makes sobriety in SLAA very personal and quite amorphous, unlike AA sobriety, which is "nothing that alters you from the neck up." So, for example, one guy confessed to fucking a prostitute, but because prostitutes weren't one of his "bottom lines," he didn't consider it a relapse and was still "keeping his time." Get it?

I smile a little and thank her, but honestly, I find this a bit far-fetched. I mean, doesn't the universe have better and more important things to worry about than my pussy?

At most of the SLAA meetings I frequent, very few people raise their hands as willing to sponsor. The fact that the program seems to have a lot of sheep and very few shepherds doesn't instill much hope in me. I also take note that unlike AA, which gives you your first chip after a month of staying off the sauce, SLAA gives chips for one day, two days, and three days of "sexual sobriety," as well as every month. This further encourages my doubt that the program is feasible for any length of time. Then again, perhaps it's just me. Besides, being newly sober off substances, I'm more concerned with not picking up a drink or drug than not picking up a guy.

Amanda, my old roomie from rehab, has recently relapsed and is back in treatment. They are forcing her to go to SLAA, too.

"I hate it, because everyone in there is gross, and they all seem to have a boyfriend or a girlfriend that they can't stop cheating on, and I'm single forever," she tells me. "Plus, I sit there and think about them fucking. Soooo gross!"

Besides all of us sexual compulsives, SLAA has the self-identified "sexual anorexics," people who have withdrawn completely from sex and love out of a fear of intimacy or a fear of relapsing. Of course, this type of celibacy is not recovery—just the other end of the spectrum of active sex and love addiction—and the program makes that clear. Still, to me, it feels pretty damn lightweight. At one meeting, one of these sexual anorexics spoke of her disdain for the many platonic hugs she was getting from men recently.

I laughed and thought, "Oh, honey, I wish my problem was just hugs. Try getting fucked by a twenty-eight-year-old AA newcomer in the backseat of your car, and then we'll talk."

# CHAPTER ELEVEN

I pray I get put on Esteban's crew, not only because he is happy and hilarious, but because he only does painting, and that's a much sweeter gig than sweeping the streets. When I'm with him, we spend most days in Glassell Park painting over graffiti. It's looking like "Cornejo" has been busy here. Every wall and garage door has "Cornejo rules," "Cornejo was here," "Cornejo is king" spray-painted all over it. A week later we come back, and "RIP Cornejo" is everywhere. Evidently, somebody besides us got very sick of Cornejo.

Esteban had come to this particular community labor outlet eighteen years before on a gun possession charge. Actually, it was two guns, and one had been a sheriff's. He had a stunning 140 days of community labor ahead of him, but the crew bosses immediately noticed his wizardlike ability to color-match paint, and, after he was off probation, they invited him to come work for them. He declined. He already had a job that paid well at a watch factory. Two weeks later, they called him again, offering him the pay rate of his choice and he took the job. That was sixteen years ago. So he was cool because he had been one of us. There was no judgment from Esteban. He understood that plenty of people drive drunk or get in fights with their spouses. We were just unlucky enough to get caught.

It's 10:34 a.m. on a Thursday. I am slaving away with the roller, skinny arms trying to balance the extension pole, paint dripping onto my sweaty face, and Esteban comes over and says, "*Tranquilo*, Amy. Take it easy. Easy," and flashes his big white smile.

I laugh. I'm getting too intense, as usual.

I go to pull a big pail of paint out of the truck. It's super heavy.

"You got it?" he asks.

"Yes." I smile, my bony shoulder drooping under the weight.

"Yeah, you're strong. You beat up your husband."

"Well, not exactly." I laugh.

We finish the job and pile back into the truck. Then Esteban starts in on the most disturbing story. He had watched a movie the night before. It was based on a true story.

"So this girl," he says. "She was only twelve years old. And her uncle take her to live with him and have sex with him in the mountains. She don't know is not okay. She only twelve. But he don't want her to get pregnant, so he take her to a *bruja*...how do you say? Witch? Yes, he take her to a witch, and the witch...she put a potato up her bagina..."

*Bagina?* "Bagina" is instantly my favorite word. Even over "pussy," which took me till my forties to say without flinching. "Bagina" is fucking hilarious. I'm using it. I don't care if I never get laid again.

Esteban continues, "So, for two years she don't have no baby. But she get sick. Really sick. And so her uncle take her to the doctor. And he look up into her bagina and see the potato. It grow root. And the root go into her stomach. And then she die. Lucky for her she was not in Mexico, because there we eat yuccas, and yuccas are very big!"

All the guys laugh hysterically. I chuckle uncomfortably. I'm the only female in the truck.

We pull into a McDonald's.

"Okay, break time!" he says. "Ten minutes, guys!"

We all pile out of the truck to smoke or grab the swill they call coffee at fast-food places.

I'm shocked when two of the guys come back with hash browns. After a story like that, how the fuck could they eat potatoes?

Toward the end of the day, we stop at a street corner to paint over some new posters plastered on the power box. It's pretty much a weekly stop. There's an old black homeless man in a wheelchair. He is always here. He has huge swollen legs and feet and stinks to high heaven. He has the most piercing ice-blue eyes I've ever seen, and when he smiles, you see that his two upper front teeth are missing.

"Do you like your job?" he asks me.

"It's not a job. It's community service," I confess.

He just smiles with kind eyes.

"Can I help you move over a bit so we can paint here?" I ask him.

"I got it. Thank you, though." He wheels himself over a bit and then begins to fix his hair with his fingers. A large silver rhinestone ring sparkles in the sun. I'm mesmerized.

I used to be very uncomfortable when I saw handicapped people. I'd either avoid looking at them or just thank the God (that I didn't believe in) that it wasn't me. That all changed when I was living in San Francisco in my twenties.


Back then, I was ripping through my trust fund thanks to my speed addiction, and my father was getting suspicious. I needed a job. I'd left the dishwashing job and been fired from the waitressing gig. I needed money. I looked in the local paper. "Video director seeking assistant." Sounded interesting. Back to my Hollywood roots. I called and got an interview for the next day.

I took the train downtown to the financial district. This "video director" lived in a big loft on Kearny Street. I knocked on the metal door. It seemed like ages before it opened. I looked around anxiously. It was eight a.m. and I was still up from the night before and the night before that. The sun was coming up. My eyes burned. I looked down and noticed that my hands were a little swollen. They felt tight. I chewed on the inside of my cheek. Finally the door opened. A frail young man in his late twenties with gnarled, bent hands sat in an electric wheelchair. He was smiling and wearing a silly knitted hat.

"Hiya! Good morning," he said.

"Uhh, hi." I tried not to look surprised. I was starting to come down. My palms felt moist, my mouth dry. My back ached. I didn't want to betray my prejudice. I had never worked for a handicapped person before. Hell, I didn't even know one.

"Come in," he said, and with that, he whipped around in his wheelchair and started to zip through the loft. "I'm Eli."

"Amy," I returned.

I took a deep breath and followed him. The smell of warm oatmeal and peas hung heavy in the cold air. We passed a large rack that I would later learn was for stringing him up so he could have the lost experience of standing again. We continued into his bedroom. The odor of stale urine hit me like a right hook. I was grateful my sense of smell had been heartily deadened by regular meth use.

"This is Sage. She's one of my assistants. She'll teach you what to do," he said.

Sage was a tiny ex-dancer with skin the color of burned toast and dark, messy hair. On the days she wasn't working for this guy Eli, she worked at a hospice for AIDS patients.

"Have you ever done any nursing?" she asked in her little-girl voice.

"Nnnno. I'm kind of a . . . no." They didn't need to know what an entitled asshole I was.

"I'm confused," I continued. "I thought this was a personal assistant job."

"It is," she chirped. "It's being the personal assistant to a quadriplegic."

"Ahh . . . okay," I said, comprehending the situation. I wanted to bolt out the door at that very moment, but then I remembered my new mantra, "Yes to everything."

"Have you ever dealt with shit?" Eli asked me bluntly. He was dead serious.

My brow furrowed. "Well I . . . have a cat," I offered.

"Good enough!" he said buoyantly. For a so-called "cripple," he was really fucking happy. It was disarming. I could walk fine and was a hundred times more miserable. Maybe there was something to learn here.

"Look, I like you, Amy. You're funny. I know you don't have any experience, but just give it a try, okay? If you don't like it, you can quit. Cool?" He had hope in his eyes.

"All right," I conceded. And with that I was hired.

I was given a set of keys and watched Sage go through the routine one time. Then I was on my own. I would show up at eight a.m. sharp. Eli would still be in bed sleeping. I'd wake him and pull the covers back. Occasionally, the pee bag attached to his catheter would have leaked onto the bed, and he'd be lying in his own cold piss for a few hours. I would stick a towel underneath him and begin the morning ritual. First I'd stretch out his atrophied legs. His legs were stick-thin and narrow, like those of a malnourished child. They would shake as I pulled them straight. I'd hold them that way until the trembling stopped and they were limp again.

I was a bit heavy then, with a heaving bosom and thick thighs. And a good thing that I was. I needed to be able to hoist his wasted body over my shoulder and then into the chair. It was there that we did his morning arm exercises. He would push against my hands in a circular motion and I would resist. But he always had to have music. His favorite was Hendrix; huge Jimi posters were plastered all over his dark, smelly bedroom.

He loved putting on this terrible ghetto accent. "My legs is broke. They don't work no mo," he'd joke.

Whenever I came to work, all the petty shit that I was distressed over seemed so insignificant. Because at least I could walk. And that made running away from myself so much easier.

"Are you knocking boots, Amy?"

"Knocking boots?" I asked breathily, as I pushed against his surprisingly strong but feeble-looking arms.

"Getting laid. Making love. Having sex."

"Oh. No. Not really."

"Better get on that shit. You never know when, all of a sudden... Boom! You're in a chair."

"I'll get right on that," I said, Hendrix blaring.

"God, I love Jimi. Foxy lady, doo, doo, doo..." he sang.

Eli used to have everything. He was beautiful and young and rich, with loads of musical talent and gaggles of girls. He showed me a video of himself before the motorcycle accident, and I wept like a bitch, seeing that wasted potential and how cruel fate could be. And then I saw myself—the life I'd lost to depression, self-destruction, and procrastination. I was only twenty-four then, but I had been in my own way forever, blocking the exits as my fear and self-hatred consumed me.

"Tell me one of your spoken word thingies," he said.

"Really? It's eight in the morning," I said as I snapped on a rubber glove. I bent down and inserted a finger into his ass and made concentric circles until he was stimulated and took a shit.

I'd always been pretty vain. I don't consider myself particularly beautiful, though I'm by no means ugly. Men seem to find me rather attractive, which has always both puzzled and soothed me. But it never touched that deep void in me, that bottomless trench of self-loathing. Eli made all that bullshit seem so inconsequential. Yes, his body was broken and maimed and rotting from disuse, but his soul was so fucking vibrant, it made his paralytic state almost immaterial. He was more alive than anyone I'd ever met.

"Are we taking a bath today, sir?" I asked.

"Yes! I think we will do a little sudsy."

I began to run his bath while he chatted to me from his potty chair. I always acted as if nothing I was doing, nothing about him, was out of the ordinary. He was so vulnerable, so dependent, that I wanted to reclaim and give back to him any dignity and honor I could. It's what I'd want done for me.

I rolled him over to the bathtub, hoisted him over my shoulder, and laid him carefully into the water. What a relief it must have been to have those twisted, heavy limbs float delicately, weightlessly in the warm water. He would dunk his ears into the water so he couldn't hear me; he could just see my ridiculously expressive face ask him what he wanted for breakfast. He would laugh and laugh. I didn't care that he was laughing at me. I was just happy to see him happy.

Eli could move his arms, but his hands were forever curled into a clawlike position. I would take a washcloth and rub it with soap and hand it to him. He would take his little pincerlike hand and clumsily rub the soapy rag over his chest. The places he couldn't reach, I would wash for him. But I never washed him like a child. I washed him like you'd wash a sick friend.

I would then heave his wet, stiff body onto my shoulder and into the chair and wheel him over to the bed, where I'd dry him off. He'd be shivering but couldn't feel the cold. I'd attach a condom to his penis, which had a tube leading down to a urine bag that was Velcroed around his ankle.

"What do you want to wear today?" I'd ask.

"My tie-dye shirt. The purple one."

"You fucking hippie," I teased.

I'd dress him and put him back in the chair. He'd follow me in his chair into the kitchen, where I'd make his breakfast.

"What are we eating this morning, master?" I asked him.

"Oatmeal...with peas."

"You are so weird."

I'd cook him up this bizarre concoction. When it was piping hot, I'd put the bowl on the table. There was this clamp thing that would hold the spoon or fork, and I'd insert the spoon and slide the clamp onto his bent little hand.

"What's your T-shirt say?" he asked with a mouth full of oats.

"It says 'slave,' and it has a ball and chain because I think relationships are like prison."

"Couldn't agree more. Gotta get in, get yourself a little somethin' somethin', and get out. That's what I say."

I laughed as I scrubbed the pot clean.

I didn't do this job for money. It really didn't pay much. And though the hours were short, they were early, which didn't agree with the budding drug addict in me. Despite all of this, I was never late. I was always on time. He needed me. I had never been needed. I had never felt useful. I had always been the black hole of want and despair that friends and family threw time, love, and money into. I had been the person that everybody needed to take care of. Yet here I had become the caretaker. That ability was in me. I was relieved and pleased.

When we'd go out in public, to run errands or eat Indian food (his favorite), people either ignored him out of discomfort or looked at him with the same kind of pity and horror they'd give a sideshow freak. Both reactions made me angry. Didn't they realize he was just a young guy who'd been in an accident? He still liked good food and good drugs and fast women. He just couldn't chase them like he used to.

One morning, I came to work, and my pupils must have been huge, because he knew. Immediately. And the jig was up.

He didn't ask me if I was on drugs, so I didn't have to deny it. There was a trust between us, an unspoken intimacy, and I didn't want to disrespect it with lies.

"Listen, Amy. I've lost of a lot of friends to speed. I can't be around it. So if you're going to do that shit, you can't work for me," he said calmly.

I was still in the first flush of my druggie love affair. Speed had me wrapped around its evil finger, and I was as loyal as a speed freak could be.

"Well, I'm not ready to put it down right now," I said bluntly, with a little impunity. And with that, I quit. Or was fired. I guess it was a bit of both.

# CHAPTER TWELVE

I take a day off from community service and go see my hairdresser, the same one I've had since before I was married. He is a buff, straight Latino guy who wears tight rock T-shirts and works at a chichi salon in Beverly Hills. Just because I'm a dirt-poor criminal and divorcée doesn't mean I have to look like one.

He takes my hair down from its ratty bun.

"Oh, my God, what is in your hair? Is that semen?"

"No, not this time. It's probably paint . . . from community labor."

A sixty-something woman with a $4,000 handbag and an aggressive facelift looks over.

"Shit happens," I say and shrug.

"You're so gonna get me fired," my hairdresser mutters.

"You love me!" I brag.

As I'm leaving the salon, I get a text from another comic I've been fucking.

"Can I cum in your pussy?"

"I can't take the romance," I shoot back.

"Meet me @ the Comedy Store. I wanna fuck u there."

"Where @ the Comedy Store?"

"There are plenty of places 2 do it."

"Sounds like u have done this B4."

"Y or N?" he demands.

"OMG, calm down, horndog."

Of course, I oblige, having the world's shittiest boundaries.

After it's over, he gives me a peck on the cheek and says, "Always a pleasure, big homie."

*Big homie?* Please don't fuck me and then call me "big homie." Jesus. I used to be a CEO's wife. But anybody with a long-term fuckbuddy will tell you the same thing: it's hot at the beginning and all business at the end.

As I drive away, I feel a burning in my crotch. Perfect. When I finally get home, I take a look-see downstairs to see what the problem could be. As I pull down my underwear, I see the spearmint gum he had been chewing.

"I found ur gum . . . in my panties," I text him.

"Was wondering where that went!"

Just then, Terry, my roommate, walks into our bedroom.

"Hiiii!"

"Hey," I say to her. "Weird question: how do you get gum out of clothing?"

"Well, what kind of clothing?" Terry asks.

"Underwear."

"Oh, my God. I don't even wanna know . . . You are *so* gross."


I know I'm really in the fold now at community service because they're letting me in on the secret super-cheap Latino markets—and feeding me homemade *chicharrón*—deep-fried pork rinds. Plus, I now know that *horniado* means "horny" in Spanish. I can't say I'm developing a taste for ranchero music, but it won't be long till I can at least boast a tolerance.

I'm in the pickup truck. Mauricio is our crew boss today. He's young, husky, and a smart-ass, but not particularly bright. He talks a lot. I think he has a mild crush on me, because he gives me endless shit.

"I do murals on the side. I don't really like to draw, but I'm into vandalism."

"Nice. So you're probably spray-painting all the shit that I paint over every day."

"You know what's funny? That you used to be a comedian, and you're not funny at all."

"You know what's even funnier? That I'm listening to a chunky twenty-six-year-old Latino who wrangles convicts for a living tell me what's funny or not."

A new guy slides into our van. He's been moved over from the other crew.

Without missing a beat I say, "I smell pot."

"You can smell it on me?" he says, not a little freaked out.

"Honey, I've been in six rehabs. I'm better than most drug dogs."

Turns out he was busted for pot (he wouldn't tell us how much), but it obviously didn't faze him, because he is sporting a baseball cap with an embroidered marijuana leaf and socks with smiling ganja plants on them.

We hit the streets (or go out to "rock the broom," as I now call it). It's the day after New Year's and we're doing the Santa Monica Boulevard route. It's particularly gnarly with streamers, flyers, and drug paraphernalia.

The new stoner is sweeping up a wadded shirt on the sidewalk, and underneath it is a pile of human shit. He gets poo on his broom and flips out.

"Why is this happening to me?! I'm a good person!"

I keel over, laughing. Just then my phone bings. It's a text from Linda: "I'm at a BBQ with a supermodel." I look around and then quickly type back: "Good for you. I'm sweeping up human poo with a bunch of criminals."

There is an abandoned building we always pass on this street sweeping route, and this older blond tweaker has taken up residence there. She wears dirty white spandex shorts that show off her twig-thin, bruised legs. She has no belongings, and her face is overly tanned and caving in from life on the streets and the decay of meth. She sits on the wall and swings her legs maniacally. I sheepishly get a little closer to sweep the leaves from the front of the building. My presence doesn't even register. She's in her own world. I know it all too well.


After I crashed and burned on speed in San Francisco at twenty-four, my parents moved me back to L.A. They had both moved out of state by then, but their thinking was: "She was sober there. She'll be sober there again." After getting back to L.A., I managed to stay off speed for a few months but I was compensating by drinking two bottles of red wine a night. Alone. At the time I was writing yet another book I would not finish while reading a lot of Bukowski, Kerouac, and Hunter Thompson. I could easily rationalize my escalating drinking because all the great writers were alcoholics, didn't ya know?

One day, I was poking around an antiques store.

"And how are you today, miss?" the perky gay man asked me. He had thick dark hair, perfect white teeth, and smooth, bulging biceps.

"Ehh. I'm okay."

"Just okay? Girl, what you need is a rail!"

I don't know what kind of energy I was giving off that day, but that store owner saw something deep inside me: that I was a junkie, and I always would be. And with that, I was back in. From one gay storeowner, I navigated the entire Los Angeles speed scene. Within months, I was buying from everyone—homeless Hollywood hoodlums to Mexican gangsters.

One of my friends from San Francisco came down to L.A. to visit. We stayed up on speed for a ridiculous seventeen days. He was a bisexual skinhead, which always confused me, but I came to find out this combo was not uncommon. He had delicate features offset by a bald head so shiny that you could almost see your reflection in it. His red suspenders hung loosely on his narrow frame. You could hear him coming from blocks away as he stomped on the pavement with his steel-toed Doc Martens, whistling Fear songs.

By the end of our seventeen-day run, we were writing a new bible based on Emerson and Nietzsche and were convinced we'd found the mathematical equation for God. We had been so high for so long we could barely speak English. The night before he left to go back to San Francisco, he pierced my lip with a large safety pin as we swigged Jack Daniel's and made a blood pact to seal our friendship. The good thing about tweaking for more than two weeks straight is that you don't really feel pain. The bad thing is that your judgment is off, and you end up with sewing paraphernalia in your face.

As I dove back into speed, I learned that most tweakers are broke and are considered the bottom of the drug addiction barrel. The tweakers in L.A. seemed less creative and more desperate than the S.F. speed freaks. They were older, had been in the game longer, had been to prison. In L.A., I had multiple dealers, as they would all get busted with some regularity, and I couldn't be without. By this point, I had a pretty big habit.

I had one dealer who'd spent most of his adult life in the pen. He was covered head-to-toe in prison tats and ran around with this extremely skinny black guy who claimed to be one of Michael Jackson's cousins or nephews or uncles or something. Who knows whether that was bullshit or not? I learned not to ask too many questions. I'd be friendly, give them my money, and get my drugs before they tried to hurt me or fuck me.

I had another dealer who was a woman who "washed checks"— where you literally wash away the original ink on a check so that you can rewrite it with a different amount to somebody else. She also sold car parts on the black market. "Hey, if you can get any parts from early nineties Civics, I'll take 'em," she said. She once suggested that I deposit some washed checks for her, and they'd cut me a percentage, but I instantly pictured myself in an orange jumpsuit being some huge black chick's "bitch" and politely declined.

I had yet another dealer who was a skinny homeless kid who sold both meth and his body on Hollywood Boulevard. No car, got around on Rollerblades.

I got ripped off numerous times. I'd stupidly give someone money to go get drugs, and they would never come back. Or I'd accidentally fall asleep when a dealer was at my house, and I'd wake up and whaddaya-know? My money *and* my drugs were gone. I was really naïve and out of my league. I pretended to be a tough girl, but I was anything but. One time, Spider and Joker, my Mexican gangster dealers, came over to my apartment to sell me some meth.

"It's good shit. This batch is strong, homes," Spider said.

"Cool," I answered excitedly as I put a chunk in my glass pipe and fired up my mini blowtorch.

Then one of them pulled out a silvery black pipe.

"Hey, *guera*, do you know anybody who'd want to buy this?"

"I don't even know what that is," I said, exhaling white smoke like a dragon.

"It's a silencer. A gun silencer."

"Ummm...yeah. I'll ask around, but nobody springs immediately to mind." I tried to act cool, but inside I thought, *I'm gonna die!*

I would dumpster-dive and find old furniture and stay up all frenzied night refinishing it. Sometimes the depravity and degradation of my life would seep below the high of the meth, and I would lie in the bathtub for hours, crying, smoking speed off tinfoil, Nirvana on loop.

After I'd been smoking speed for a while, I noticed that most of my dealers shot it. Why? It must be better. I wanted to try, but they all discouraged me.

"It ruins life for you. You won't be able to enjoy anything ever again," one said. "Not puppies or sunsets or flowers. You won't feel pleasure anymore."

I wanted to say I wasn't that fond of puppies or sunsets or flowers, anyway. And I was already a depressive. Pleasure wasn't that big a force in my life. But I didn't say shit.

The O.J. trial was happening at this time, and lucky me, my phone number was one digit off from Johnnie Cochran's office number. This was pre–cell phones, so I'd come home and there'd be multiple messages on my answering machine for Mr. Cochran: "Johnnie, how *dare* you use Hitler in your closing argument!" or "Mr. Cochran, I want to thank you for the incredible job you are doing defending our brother, O.J. This case is a racist travesty..."

I was letting some actor kid, Pete, crash with me. He was mid twenties, like me, probably good-looking, but it was hard to tell because he was so strung out on meth. He looked perpetually dirty, hair unkempt, pants falling down. He would stay awake for so long that he'd fall asleep sitting up. He made money by sneaking into old buildings that were abandoned or being renovated and stealing copper and old glass doorknobs and then selling the stuff. He had a shitty old white pickup, and the truck bed was filled with junk—junk he'd found in the trash, junk he was trying to peddle, junk he'd stolen from other drug addicts. Eventually, he started getting small royalty checks—$8.24 or whatever for reruns of shows that he'd acted on. I never asked him when he'd started having his mail forwarded to my place, nor about his prior acting career. Tweakers never ask each other what their life was like *before*. Life before tweak is like an alternate universe, a taboo time capsule that, essentially, ceases to exist. It is too depressing to think about what your life had been like or could be like if you hadn't fallen down into the black hole that is meth.

One day somebody called for "Johnnie's office," and Pete took the call and pretended to be Cochran. The woman on the other end of the phone was so thrilled to be talking to the famous attorney that Pete made a plan with her to go bowling or golfing or something... I was too busy smoking speed out of my glass pipe and laughing to know for sure. I just remember him saying, "Thank you, thank you" a lot. Eventually, Pete met a woman, an older mother of three—also a tweaker—and they moved into his Orange County storage unit together. Ain't love grand?

On more than one occasion, I was convinced I had bugs in my skin, which can be a side effect of meth. But one of the gutter punks in S.F. had had scabies, so the idea that I actually had bugs in my flesh wasn't that far-fetched. I would feel things crawling on me, like the lightest invisible feather, and I would scratch ferociously, and black spots would appear on my skin. I collected the black flecks that I dug out of my arms and belly and put them on a napkin and went to see a dermatologist. He concluded that it was just "debris."

"What the fuck? I never had 'debris' coming out of my skin before," I said. I failed to mention that I never had been a raging drug addict before, either.

I saw a psychiatrist and tried to swindle a prescription out of her for some pharmaceutical speed. I figured it would be stronger and definitely cleaner than the crank I'd been scoring. I told her I was lethargic, had ADD, possibly narcolepsy, anything I had read in the *Physicians' Desk Reference* that should or could be treated with amphetamines. She was suspicious but gave me some slow-release tablets and sent me on my way. The slow-release tablets were useless. You couldn't get a rush. I went back for a second round. She quickly saw me for what I was and suggested I go to AA. I suggested she go fuck herself.

I recounted the experience with the shrink to my father. I was twenty-five at the time, and I had not been to AA yet. I told my father, "I'd rather die a junkie than go to those creepy meetings." So, desperate and running out of options, my dad made an appointment for me to see an "addiction specialist." This "specialist" interviewed me for about an hour and deemed me an "atypical addict." Hah. Fooled some "professional" again. I was high in the session and talked circles around the man. I rationalized my drug use to him as self-medication for an innate mood disorder. I came in prepared with loads of studies citing amphetamine use for medicating severe depression and borderline personality disorder. He bought it.

This entire time, I was seeing an expensive Brentwood therapist once or twice a week, paid for by my dad. My dad had chosen him specifically because he was known among the L.A. therapeutic community to be "very tough" on addiction. I was high the whole year I was in therapy with him. I'd usually snort speed in the bathroom in his office building right before my session. Not only did I never get better, but he never noticed I was on drugs. Or, if he did, he didn't confront me about it. We talked about my depression. And, sure, I was depressed. But how much of it was due to the fact I was smoking a teener of crystal meth every thirty-six hours, we will never know.

I was absolutely mesmerized by the drugs. You know those tiny little tins of Tylenol you can get at 7-Eleven or the airport? Well, I had taken one of those and removed the red and white paint with paint thinner. I lined the inside with holographic sticky paper and glued a small tin skull on the front. I knew I was addicted to poison, to death, but why not make it a little stylish?

My drug habit was expensive...at least $170 every two days. My "sorry, I misbudgeted" wasn't flying with my dad anymore, so I started selling speed. I bought a tiny scale and some plastic bags. Meth is cheaper in bulk, so I'd buy a teener (one-sixteenth of an ounce) or an eight ball (one-eighth of an ounce), sell enough quarters (quarter-of-a-gram bags) to break even, and then have the rest of the drugs for myself. I did have a stream of weird raver kids knocking on my door 24/7, but it was a small price to pay to get high for free. I was always up anyway.

As my parents sensed me deteriorating both physically and mentally, they each called me daily to urge me to go into rehab. I always refused, but I could feel the ride was ending. I'd heard an old druggie adage: *You know why there are no old speed freaks? Because they're all dead.*

My mother came to visit, but I knew she was really on a recon mission. The day she arrived, I hadn't gotten high in two days, and I was bedbound and gray. My mother stocked my refrigerator and cleaned my little studio apartment, which I gather was beyond disgusting. Tweakers are notorious for getting high and cleaning things or tinkering with electronics. A few lines in, they're taking apart stereos or feverishly scrubbing the grout in the bathroom with a toothbrush. I've never been into cleaning, and that didn't change when I got high. It turns out that being raised by maids, as I was, doesn't make you grateful and neat. It makes you spoiled and messy. So I was the dirtiest speed freak around.

As soon as my mother flew home to Santa Fe, I was right back on the pipe. One afternoon, I was in the market a few blocks from my place. I had been up for about five days straight. I grabbed my dietary staples—a large bottle of Mountain Dew and a Caramello bar—and headed toward the register. That was the last thing I remember. Next I knew, I was on a gurney in an ambulance.

"What the fuck?" I tried to sit up, but I was strapped down.

"Calm down, miss," the paramedic said.

"Can you tell me what day it is?" another paramedic asked me.

"What?" I felt confused, foggy.

"Can you tell me who the president is?"

"Of course," I snorted.

"Who is it?"

I drew a blank.

"Have you done any drugs tonight?"

"Yeah...obviously some really shitty ones, because here I am!" I said defiantly. And with that, we were off to the hospital.

Doctor's guess: a massive seizure. They did a head CT scan, made me choke down some charcoal for a possible overdose, and released me.

When you are a drug addict, you know that you will eventually have to pay the piper. You can run for a while, but there will be a point when you have pushed things too far. You can't really fuck with Mother Nature for that long. Eventually, she'll take your head and slam it to the ground and remind you who's boss in this game called life.

Back in my apartment, I called my dad and quietly said, "I'm ready to go into rehab."

"I know. I'm already on my way down." He'd had a paternal premonition.

I agreed to rehab, sober living, everything. Whatever it was, yes.

My father was so frightened by my speed addiction and so disgusted with me that we couldn't be in the same room together for ten minutes without getting into a heated argument. So my stepmother, at the time, flew into town. (I think it was wife number three. There would be a fourth marriage, which would also end badly.) She and I checked into a tiny hotel on La Cienega. I kicked in that hotel for a week, sweating profusely, too weak to get out of bed, completely delirious. Most of the time, I just slept. I was so tired. Almost two years of staying awake had taken a toll on me.

Once I was physically off the stuff, the mental detox began. That was the hardest part. Speed sucks you into this weird netherworld of hyperactivity and perceived synchronicity, which is very magical, inviting, and hard to shake. When you're on speed for days at a time, you start to see "signs" everywhere, hidden messages about what you're supposed to do or where you're supposed to go. You feel like you're really plugged in, wise to some mystical secret, in line with the universe. Of course, it's all just delusion, the beginnings of psychosis, really. Even knowing this, life without methamphetamine seemed dull and pedestrian and exhausting.

I was sent to a "dual diagnosis" treatment center for two grueling months. "Dual diagnosis" is the clinical term for unlucky fucks who, like me, are double trouble because they have mental illness (or a personality disorder) *as well as* substance abuse issues. The place was very institutional, with linoleum floors, pale blue walls, heavy metal doors, and fluorescent lighting. There were some other drug addicts there, but the majority were seriously and chronically mentally ill. During my time, a variety of people checked in and then checked themselves out: a depressed woman with lupus; a twenty-something Swedish heroin addict who wore a really bad wig; a teenage Iranian crackhead from Tennessee who was already brain-damaged from the drugs he'd done; a skinny manic-depressive kid who didn't think he needed medication; a young, pretty-boy rich kid from Brentwood with anger management issues; a quiet depressive girl with a big moon face who trembled and had had multiple sessions of electroconvulsive therapy. She ran away from the center almost weekly. She and I instinctively avoided each other.

The depression and rage that descended upon me once I got clean were monumental. I had screaming matches with my therapist, a megalomaniacal, short, bald Jew. I kicked chairs across the room and threw frightening tantrums. Bizarrely, he seemed to delight in goading me during group therapy. I was by far the most melodramatic of the patients (the others were too shy or too medicated), and I always provided a provocative starting point for discussions.

This therapist's big thing was cognitive behavioral therapy: *Don't wait for the feelings to change. Act and* then *the feelings will change.* The way he saw it, the key to everything was knowing who you were, because then nobody could have any power over you. He explained it this way: "I mean, I'm a short guy—five foot six. If somebody calls me a 'midget,' I'm not hurt, because I know I'm not a midget. If I wasn't sure if I wasn't a midget, then I'd get upset." He had a point. We really only get triggered by things we know (or fear) are true. I was afraid people would see that I was irreparably broken, ugly, unlovable. I don't remember much else of what he said, but I do remember that.

# CHAPTER THIRTEEN

Terry and I drive to the small park in the valley where Brendan's memorial is being held. Despite my twenty-plus years in and out of the program, I have not been to many memorials. I've been lucky that most of the people I'm close with are still alive, despite doing their damnedest to kill themselves. And I feel weird being at this memorial: not just because I fucked somebody who's dead now, but because I fucked somebody who's dead now *and* we didn't end on the best terms. Would he even want me here?

I see Amanda, my hooker roomie from treatment. We hug.

"This must be so weird for you," she says.

"It's pretty surreal. I'm not going to lie...You still in treatment since your relapse?"

"Yep. So lame."

"How's your roommate this time?"

"Not as cool as you."

"Good answer." I smile.

The memorial was organized by Brendan's men's AA stag meeting so it's 98 percent men. To be fair, Brendan had a "problem" with hookers. I was really the only woman he'd been sleeping with who wasn't a pro, and from the look of the crowd, pros don't go to johns' memorials.

There was a big picture of Brendan on a stand—an acting headshot, no less. It *is* L.A. And for some reason, they are videotaping the whole service for his parents.

Various people get up and speak. More than one says, "He died struggling to 'get' this thing." I have on big eighties *Playboy* sunglasses— very funeral appropriate—but I'm wearing them so nobody can see my eyes rolling. I get that this is an AA memorial, but does the entire focus have to be on this guy's inability to get sober? Okay, so he died of alcoholism, but at no other memorial do people harp on *why* the person died. Imagine a similar service for a person who died of, say, lung cancer: "Well, he tried hypnosis and Chantix and the patch, but fuck, man, he just *could not quit smoking*." Or how about AIDS? "I warned him to use protection, stay out of those bathhouses, get off Grindr, and not share needles, but he wouldn't listen. He hated condoms and just *loved to fuck*." Of course that would be atrocious and in very bad taste. And I feel the same way about this.

His myriad of sponsors from his many different twelve-step programs—GA (Gamblers Anonymous), SAA (Sex Addicts Anonymous), SLAA, AA—mention that he "didn't want to do the work" and, especially, how "he couldn't be honest." One even mentions his love of hookers. Really?

I turn to Terry. "You gotta be kidding me! His parents are from the Bible Belt!"

I get up and walk away from the crowd to smoke, muttering to myself, "Outrageous. Pompous AA fuckers..."

I come back just in time to hear the kicker—when one friend says, "I'm glad it wasn't me." Nice! Sorry, but I have never heard of anybody coming back from Afghanistan after watching their buddy be blown to smithereens and saying, "Better him than me." If anything, they have survivor guilt.

Terry and I get into the car, and I am absolutely fucking livid.

"That was so fucked up. That memorial should have been about what he did right in his life: his enthusiasm, how alive he was, his passion, his humor, his wit—not how he liked to gamble, bone, and drink."

I rummage around in my purse for my stupid vape juice to fill up my even stupider vape contraption. I notice my hands are shaking from rage.

"And that one asshole reading from the Big Book?" I continue. "Oh, my God. I really thought I was going to hurt him."

"Why didn't you get up and say something?" Terry asks.

"What was I going to say? Oh, yeah . . . 'Brendan and I were both comics and sex addicts and we fucked each other senseless. It's nice to be here'?"


The next morning, I'm doing community service, and I'm sweeping a corner near a taco stand when I spot a syringe. We are specifically instructed that if we see a syringe not to pick it up. The crew boss must come take a picture of it, document it, and dispose of it.

Before going to find the supervisor, I bat the thing around on the sidewalk with my broom. The syringe looks old. The markings are worn off. But there's residue in it. I get a weird rush: nausea and longing.

I flash back to ten years ago, being alone in my quaint deco apartment after my second stint in rehab. I was doing coke to a sound track of the Twilight Singers, wondering who I could get high with. I cracked open my rehab-supplied Alcoholics Anonymous Big Book. In the front, like a high school yearbook, were sweet inscriptions from fellow clients along with their phone numbers. I used my deductive reasoning to decide which among them would already have dropped the ball and be down to party. I picked a handsome rich-kid junkie—a chronic relapser—and picked up the phone. Bingo. Within a few hours, he was at my house with cocaine, heroin, and syringes.

As he shot speedballs, I snorted long, thick lines of coke off my big mirrored coffee table.

"Why aren't you shooting?" he asked me. "It's so much better, and you use so much less."

Why *wasn't* I shooting? That was a very good question, and I didn't have a very good answer. Because . . . because I didn't? Because I was afraid? Because it was taboo? All of these responses seemed weak in the face of this new, exciting prospective experience. *Why not?* I thought. Why not? Possibly the worst reason to do anything.

"Okay," I said quietly.

He mixed up a concoction of cocaine and water in a spoon and drew it up in a syringe. He took the belt of my pink velour robe and tied it tightly around my upper arm. My veins bulged. He inserted the needle and then drew back. Blood shot into the barrel, and then he slowly pushed the plunger in. I watched in fascination and horror. My heart was pounding furiously. And then the coke hit me. The feeling was overwhelming. It was a strong rising flush, like you were about to have the biggest orgasm of your life while riding a terrifying roller coaster. *Oh, my God. I get it now.* And from that moment, I was a true junkie.

For the next few weeks, this guy and I shot coke, drank milk shakes, and scored dope together while camping out at his place. My pants got looser and looser. He got sweatier and more paranoid. I would wake up to find him in his backyard armed with a gun and a flashlight, waiting for the cops to come arrest him. Cops who weren't there, and, moreover, weren't coming.

I never shot heroin (though I smoked it once and promptly fell asleep) because I'm an upper girl at heart. Plus, I wasn't ready for the commitment. I knew that with coke, you just slept it off for a few days. There was none of that kicking sickness. Though with the epilepsy I developed in 2001 from my meth abuse (I now have what numerous neurologists have described as "hyperactive lesions on my frontal lobe"), shooting heroin probably would have been a smarter bet. Shooting coke, with or without a seizure disorder, is dicey. That shit is dangerous: seizures, heart attacks, strokes, and that's if you're normal and healthy. Even people without epilepsy overshoot the mark and have convulsions. But I was deep in it now, and I felt invincible. Or maybe I just didn't care anymore. Whatever, the result was the same: confident recklessness.

The rich-kid junkie had been shooting me up this whole time. I was still the novice. He marked my syringe with Wite-Out on the tip so we wouldn't share needles. This guy had been doing this for years. He knew all the tricks.

One night, we scored some coke off a new dealer, and right after he shot himself up, he darted outside.

"Hey. Wait. Hit me!" I demanded.

"Wait a second!" he barked.

I didn't want to wait. We drug addicts aren't good at deferring gratification.

"Aw, fuck it. I'll do it myself," I said.

I drew up the syringe and plunged it into my arm. Immediately, I slid off the chair and went into violent convulsions. Miraculously, I didn't totally lose consciousness. As I thrashed about on the floor, I kept muttering, "I'm gonna die. I'm gonna die. I'm gonna die." I came to, and the rich-kid junkie was nowhere to be found. Turns out he was in the yard, throwing up and having a moderate heart attack. Yeah, this coke was no good.

I wish I could tell you that I got clean after that terrifying episode. But I didn't. The odd thing about being a drug addict is that if you overdose, you just chalk it up to experience and try to be more careful the next time. It doesn't scare you into getting clean. If shooting coke was going to give me seizures, well, I'd just have to practice some harm reduction. A seizure, if you come out of it, will not generally kill you. What can kill you is if you go into *status epilepticus,* which is basically back-to-back seizures with no breather. Or if you seize in the shower, you could face-plant and drown in just a few inches of water. Or if you seize and hit your head, you could get a subdural hematoma and die. So head injury was my primary concern. Hey, I could shoot up while lying in a pit of pillows! But that limited me to the bedroom or the living room, and I really preferred shooting up in the kitchen. Hmmm... Wait! If shooting coke was a high-impact sport, I needed to wear protective gear! I remembered a red bike helmet that an AA friend who also had epilepsy had given me. It had a Grateful Dead sticker on the front. I hate the Dead almost as much as I hate bike riding, but whenever I felt seizurey or had been up for days getting high, I'd put the thing on. Yes, just skinny blond me in a long seventies polyester nightgown and a red bike helmet. Looking back now, it seems ridiculous and deadly, and it was. It was passive, nonchalant suicide.

I really liked drugs. Let me correct myself: I loved drugs. I just didn't like the consequences. Any drug addict who says they hate drugs is a liar. As the line goes, *you know what I liked about drugs? Everything.*

With drugs, you can circumvent all the productive work and fulfilling relationships that you'd normally need in order to have a feeling of wholeness in your life. Drugs let you be bored and lonely, broke and homeless, and still plug right into feeling good. I'm lazy. I liked that.

Now that I was officially a junkie, it was a whole new hell. You don't just become addicted to the drug. You become addicted to the entire ritual of shooting up. There is something soothing about a repetitive series of events, especially one that you know is the route to the high. I used to feel high just waiting to meet the dealer. Your brain knows what's coming. It's no dummy.

One of my most frightening memories is me crouched in the bathroom sink, the belt of my robe tied around my throat like a tight scarf. I was leaning into the mirror, poking a needle into a swelling neck vein. Spray marks of blood went onto the ceiling. There were already brownish-red splatters on the wall. I tried to wipe them off with a wet rag. I was noticeably trembling, fumbling, in a hurry to shoot myself up again. When you shoot coke, you get an immediate rush, but it's gone within minutes, so you have to shoot up again and again and again. Feed the monkey. Every twenty minutes. I had become a human pincushion. I had track marks everywhere. I tried to shoot up in my feet, breasts, groin. Nowhere was sacred.

Shooting up is a loner activity. It is not social. You can't show up at a party with a six-pack of beer and some syringes. I did, however, have one guy, this young Southern kid who was a self-proclaimed drunk and crackhead, that I'd get loaded with. I'd haul over to his apartment, and we'd get high together and have mediocre sex. However, even he was tripped out by my new routine of shooting up, which I found both odd and hypocritical.

"I can't watch you do that," he said one night.

"You're a fucking alcoholic and a crackhead and you're tripping about this. Really?"

"It's just kind of scary."

"Well, this is what I'm into now. So either you're cool with it or..." I moved toward the door.

"Nah, nah...it's cool." There was an awkward silence. He looked at me and said, "Wanna fuck?"

"Sure. Let me just shoot up first."

I was sitting on his bed in a black bra and jeans, tying off. He stood over me in his boxers, shirtless, drink in hand, watching. I injected the coke and lay backward as the intense feeling rushed through me. Every time you shoot coke, you feel like you just might die. But then you're dragged back from the brink, just in the nick of time. And that's half of the fun: taunting death. Every junkie will tell you that.

A few months later, I was shooting coke in my kitchen. By myself. Party of one. Spoons with white residue and used syringes littered the canary-yellow countertop.

There were blood splatters everywhere.

I'd been up for three days. I was shaking. I took the pink tie of my robe and wrapped it tightly around my slender upper arm. Veins bulged. Most were purple and swollen from overuse. I tried to hit a vein in my forearm but, as usual, it "rolled," meaning it moved from side to side, so I went back to "Old Faithful." This was the one fat vein in the crook of my elbow. I shook as I pushed the needle into it. My nerves were shot, and I promptly pierced right through the vein and scratched the bone.

I shuddered, attempting to shake off the feeling. Then I tried a bit higher up, got in, registered, and shot. My legs immediately wobbled beneath me. I was having a seizure. I crouched down to steady myself, yelling at the seizure to go away. I'd read somewhere that you could scare a convulsion away, like a ghost. I kept repeating the mantra, "I'm okay, I'm okay, I'm okay." My whole body quaked, but I did not lose consciousness. And because of that, I considered it a win. I mean it wasn't a "real" (AKA *grand mal*) seizure. But the convulsion had fucked up my rush. I figured it was just too strong of a shot. I mixed another dose with more water, shot up again, and promptly had a second seizure. When I came out of that convulsion, I had my "moment of clarity." I saw my future. This was going to end badly for me. I was going to die or, worse, end up zipping around in a wheelchair like Eli. I just knew it. I *had* to get clean. This "thing" that I thought I needed to be able to live on the planet was going to kill me. I wasn't going to be one of those old junkies. I was going to be that thirty-eight-year-old woman who died alone in her kitchen because she couldn't stop getting high. Fuck. That.

Just then, I heard somebody calling my name from a ways off. Great timing for a visitor. But then I remembered that I had called a sober guy to please come help me right before I had done those last two shots. I'd seen him around the rooms for the past twenty years. I heard my name again, and I went and looked out the window, and there he was.

"Why didn't you buzz the doorbell?" I asked.

"I did. For twenty minutes. I was about to leave."

"Oh. I didn't hear. I just had a seizure."

"Let me in," he demanded without a beat.

He entered, all black ski cap, big leather jacket, calm.

"Hi," I said sheepishly.

"This house smells like death," he announced.

"Ewww. Really?"

He looked at me and said, "You know, this was one of the moments where it could have gone either way: you could have lived or I could have left as I was about to and you could have had another seizure and died. I can just hear it now: 'Remember that girl, Amy? Well, she overdosed and died yesterday.'"

I just stood there, nodding, filled with shame.

"Do you want my help?" he asked.

"Yes," I answered.

"You have more shit?"

"Yes, it's in the kitchen." He followed me into the kitchen, and I reluctantly handed him four small bags of coke—about $200 worth.

"We're gonna flush it."

"Dude, that's a couple hundred bucks' worth. Can't we sell it?"

He flashed me a reprimanding look and walked into the bathroom, and I heard the toilet flush. The sound alone pained me. I couldn't watch. It would be like watching a bonfire of money and pleasure.

"I think your kitty would appreciate it if you cleaned his box," he said, returning to the kitchen.

I nodded. "Does it smell? I can't smell. I'm congested because—"

"You could have more shit and not be telling me," he said.

"I don't. That's all. I swear...Can't I do one last shot?" I pleaded again.

He raised an eyebrow at me, and I sighed, and then we poured out the last spoonful of my water-cocaine mixture.

"Okay...now...You got more rigs than these?" he asked.

"Yep." I showed him my stash, and we filled up a bag with more than thirty used and unused syringes. He took the bag out to his truck.

When he came back in, he said softly, "Let's clean up your kitchen a little bit."

We wiped down the counters in silence.

"Let's see your arms. Whaddya do?" he asked as he gently grabbed my forearms to inspect the damage. "You suck at this, you know that? What a fucking mess."

I was quiet, with big, penitent eyes.

"Well, it doesn't look too too bad. We'll know in a day or two if you've got blood poisoning or staph," he continued.

I kept my head bowed down, like a little girl who has been naughty.

"No more getting high tonight, right? Can you sleep? Just try. Okay?"

"Okay," I said mechanically. I was coming down from my high. My head was throbbing from the seizures. I was hungry. My mouth was like cotton.

"Call me in the morning."

A hug and he was out the door. I closed the door behind him and locked it. He became my sponsor for the next two years.

The following day I wrapped my purple-spotted arms in Ace bandages and went to an AA meeting. It was in the lower bar of a big cheesy metal club on the Sunset Strip. There, hipsters talked about the joys of sobriety while staring at rows of pretty colored bottles behind a low bar. I was skinny and trembling, wearing a parka in the summer and shivering from the snow still coursing through my veins.

# CHAPTER FOURTEEN

I'm sweeping the Santa Monica Boulevard route today with some young Mexican kid named Carlos. I brush the leaves and cigarette butts into a big dustpan, and he trails behind me with a huge trash bag that I dump these gutter treasures into.

I'm happy today. I've had an epiphany about my community labor. Last night, I was watching some documentary on Netflix, and this black preacher from Georgia said something like, "The trial that you're experiencing has nothing to do with what you've done. But it has everything to do with who you're going to become." Boom. Yes. That was it. Holy shit. I realized at that moment that community labor could be the *best* thing that ever happened to me. It could be the best thing or the worst thing, and it was *my* choice. This court-ordered 240 hours had to be done, so I could be miserable about it or I could find something good and worthwhile about it . . . aside from not going to jail.

When I was seven, my mom asked me why I didn't put the dishes in the dishwasher, and my answer was "That's what maids are for." She was horrified. But I got away with that attitude and much more as the years went by. When you grow up spoiled, everything is given to you, so you never learn to do things for yourself. And after years of that, you actually can't. It's like muscles. If you don't use them, they atrophy and die. Your learned ineptitude becomes crippling. On top of that, it's impossible to have pride in something that you didn't earn. So here I am at forty-two and I have nothing to show for it and no idea how to achieve anything. All I have is years of dependence and empty blowhard entitlement. I thought the rules didn't apply to me. I thought I was special, exempt.

Evidently the Beverly Hills court system and fate had colluded to make sure those days were over and that I would meet my destiny on the road I had taken to avoid it. Dodging hard work? Here you go, girl. Having trouble completing things you start? Complete this or go to jail. Need humility? Welcome to a month of being scorned and ignored by everybody except for shit-faced hobos.

This is fucking great. I'd finally develop a work ethic. I had always known that anything worthwhile took time and effort. But I had been afraid to do things I wasn't immediately good at. I didn't want to look foolish. I didn't have the faith that I would or could get better. And as I've said before, I was lazy. I had always taken the easy way out. My addiction was a symptom of that. I didn't want to feel bad. I didn't want to do the work to make myself happy. I wanted to feel numb or good 24/7, and drugs let me do that.

I would expunge the guilt I had for being a bad wife. I would shed my entitlement. I'd meet new people. I'd get the lean, sun-kissed castaway look everybody in L.A. is vying for. This is like Barry's Bootcamp and a Tony Robbins seminar all rolled into one.

So I'm sweeping up cigarette butts, gum wrappers, and condom packets on Santa Monica Boulevard, just in the zone, singing Steve Winwood's "The Finer Things": "The finer things I feel in me. The golden dance life could be..."

To an outsider, I must seem insane—or even high—so happily crooning away as I sweep trash and leaves from the gutter. I just pay attention to the way my hands feel gripping the broom, the sun beaming down on my face, the muscles in my arms aching, the layered smell of the city streets. There is nothing to figure out right now. Just sweep. *Sweep the leaves, Amy.* For somebody who lives in their head and is essentially terrorized by their thoughts, this is a sweet reprieve. Just to be in your body, mindless. And when I get home tonight, I'll be so tired that I won't have the energy to go on my usual mental jaunt—the "greatest hits" tour of my worst fuck-ups and missed opportunities of the last few years.

I have a dustpan full to the brim of trash and leaves. I have no Carlos.

"Carlos? Come on, man! Keep up."

"Hold on, girl. This man needs directions."

I look a few feet behind me, and he's talking to some guy in a suit. He's trying to help the guy find an address on the street. I drop my broom on the ground and mop my sweaty face with my forearm, as my hands are covered by cheap plastic gloves. Fuck, it's hot. I look over at Carlos and the guy he's talking to. Wait...he looks familiar. I squint and wrack my brain. Oh, my God! It's Michael. He's in AA. I fucked him! Like, eight years ago.

I turn my back and look down. I'm mortified. I jokingly think about going up to him and saying, "Hey, it's Amy. Remember me? I just got out of a bad marriage, jail, and rehab. Aren't you bummed you didn't stay on *this* ride?" But of course I don't. I just wonder what it must be like to be able to stay on track for any length of time. If I had, where would I be now?

I met Michael in 2005. I had been sober for almost nine months, but my epilepsy had become rebelliously active again. I had just had another *grand mal* seizure after going on a new depression medication. For an epileptic with major depression, getting the dosage right is a real balancing act, because antidepressants can lower an epileptic's seizure threshold. You don't want to be undepressed but seizing, or seizure-free but suicidal. Medicating is an art, not a science. There's a lot of trial and error involved—which is not exactly reassuring when your life's at stake.

In the ER, the doctors wanted to give me Ativan—typical seizure protocol. I called my sponsor to get his okay, and he said, "Just let the doctors do what they need to do." So I did. If you have never had the experience of intravenous Ativan, well...my condolences. It is fucking awesome. They shot me full of Ativan, and I asked for more. They gave it to me, and I asked for more. They gave it to me again, and I again asked for more. At this point, they refused—wisely—as I was singing, putting on makeup, and calling people while still lying on the gurney.

The whole next week is a blur. I'm guessing I convinced my gullible new psychiatrist to give me a scrip or two for Ativan, which I then gobbled up with the fervor only a drug addict can muster. I've *heard* that I was in AA meetings—loaded, kicking over chairs, yelling, "I'm a princess, motherfuckers!"—but I don't remember a moment of it, thank God.

I apparently called my father, multiple times a day, in an Ativan-induced blackout. "I wanna get loaded and die," I'd chant over and over. I vaguely remember pouring pills into my mouth like Tic Tacs from an open prescription bottle and chain-smoking Parliament Lights. Finally, my papa said, "Ames, you need to go somewhere and cool out."

"You mean like a spa?" I slurred.

"Kind of."

"Okay. I'll pack... But first I need to wash my hair and get laid."

"Whatever you need to do, Ames."

I washed my hair, but I was so out of it, so fucked up on pills, that even the most lecherous creeps in AA refused to come over and service me.

I called a cab and vomited in it on the way to the "spa." The next morning I came to, only to realize that in my blackout, I had signed myself into a seventy-two-hour hold at the Thalians Mental Health Center. Idiot.

My roommate was a thirty-two-year-old mother of six, and she didn't know how the fuck she got to the "spa," either.

"I had one glass of wine and a Valium to relax. I did not try to kill myself. I have six children: two sons and quadruplets. Why would I want to kill myself?"

"That sounds like six reasons right there," I muttered.

Let me explain something, when you're in a green paper gown in the psych ward, anything you say can sound crazy. I told a nurse, "Well, I thought this was a spa... that's why I brought my bathing suit." I was dosed with extra meds immediately. Or "Umm, nurse, I'm worried my cat isn't eating."

"Uh-huh." She listened with mock concern. "Did he tell you that?"

"If you want to get out of there, you better act like somebody who can get the fuck out of there," my father said through the pay phone.

"Papa, I—Will you shut the fuck up?" I blurted out to a patient walking by who was chattering loudly to himself. "I'm talking to somebody who actually exists!"

I got off the pay phone and wolfed down a bagel, warily eyeing the other patients. Some looked totally insane. Others just looked pitiful. A few looked as if they had, like me, just fallen on hard times.

Every day we had to go to "goal group" and talk about our goals for the day. Like there were so many fucking options. Hmm, maybe I'll make an ashtray. Or maybe I'll eat another bagel. You know what? I think I'm just gonna curl up in a ball and rock in the corner of my room for three hours.

We were sitting in a circle of chairs, and in walked the social worker who'd be leading the group: dark, wavy bob, black pants, white top, plain face. She couldn't be more vanilla.

"Hi, I'm Megan and this is goal group. Please remember there is no touching, sexual or otherwise. We let words warm us from the inside."

"Well, that sounds boring," I said aloud. She shot me a look.

The mother of six had been discharged that morning, and my new roommate was a pudgy bipolar girl who kept getting reprimanded for wearing clothes that were too revealing. I remember a doughy white shoulder peeking out of a black top but nothing untoward. She had checked herself in voluntarily while her doctor switched her meds over. I doubt she'll ever make that mistake again.

First up in our circle was a Russian woman. She was toothless and gurning and growing a small goatee. She had a ponytail on the top front of her head like a unicorn. I've come to believe that ponytails are the crazy dial of humanity. If it's up at the front, like this woman's, you're nuts. If it's at the top of your head like Pebbles, you're just perky with manic tendencies. If it's just a regular ponytail, you're some sorority bitch going for a run. And if it's tied low at the nape of your neck, you're depressive, a lesbian, or a sister wife.

She pointed a bony finger slowly toward the whole group. "My goal for the day is to pray to the baby Jesus because you're all talking about me and it's all negative!"

I collapsed in silent laughter.

"Stop it," my new roommate said, nudging me. I wiped away tears from laughing and tried to collect myself.

Next to the Russian with the beard was an enormous woman with a huge belly, arms folded atop. The bearded Russian had her arm linked around the enormous one's.

"I'm going to pray with her," the big-bellied lady said.

I clapped. "Good goal, good goal."

The bearded one smiled a gummy smile and rested her head contentedly on the fat one's bulging shoulder.

Next up was a black guy in a wheelchair. His legs were really thin and burned, but they were beautifully folded over each other. I didn't know his name, so I called him "origami man." I had fantasies about sneaking into his room at night and folding up his legs into a swan or crane. I had spoken with him briefly at breakfast. He was reading the newspaper and seemed relatively normal till he began to launch into government conspiracies, UFOs, and brain control. That's when I hailed for the check, so to speak. His goal was something about keeping informed on the latest secret something. He was not half as amusing as I had hoped.

During this entire group, there was a guy who, obviously gravely stricken with OCD, was picking up tiny specks of different things off the carpet. I kept seeing him disappear as he bobbed down behind the social worker's chair, put something in a napkin in his hand, and then bobbed back up, only to disappear again five seconds later. I was mesmerized by his focus.

Third up to share was a blind, fat lesbian. She teetered back and forth, eyes closed, saying almost in a whisper, "My goal for the day is to make a friend, because it's dark and lonely in here."

I turned to my roommate and whispered, "Isn't that a Morrissey song?"

My roommate ignored me but Megan, the social worker, was paying attention.

"Okay, Miss Chatty Cathy..."

"It's Amy. Not Cathy."

"What's your goal for the day, Amy?"

"Well...umm...*my* goal for the day is to get the fuck out of here. And I can't believe I'm the only one who said that."

After the group, I was eating a small container of pudding when an old German man came up to me.

"You think you are so different from us. That we are crazy but you are not. But you are here for a reason, too." His eyebrows went up slightly as he looked deeply into my eyes and then walked away. I was speechless. He was absolutely right. I was an asshole.

The memory of the rest of my stay was clouded by the heavy psych meds. This is probably a good thing because I spent five days with people who were pretty tortured and out of their minds. One even thought he was Thomas Jefferson. I also lost seven pounds, thanks to the inedible food. It was like a cross between *One Flew over the Cuckoo's Nest* and Jenny Craig.

Finally, I had a meeting with the head psychiatrist, a quiet Jewish man with glasses and a yarmulke. I was hoping it would be my exit interview.

"Your problem is that you think you are smarter than everybody else," he said.

"No I don't *think* that. I *know* it," I said, smiling.

He wrote something down in my file.

"I'm just kidding," I added.

He wrote something else down.

"You also like to get attention, which you do by getting negative attention."

I shrugged. "Okay. Food for thought," I said. "Now that I'm not shooting coke in my neck, I'll look into it."

Incredibly, he discharged me. I might have been a sarcastic ass, but I wasn't certifiably "crazy."

I was thrilled to be released into the free world, but they had fucked with my meds and taken me off my normal seizure protocol. I felt disoriented and depressed. I went to an AA meeting that was held at this weird coffeehouse on Vine. They served overpriced lattes, Mexican tortas, and fruit shakes. The walls were covered in shitty amateur art that was for sale. I was super skinny, no makeup, greasy hair. Leon, a queenie costume designer who sounds like Harvey Fierstein and can't stay sober to save his life, was there. He had on some getup that was very Britney Spears crossed with Courtney Love crossed with . . . a five o'clock shadow. He, at least, thought I looked great.

"You look like a pretty young boy. I'd totally fuck you," he croaked.

"You're a freak, Leon. But you have good taste," I retorted.

He laughed.

It was there that I met Michael, the guy asking Carlos for an address on the street we were sweeping. He was short and Jewish, neither of which I find attractive, but he was nice to me, a great photographer, and pursued me with a terrifying fervor. I eventually caved, and we fucked once. It was awful. He had a small dick and had trouble getting hard. He was nervous and embarrassed. I was insulted and offended. When he finally got a boner, he tried to fuck me in the ass. Listen, I'm not against anal sex, but not the first time I'm with somebody. And, honestly, his dick was so small, I probably would have let him fuck me in the nose if he hadn't been so presumptuous. But who fucks a girl who just got out of the psych ward and off a relapse? My vulnerability alone would make it too easy, like shooting fish in a barrel. Oh—I'm sorry. I mean, welcome to AA.

# CHAPTER FIFTEEN

My court date is coming up and I'm only half done with my community labor. I've heard from my other fuck-up friends that a first extension is easy to get. However, my lawyer has long since abandoned me, so I'm doing the self-service legal thing now. I have no idea who my judge is or which court I'm supposed to go to. Trina, my bail bondswoman buddy, gives me my case number, and I call the courthouse. Turns out that criminal cases are no longer heard at the Beverly Hills Courthouse. I have to go to Airport Court. And a new judge has my case, and—praise Jesus—it's a man. This is good. Men like me better.

Still, I'm nervous. If the judge, for whatever reason, chooses not to give me an extension, I go to jail.

"Call me tomorrow after court and let me know everything went okay," Trina says.

"Yeah, I'll be calling you. Either to tell you it all went fine or to ask you to bail me out...again."

I put on my hippie shirt (it's the most court-friendly thing I own) and drive down to Airport Court. I really feel like I'm going to have a heart attack. Why do I always think it's a good idea to drink a five-shot latte and vape my brains out when I'm already nervous? So fucking stupid. I call Linda and cry briefly on the phone with her.

"What if the judge doesn't give me an extension and I go to jail?" I whimper.

"That's not going to happen," she says calmly.

"How do you know?"

"It's going to be okay, I promise."

"If he's having a bad day and throws me in the clink, will you come visit?"

"Of course."

"Will you smuggle little bags of coke up your vaj like they do in the movies?"

"Whatever you want."

I hang up and look at myself in the rearview mirror.

"You got this," I whisper.

I wait my turn in the long, crowded line at the building entrance. My bag finally goes through the X-ray machine, and I walk through the metal detector unscathed. We're good to go.

I take the elevator up to the fifth floor and enter the courtroom. I sign in with the bailiff and sit down and wait for my case to be called. I'm fussing with the papers I brought: a letter from the rehab saying that I was in treatment for seven months, the paper that proves I completed the year of domestic violence class with stellar ratings, and my sign-in sheet from community labor, showing that I have completed about 120 of the 240 hours of community labor.

A full-blown debate starts waging in my head: *You should have brought a bag of clothes and stuff, in case you go straight to jail.*

*Okay...no...that's ridiculous; this is the first extension, and I'm half done with the hours.*

*But really...what if you go to jail? Your car is just on a meter.*

*Oh, come on...I'm not going to jail. I didn't even violate the restraining order.*

*But look at it from the judge's point of view: even though you were in treatment for seven months, that should have been enough time to do all the community service.*

*OMG, would you shut the fuck up?*

Just then, they call my case. I nervously scramble up from my seat. I can hear my heart pounding in my ears.

"You're here for an extension, Ms. Dresner?" the judge asks. He's an older man, with white hair and glasses, narrow face, calm demeanor.

"Yes, Your Honor. I was in treatment for seven months and I have a signed letter from the rehab. I have completed half of my community labor and all of my domestic violence classes."

"May I see the papers?"

"Yes, sir." I hand the papers to the bailiff, who brings them up to the judge. The judge pulls his glasses down the bridge of his nose and looks at the papers. He nods and hands them back to the bailiff, who returns them to me.

"How long do you need to finish the community labor, Ms. Dresner?" the judge asks me.

"Four months should be fine, Your Honor."

"I'll give you six. See you then, Ms. Dresner."

"Thank you."

I smile politely, and as soon as I walk out of the courtroom, I punch the air.

YESSS!

But hold on a minute there, Ms. Misdemeanor. Just imagine if the judge was having a bad day? Say he got a parking ticket, or his hemorrhoid flared up, and he had said no to your extension. You'd be in jail again. Just like that. It seemed terrifyingly easy to get caught in the sticky web of the legal system. And without money to hire yourself a crooked, ruthless lawyer, you are seriously fucked.

For the first time in my life I feel determined. Determined to finish something. I am taking full responsibility for the consequences of my actions, and although it isn't easy, it does feel good. Well, "good" probably isn't the right word. I don't feel like hiding from the world under the protective tent of my long rocker bangs. I don't feel like shoving a chopstick into my eyeball when I look in the mirror because I am such a spineless junkie piece of shit. Hey, maybe it isn't Tony Robbins's style of transformation, but it's a step in the right direction. And for the first time since I can remember, I feel really committed to something. I am committed to never getting arrested again, which means staying sober and controlling my temper. Again, it is a start. I wonder if all those years that my parents had bailed me out and "saved me" had really saved me at all. Maybe their patience and generosity and love had just prolonged this necessary and painful learning curve.

You know that saying, *Fool me once, shame on you! Fool me twice, shame on me?* Well, for me, it's more like *Fool me three hundred times, Hell...lemme take one more crack at it.* I guess I am just one of those stubborn assholes who has to burn their house to the ground to realize you shouldn't play with matches.

Tinder is killing me. It's so addictive. It's set up like a video game or a slot machine with that stupid *BING!*, like hitting the jackpot, when you get a new match. Add that to the thrill of a bit of "strange" and the rush of validation and hope, and you've got a deadly combo for a romantic thrill-seeker like me. Still, as an ex-criminal, I am a little uncomfortable with how many cops are on Tinder.

A very attractive guy, a New Yorker who comes to L.A. regularly for business, hits me up. He is extremely clear about what he is looking for.

"Listen, here's the deal. I've got hoes in different area codes..."

"You are *not* quoting Ludacris to me..."

"Yeah, but it's true."

"Umm, okay...so am I applying for 213, 323, or 310? Is 818 already taken?"

I'm a writer, and I was a comic, so verbal banter, even if it's bullshit, is my forte. I appreciate his honesty and delude myself into thinking I can handle the situation.

"Meet me at the Beverly Hills Hotel at eight p.m. tomorrow night. That's where I'm staying."

I think I've been to the Beverly Hills Hotel once in my life, back when my ex was trying to impress me. He took me to the Polo Lounge—as if to say, "Look at the life I can give you..." Sad to say, it worked.

I need something to wear. I have T-shirts with holes in them and flowy seventies Stevie Nicks stuff. Nothing in between. Terry might have something. She was rich and she's a grown-up.

"Hey, Terry, I have a date tonight. Do you have a hot top I can wear?"

"I don't get it. You stay in your room all day, and you have more dates than anybody I know. . . ."

"It's all marketing." I smile. "Thank you, Wendy Hall Photography, for helping me lure poor, unsuspecting men into my poisonous lair."

"You are so weird," Terry says. She holds up a lace Isabel Marant number. "How about this?"

"Bitch, you know me!" I say as I gleefully grab it and put it on.

I slip on my uniform black corduroy jeans and then some socks.

"Your socks don't match," Terry says.

"I don't care. You think he's not going to fuck me because of my socks? Pleeease. It's Tinder, girl."

I put on a vintage black fur.

"You look gorgeous—aside from the socks," she says. "Go have fun."

I do look pretty amazing. Now, if I can just throw my voice up an octave, not say "dude" or sit like a man, I should be good.

On my way out, I'm caught by Mariana, the house manager.

"You look nice. Where are you off to?"

"Uhhh . . . coffee . . . with a friend," I lie badly.

"Riiiiight . . . Just be back by curfew."

I give her a thumbs-up.

I drive my bird shit- and leaf-covered VW Passat to the hotel. You can *only* valet there, the thieving motherfuckers. Driving up, I look down at the floor of the front seat. It's covered in empty water bottles, Styrofoam Body Factory cups, and Yerba Mate cans. Classy.

I am walking through the lobby, all dolled up in my fur, when a guy walks by and says aloud, "This place is *full* of hookers tonight." Oof. I thought I looked glamorous, like a seventies supermodel, but evidently I look like a seventies streetwalker.

Lucas, my Tinder date, told me to meet him in the Polo Lounge, but I make a brief pass through, see a lot of old rich men and underclad young girls, and I immediately exit. I feel anxious. What if he doesn't think I'm as hot as my pictures? What if I don't think he's as hot as his pictures? Why am I doing this at all? Ugh.

I text him that I am "outside the Polo Lounge." I'm sitting on a couch in the hallway, all wide-eyed and shaky.

He comes down and he is...gorgeous. Brown hair, blue eyes, square jaw. Totally out of my league. We go have a drink at the bar. Well, he has a drink, and I have a Diet Coke. I'm nervous, so I start spewing—jokes, my story, anything to amuse, impress, or deflect. He's laughing. He's surprisingly nice and down to earth for somebody who looks like they just stepped off a goddamn runway. Turns out he has a girlfriend in New York, but their relationship is "open" at the moment. Okay...but does *she* know that?

We go outside to have a quick smoke. We make fun of how creepy Tinder is, which is a way of saying, "I never do this" or "I'm different" or "You're special." It's all bullshit, but it works to create some instant false intimacy. We share horror stories, stories of famous people we fucked, and then head up to his room.

"Do you mind if I smoke a little pot?" he asks.

"No, no...do your thing."

He smokes a joint, turns on some music, lights the fireplace, and says, "Okay, let's make out." Pretty blunt, but we're both here for the same thing. It's more like a drug drop than a date.

We start fooling around on the rug in front of the fire.

"How do you stay so skinny?" he asks me as our clothes come off. "You work out a lot? Or just don't eat?"

"Work out?" I stifle my laughter. "Um...no. Poverty and anxiety. It's actually a pretty efficient weight-control system. And lanky Jew is my natural body type."

"Nice..." he says as he goes down on me.

We move to the bed.

"Do you have a condom?" he asks.

"No, do you?"

"No...Fuck! Do you have anything...weird?" he presses.

"No. Do you?"

"No...and...I never raw dog, but..."

He pulls out a bottle of Rush and starts sniffing. (Rush is a liquid you inhale that gives you a head rush, thus its name. It's more commonly known as "poppers," and it's big in the gay scene. I've never done it.) So by this point, he's had a few drinks, some pot, and now some Rush. I, on the other hand, am stone-cold sober. I try my best to match his chemical-induced abandon. It seems unfair, like he's cheating. I'd sure like to snort something to feel more at ease with the ill-advised idea of fucking a stranger without a condom. In the end, he does make up for that. The sex is great, and I make it back by curfew.

We try to hook up again before he leaves town, but our schedules don't match up. Once he's back in New York, we talk a few times, and, unsurprisingly, he ends up in rehab. I also learn that he and his girl-friend ended up "closing" their relationship so they were exclusive now. I'm no psychic, but I saw both of these events coming.

My father is in town from Ashland, Oregon. I meet him at an over-priced sushi restaurant on La Cienega that has paparazzi perched like vultures outside. Think West Elm with a lot of bamboo, koi ponds, and scantily dressed starlets.

I walk in and hug him.

"Hi, Ames . . . You smoking again?"

Damn, I'm not even sober nine months and he's already on me about my smoking. One thing at a time, man.

"Yeah, I'm smoking. But I really wish I could have a drink."

"Not funny."

"Papa, listen to me," I say to him. "Whatever I'm doing, dating pricks or smoking cigarettes, if I don't have a needle in my arm, I'm a fucking success. Don't you get it? If I lay my head on the pillow sober tonight, I'm a winner for that day."

"I know you have to believe that in the program." My dad is a cynic, not just about AA, about everything.

"Have to believe it? I know it. I've been dying to get high for the last two days! You think I'm home free because I have a few months? Wake up. People relapse at five years, fifteen years. They get high and they fucking die. So let's not get ahead of ourselves."

My father is quiet. We stare at each other. My father looks concerned. I'm livid.

He takes a drink, wipes his mustache, and says, "Can I ask you a question? What is the difference between hope and expectations?"

"Hope is a feeling that things *can* change for the better. But expectations... well, when you have expectations, you are presuming that things will turn out a certain way, and you're bound to be disappointed if they don't."

He nods and takes another sip of his wine. "Okay, so what do you need from me?" he asks.

"Compassion. And tolerance. Just try to operate from the premise that I am doing the very best that I can to be happy and productive; however from the outside it may look to you."

"Do you have compassion for me? Can you imagine what it's like being your father?"

"I can't imagine. Heartbreaking and frustrating, I'm sure."

He reaches across the table and grabs my hand. I start to cry.

"I'm doing the best I can, I swear. So, I'm still dating assholes. The latest has your dry wit and dismissiveness and the emotional coldness of my mom. It's the perfect comfort food recipe from the combo plate of my parents."

"That sounds clever, but it's trite," he says. "That's theatre dialogue."

"Whatever. What I'm trying to say is that I'm operating off old programming and it's going to take some time to rewire everything. You just need to be patient."

He signals to the waiter for another glass of Chardonnay.

He looks across the table at me. "We've been doing this a long time," he says.

"What?" I asked.

"You at the bottom of the well," he answers.

# CHAPTER SIXTEEN

Trina calls regularly to see how things are going. She likes to remind me that "Community service is a *privilege*." Well, lucky me, I'm off to be "privileged" for yet another day. Last night, I hard-boiled some eggs for my sack lunch. Cooked eggs sitting in a hot van for four hours should make me some friends.

Much to my relief, this morning at community service, I am finally put on the graffiti removal crew. This job consists of spraying some stinky yellow liquid on the pavement and giving it a scrub, and then the crew leader pulls out a pressure hose, lets loose a violent jet of water, and away go all the gang tags. The hose seems like the most fun part, but I guess if you aim that thing at somebody, it could take their skin off. Plus, the pressure alone could knock you on your ass. I gather they've had some problems in the past with crew members getting hurt and suing, so we are only allowed to spray the yellow stuff and scrub the sidewalk with long-handled metal broom brushes while the power washing is left to the supervisors. It's boring work, but not exhausting.

The crew boss for graffiti removal is a tiny Guatemalan guy named Felipe. He doesn't speak much English.

"You espeak Spanish?" he asks me.

"No. So you can totally talk shit about me, and I will never know."

He smiles. He has no idea what I'm saying.

That morning, the graffiti removal crew is me, Felipe, and one other guy, an Asian kid. The Asian kid is short and stocky, with well-muscled arms and that swagger that tigers, gang members, and guys with big dicks all have. We ride together in this tiny truck with a water tank on the back. Every hour or so, we stop at a hydrant in a residential area and refill the water tank.

We are hosing down a bus stop. A woman with roller-set hair and eighties glasses is waiting for the bus. Suddenly, she comes up to me and says, pointing to the hose, "I have terrible allergies."

"It's just water, ma'am," I reassure her.

"Oh, good." She smiles and goes back to the bus stop.

Two minutes later, she comes back over, and as I prepare to answer another of her questions, she hands me a piece of candy. It's that kind of weird good candy that only old ladies have; the stuff they've been eating for forty-odd years. Her steel blue eyes are magnified by her thick eyeglasses. They look serene and kind. She smiles as I take the candy from her hand. I smile back and let out a weird childlike "Yum. Thank you!" Did she give me candy because I reassured her that it was just water? Did I look hungry? Did she feel bad for me? Maybe she has a grandson in Rikers? I have no idea what the deal is, but it's the little moments like these that are the surprise bonuses of all this court-ordered bullshit. I love these random connections with strangers. They are so rare in L.A., where you spend 98 percent of your time in your car, on your iPhone, screaming at shitty drivers, or drinking cold brew coffee and having a quiet existential crisis.

We stop for lunch at Burger King. It's just the Asian kid and me. Felipe eats his lunch in the truck.

"How much time you get?" I ask him.

"Six months."

"Six months?! Jesus. What'd you do?"

"Long story," he says.

"I got time." I smile.

"I'm a boxer, and I was at this club, and this dude comes up to me and picks a fight. I don't even remember what it was about. We were both pretty drunk. He throws a punch at me and I defensively block him and punch him back. Well, I guess I hit him really hard, because he fell backward and hit his head on the corner of a table. Fucked him up real bad. He was in a coma for almost a year, during which time I was facing manslaughter charges and looking at major prison time. But then he woke up. And now he's suing me for a million bucks...medical bills, emotional distress, damages...all of it."

"Whoa. I'm sorry, man."

"Yeah, it sucks."

I could tell that this kid had told this story a million times to thirty other nosy community service laborers like me. But this kind of thing is always our first entry into conversation with each other: *How much time did you get? What are you here for?* It's the one common bonding element among us. Reflecting on what this Asian kid told me, I remembered hearing that if you're a trained boxer and you hit a civilian, you can be in big trouble. They can charge you with "assault with a deadly weapon" because your hands are really deadly weapons. I felt bad for him. He was just defending himself, and now because the other guy was drunk and a bad fighter and fell over and landed perfectly on the edge of a table, he was *fucked*.

And that's really all it took to put my shitty situation into perspective. Suddenly I was the lucky one. My thirty days was a breeze! It's like that modern take on the famous Persian proverb: "I cried that I had no shoes until I met a man who had no feet." Well, I just met a guy who had no feet, and suddenly being barefoot was pretty fucking great.

I've pretty much lost everything: my home, my marriage, my sobriety, my sanity. I even lost most of my belongings. My ex was kind enough to put a few of my things into some garbage bags that Linda retrieved, but he donated the remainder of my stuff. The real kicker was that I also lost my health insurance. Gone were the Beverly Hills doctors with their designer waiting rooms, fresh-cut flowers, expensive art, and chi-chi clientele. As I had a pretty colorful mental health history and was well beneath the poverty line now, my psychiatrist suggested I apply for MediCal disability. And despite a twenty-year struggle with drug abuse, I was advised not to lead with or even mention my addiction.

Although addiction is considered a "disease" by most medical associations, it is not considered a disability. (Frankly, my drug use was equally, if not more, disabling than any of my other issues, but I don't make the laws.) The MediCal bureaucrats initially refused me, but I appealed and won.

My experience with the MediCal system has not been that bad. Every test a doctor has ordered (from MRIs to EEGs to mammograms) and any specialist they have referred me to (neurologist, psychiatrist, gynecologist) has been approved. Granted, I have to drive forty-five minutes or more to an "urban" area (fuck it... I like taquerías), and I'm usually the only white or English-speaking patient in the clinic. The waiting rooms are small and cramped, with cheap, rickety furniture, linoleum floors, ancient fitness magazines, and dusty fake plants. And even with an appointment, you have to wait. It can be as little as thirty minutes or as long as two hours. Also every MediCal doctor—and I do mean every—tests you for HIV, so that's obviously a big government concern.

My primary care doctor is Russian, and so is every single person who works in her office as well as every patient I've ever seen in her waiting room. Once, attempting to fit in, I said, "Well, I'm part Russian Jew, I look a little Russian, and I once dated a Russian electrician." I smiled. Nobody was amused.

"You must to learn Russian," the nurse told me. "Iz good!"

I wasn't really paying attention, as I was mesmerized by her loud eighties abstract sweater, huge plastic earrings, and turquoise eye shadow.

My first MediCal gynecologist was pretty (like that should matter) and infinitely capable. Her waiting room was unremarkable, aside from the huge television blaring Spanish cartoons. There were a few questions on the medical intake questionnaire that I wasn't used to: "Have you been physically abused?" and "Do you have a gun in the house?" I scribbled "no" to each as Marvin Gaye's "Sexual Healing" played over the sound system. Bad musical choice.

My only real complaint has been with the psychiatrist I was referred to—also Russian. (Evidently, I'm in the Russian medical mafia.) The psychiatrist's office was on the second floor of a shitty mini mall on the shitty end of Sunset. Every single sign or flyer in the office was in Russian. Smiling but uneasy, I sat down between a very old woman and a skinny lecherous-looking guy and immersed myself in my phone.

I have a new message on Facebook. It's from that New York actor-comic Bradley who said Facebook told him he should poke me. What does Mr. Poke want now?

"Hey, Amy, I've been reading your articles. I really enjoy them. I actually have a question for you about mental illness, bipolarity specifically."

I've got time to kill. Fuck it.

"Sure, Bradley. Hit me. I'm happy to help if I can."

Bradley goes on to explain that he has a teenage daughter from a one-night stand and that the baby mama is bipolar and won't stay on her meds. He's concerned and doesn't know how to help. There are also some financial issues regarding her health care and her unemployability.

It is not unusual for me to get strangers writing to me, confiding their problems or asking advice. In 2012, I was tapped by the then editor of the online addiction and recovery magazine *The Fix* to write a piece about sex and dating in AA. I'd like to think it was because I was funny and ballsy, but I'm sure my reputation as a program fuckbunny didn't hurt, either. I hadn't written for a magazine since my college days twenty years prior, but I wasn't doing much apart from the occasional stand-up gig and chronically relapsing, so I jumped at the chance. This piece ended up being so well received and the editor was so impressed that I began regularly freelancing for them.

The majority of my *Fix* pieces over the five-plus years I've been writing for them have been extremely personal and shamelessly confessional, chronicling my, well…everything. Was I exploiting myself? Maybe. Was I helping people know that they weren't alone? Absolutely. When you write with relentless honesty, people feel as if they know you. They feel safe divulging things to you that they keep from even those closest to them. And it's incredibly flattering when strangers consider you as trustworthy as any dark confessional.

So anyway, I answer Bradley as I would any reader who reached out for help, explaining that I'm no doctor, but I do know that it's extremely common for people with bipolar disorder to go off their meds, either feeling that they don't need them anymore or wanting their fun, super-energized mania back. I also suggest that his baby mama apply for disability, as it would help with medical costs, and she might even be eligible for disability benefits.

Just as I finish the message, Dr. Fedoseev (not her real name, which had even more vowels and was even less pronounceable) calls me into her office. She has orange-red hair, a white lab coat, and looks classically agonized in that old-school Soviet Union way.

"Tell me about your problem," she demands in a thick accent.

"Well, I've had depression since I was nineteen and have been diagnosed with all sorts of mental illnesses, including borderline personality disorder and bipolarity. I'm also a recovering drug addict and alcoholic."

"No, tell me your physical problem."

"Uh...I have epilepsy from my methamphetamine abuse."

"Why you think that?"

"That's what the tests reveal: hyperactive lesions."

"When you start with seizure?"

"Thirty-three."

"When you start drink?"

"Nineteen."

"When you stop drink?"

"The first time? Twenty-eight."

"See...you not drink; you not have seizure."

"Yeah...uh...that's not really accurate. I was five years sober when I had my first seizure."

"When?"

"At thirty-three."

"You drink now?"

"No."

"How long?"

"Seventeen months."

"So, like year and half."

"Yes."

"Where you live?"

"With friends." The girls in sober living *are* my friends now, so it's not completely inaccurate.

"With friends? You are not teenager anymore."

"Thank you. I'm aware of that, and so is my Botox doctor."

"Why you not have salary?" she asks, looking at my paperwork.

"I'm a freelance writer. I just wrote a television pilot. Also, I'm still getting on my feet after a divorce... I'm not really sure what this has to do with my depression."

"Your ex-husband don't give you money?"

"No. Long story."

"You have mood swings?"

"Sometimes, but not so much anymore."

"You try Depakote?"

"I'm epileptic. Of course I've tried Depakote. I've been on everything. Depakote didn't work for me, particularly the thirty-pound weight gain part."

"You are young, pretty... I don't understand why you need Prozac."

"Yes... youth and beauty completely cancel out any biologically based depression," I say. *Look at all the happy, well-adjusted models,* I think.

"You've seen psychiatrist before?"

"Only every single one of merit here in Los Angeles, Paris, London, San Francisco, and Boston over the last twenty-plus years."

"You don't seem stable."

"Why would you say that? I'm more stable than I've ever been. I'm sober. I'm working. I exercise. I'm not engaging in any compulsive or self-destructive behavior."

"You seem high to me."

I frowned. "I'm just feeling good today," I say.

"Why you have disability?"

"Because I have a long-standing history of mental illness, suicide attempts, and epilepsy," I tell her. *You would have gleaned that from this interview if you hadn't been so concerned about my remarkably youthful demeanor or lack of salaried work, you cunt,* I think.

"They have many new medication now for depression: Brintellix, Viibryd . . . ."

"That's fantastic, but why fix it if it ain't broke?"

"Okay. I not change your medication right now." She pulls out a pad and scribbles on it. "I write you a prescription for Prozac."

She hands me the scrip. "I see you in three months. Good luck to you."

"You don't need luck if you're good," I say as I walk out the door.

"Good luck to you" is like "God bless you." It can be both a warm sentiment and a condescending way of saying "Fuck you." After I get back to the sober living, I notice that I am wearing one of my standard holey T-shirts and that I have a bit of toothpaste in my hair, which might not have contributed to the best first impression. Still, I am aghast at her prying into my financials and her assumptions about my epilepsy. I've spent enough time in psychiatrists' offices to take stock of all the things she neglected to do. She never took a real mental health history. She never asked for a list of my prior medications or the records from my previous psychiatrists. She couldn't have been less interested in my suicide attempts or multiple psych ward visits. What she told me ran contradictory to the diagnoses of every neurologist I've had in the last fourteen years. On top of all that, she insulted me and minimized the hard work I've done to get sober and stay in recovery. That's a proud seventeen months sober, while recovering from a divorce, a nervous breakdown, and a relapse. So, how am I doing? I'm doing fucking fantastic. Fuck you, lady.

---

# CHAPTER SEVENTEEN

Another day on the chain gang. Yeehaw. I'm still not sure what all the lasso hand gestures or dog whistles that the crew bosses use mean, but I'm getting some of my Spanish back. I was bilingual when I was two, living briefly with my mother in Mexico, and although I've forgotten most of what I knew, I still understand it pretty well—much more than I can speak. In fact, I actually understand more than I'd like to some days. For instance (if my piss-poor Spanish serves me), "Coco" gives the best happy endings at the Thai massage joint on Vermont. And Cheetahs is awesome because even if you're there for two hours, you never see the same girl twice. Also, I think *chichinitas* means "big tits." (Obviously, they were not referring to me.)

While we are sweeping, we see a guy wake up naked and drunk under a freeway overpass. Everybody thinks it's hysterical except me. They point and take pictures and holler. The guy runs off.

"He's an alcoholic, you guys. It's not funny. It's sad," I say to nobody in particular.

"Oh…that's right, you were a waste case too, huh?" one of the guys says.

I don't bother answering. I don't have the energy for a debate about the true nature of addiction or how it's not an issue of morals and will-power. Also, I need to fit in, not stand out. I have nothing to prove here.

There's a super-cute guy on my crew today. He's slender with a head-ful of perfect dark hair and a smile that could give you arrhythmia. Of course, he's gay. I was hoping I was wrong about that, but as soon as he said he was in "fashion" I thought, "Yeah, definitely not on my team." He's there for a DUI. What's new? We agree to become friends on Facebook, but he asks me not to tag him in anything "related to this shit." His Facebook feed is full of red carpet events, fashion shows, and pictures of the beautiful people and the pseudo-famous. I get it. He's using "discretion," trying to be "professional." I wish I could manage that, but instead, I comically flaunt my newly acquired criminality on Facebook. I'm not proud of what happened, but I also refuse to be ashamed. Shit happens. And if you can't laugh at it . . . how else can you get through it?

Mr. Fashion promises to introduce me to all these people who will help my writing career, but we both know he's lying. We will never speak again. He doesn't want to remember me because he doesn't want to remember any of this.

At lunch at Yoshinoya, he goes outside to make work calls, pretending to colleagues that he's on a "business trip." The rest of the crew is watching what I will admit are pretty impressive videos of a girls' banana eating contest.

"Hey can you do that, *guera*?" one of them asks me, laughing.

"Leave me out of this, guys."

I get up to throw away my lunch stuff, and I hear them carrying on.

"That can't be real, bro. If that shit's real, I'll marry that girl."

I don't seem to be able to get any recovery in SLAA, and my behavior is escalating. Just like with drugs, you develop a tolerance, and you have to up the stakes: fuck more people in weirder ways, in more outrageous locations. I've had sex with a different guy each day of the week. I've fucked two guys in one night. I've fucked guys in parking lots. I've fucked guys with their girlfriends. I've created a little stable of men that I have sex with when the urge hits me. And the urge hits me a lot.

Now I'm no longer just having sex with people I'm attracted to. I've started having sex with anyone: people I'm repulsed by, people who intrigue me, people who irritate me, people I know, people I don't know. It doesn't matter. I just need the validation and to lose myself for those few brief moments. Because of that, I always have my eyes closed. I don't want to see them—these people that I'm using who are using me.

Despite my physical sobriety from drugs, I am far from "emotionally sober." I feel extremely out of control, and I'm aware that my sex addiction is the newest incarnation of my alcoholism. Instead of drinking and drugging my feelings away, I'm sexualizing them all now: fear, sadness, anxiety, boredom. Any feeling I'm overwhelmed by or just don't want to handle gets fucked away—including the feeling that I've just transferred my compulsion to get high to a compulsion to get laid. I'm still sick; it's just a new sick.

In my desperation, I decide to try SAA, which stands for Sex Addicts Anonymous. I'd heard it was more "hard-core" (whatever that means) and that there was actually more recovery there.

I find a meeting online. Of course it's in a church, which makes it all the more creepy. I walk into the small, dim room. There is a circle of chairs. It is twelve men and me. They are all quite welcoming, but I still feel very anxious and uncomfortable. As soon as the meeting starts, I begin to cry. Perfect. One woman finally comes to their fucking meeting, and she bawls through the first half of it. Good job, Amy.

The men share openly and honestly, trying to be respectful of my presence while not inhibiting the honesty of the meeting. I appreciate that. Most of them are porn addicts who can't stop jacking off to the Internet for hours and hours at a time. It's affecting their work, marriages, relationships. The rest of the guys talk about prostitutes... how they love the seediness of hookers or the shadiness of Craigslist encounters. I don't relate. What I do relate to, however, are the feelings of shame and the incredible loneliness that every single person in that room expresses.

After the meeting, I canvas all my sex addict friends (98 percent of whom are men) and learn that, in all of Los Angeles, there is but one all-women SAA meeting. It's on a Wednesday night in Santa Monica. I decide to give it a shot.

I've never been particularly fond of women's meetings. There is either too much crying or too much clapping. I'm not down with yays and hugs.

I've also heard that other women find me "intimidating" and "terrifying," but what they're seeing is just my defensive façade because *I* feel intimidated and terrified. Granted, in my very early stints of sobriety, I was powered by rage and heavy black eyeliner, and I'd be chain-smoking and stomping around in my vintage furs. I'd like to believe I've mellowed with time. Plus, I think my extended time in the sober living sorority has softened me a bit.

This meeting is in the conference room of a posh high-rise in Santa Monica. The leader is a woman who's probably a few years older than me, but looks exhausted, dry—like somebody left her in the oven too long. Though she's been in the "fellowship" for many years, she still seems pretty fucked up, if her very recent stories are any indication.

The group is a small one—maybe seven of us total—and two are newcomers, who refrain from sharing. I had expected to feel more comfortable around all women. And, though they, like me, were sex addicts seeking validation and love in all the wrong places, I do not feel at ease among them.

"Do you want to share?" the leader asks me.

There is a strange, almost reverent vibe in the air, which makes me uncomfortable and seems wildly at odds with the nature of this compulsion. Why all this weird prudish bullshit? Aren't these the same women who are blowing strangers in the self-help section of Barnes and Noble?

"Sure. Fuck it," I say. Because I'm so ill at ease, I can feel that I'm going to be more shocking and vulgar than necessary. Oh, God, here I go...

I talk about how Tinder is "like Domino's delivery for dick" and how I "boned" a thirty-year-old newcomer in my car two days prior. There is not a snippet of laughter—not even nods of identification. Immediately, I sense that my using "bone" as a verb is seen as juvenile and disrespectful in light of how painful and powerful they see this compulsion. When I finally finish my filthy, Kinisonesque rant, the leader says awkwardly, "Well, thanks for sharing all that, Amy. Keep coming back." I never did. I knew I needed help, but I also knew these ladies were too stuffy and square to be my sober pussy posse, if you will.

# CHAPTER EIGHTEEN

I've been going to this small noon AA meeting on the second floor of an infamous Sunset metal bar, the Rainbow Bar and Grill. I never drank there. Generally speaking, I tried not to drink in public because a) I tended to black out; b) booze always made me naked and violent; and c) I tended to black out. When I wasn't drinking or using by myself, I didn't really go out, because people alternately bored or scared me. So, no, I didn't go out a lot.

When you walk into the Rainbow Bar and Grill, you can see why it would be a lush's paradise. It's dark, even during the day. There's a fireplace. The fake plants are covered in dust and God knows what else, lending even more eeriness to the time capsule element of the place. The wood-paneled walls are covered with candid photos of famous musicians: Axl Rose, Lemmy, Ozzy Osbourne, Alice Cooper, Vince Neil, Robert Plant . . . you name it. The place smells cozy but sleazy, like a cabin they used to shoot porn in. The lower dining room is a sea of cheap red vinyl booths and a floral maroon carpet that stinks of spilled well drinks and decades of stale cigarette smoke, all stamped down by the stacked-heel boots of rockers and the patent-leather stilettos of groupies.

The room where the meeting is held is decorated like an old ship, with nautical paraphernalia: compasses and old gauges, weird plaques and the like. I'm guessing it's where everybody went to do coke back in the day, because the guaranteed chirp of the new guy is inevitably: "I used to do so much blow up here, man. Weird to be in an AA meeting in the old stomping grounds . . ."

I notice a new guy in the corner: dark hair and a lush beard, which he strokes seductively. He's wearing sunglasses. Inside. Fucking douche. I hope he's either high or crying, because the remaining option is poseur dickwad extraordinaire. It's probably that last one, because he's reclining, feet up, in heavy black boots, resting on the railing. It's a very confident pose, and he looks kind of short, so I immediately wonder what he's so arrogant about.

"Hi, I'm Xander, and I'm an alcoholic."

"Hi, Xander," the room answers in unison.

"What kind of fucking name is Xander?" I whisper to nobody in particular. "Like a new artificial sweetener or some alien god out of Scientology."

Xander goes on, rather poetically, to share about his emotional enmeshment with his mother, how he was her surrogate spouse. Bingo. I had the exact same thing with my dad. And from that moment on, I know something awful and untoward and magical is going to happen between us. Yes, trauma bonding, the instant intimacy and Super Glue of alcoholics.

Turns out Xander is Italian, from the Midwest. Carried his mommy issues all the way out here from the Heartland. And if that's not bad enough, he's only thirty years old. I mean, Jesus, I have vintage T-shirts older than this guy. Of course, the cherry on the cake is that he's a "newcomer" with only seven months clean. This will be a bloodbath. Fucking count me in.

After the meeting, I'm standing on the Rainbow patio, which is furnished with cheap green plastic chairs and strung with colored Christmas lights twelve months a year. I'm aggressively sucking on my vape pipe, a ridiculous Doctor Who screwdriver–like contraption when Xander comes swaggering out.

"You're very...*Serpico*, aren't you?" I say.

"Oh, why, thank you."

"How did you know it was a compliment?"

"I chose to take it that way. Life is all about perception."

I nod my head slowly. He doesn't break eye contact.

"I related to your share," I tell him. "I was...my dad's...emotional wife."

He smiles and cocks his head flirtatiously.

I look at him and laugh. "This is a terrible idea...whatever this is."

"Oh, it's a horrible idea, and it has to happen."

I get home from the meeting, and Terry isn't home. I know she had court today—a big custody hearing. I'd sent her a text wishing her good luck. A few hours later, I sent another asking how it went. No answer. I call her cell. It goes directly to voice mail.

I call the house manager, Mariana.

"Have you talked to Terry in the last few hours? She hasn't returned my texts."

"Yeah. I'm at Cedars with her right now."

"What? Why?"

"She had a rough day in court."

"Oh, fuck. Should I come down there?"

"No, no. They're releasing her soon. I'm bringing her home."

Terry had lost the hearing to get custody of her kids back, and she totally flipped out. She went straight from the courthouse to the liquor store, bought a pint, and got shit-faced. She then went over to some guy's place—and passed out in the bushes. That's where the guy found her—face-planted, ass up, skirt ripped, court blazer covered in vomit. Like any good alcoholic, even after almost a year sober, she gave herself alcohol poisoning the first time out. After hours of dry heaving, her fuck friend had taken her to the hospital. She'll be fine...as long as her ex-husband and the court don't find out.

Mariana doesn't throw Terry out for relapsing, but Terry decides it's time to move out anyway. She has to get out of sober living and into a child-friendly environment if she ever hopes to see her kids without some weird court monitor taking exhaustive notes of every little thing she feeds them, every word she utters, and every move she makes.

I'm sorry to see her go. We've shared a room for almost a year, and

despite being almost polar opposites, we have gotten along spectacu-
larly. We have sort of pulled each other a tiny bit toward the other's orbit.
Maybe I have become a little more maternal...cleaner...better about
going to the gym? She's become a little sluttier and more foul-mouthed
and learned to take herself less seriously.

Upside is I have the room to myself for a while. It's a minor reprieve.
I still have the same shitty single bed, but at least I can retreat into my
room and have...what's it called again?...oh, yeah...privacy. Still, I'll
have another roomie in no time. Mariana's house is always full, as most
women's sober livings are horribly regimented, overpriced, and overpop-
ulated. That's how you make money: pack as many junkies into a room
as possible—even if you have to stack 'em up like slaves on a cargo ship.

It's only three weeks before my new bunkmate arrives. Elizabeth is
in her early thirties, an Amazon at nearly five feet ten inches, and very
pretty, but her overzealous use of Botox and fillers makes her look like
a cross between a porcelain doll and the Joker. She speaks in a breathy
whisper, acts stupid, and smiles when she's upset. All façade. I'm the
exact opposite. This should be interesting.

Elizabeth doesn't have a job. She is supported by her father and the
various rich Persian men she dates. She isn't a hooker, per se, but let's
just say she sees sex as a bartering technique. One night, she comes
home late, and I say—with my usual finesse—"Did you fuck him?" She
answers, in all seriousness, "Why would I sleep with him? He didn't buy
me anything."

# CHAPTER NINETEEN

Just when I thought community labor couldn't get any worse, I get the chance to do it on my period, in the pouring rain: eight hours sweeping up wet trash while doubled over with cramps. However, I'm starting to pick up on my lesson's theme: "Look, Amy! It could always be worse." And of course, now, sweeping in the sun, cramp-free, will seem like goddamn paradise!

We pull up to a 7-Eleven to take our ten-minute morning break. There are two black homeless guys duking it out over "turf" out front. They're both drinking something out of paper bags.

"You stay on your fucking side, man," says the first guy. "Don't move, brother! Stay on *your* fucking turf."

"Fuck you, man. I was here first," the other guy says and wobbles to his feet.

I squeak past them to go inside and use the bathroom. On my way back out, I spot a guy who's obviously a tweaker: gaunt face, gray skin, manic gesticulation.

Just as I get to the door, the guy points to me. "Stay right there! You're my lucky charm!"

"I'm nobody's lucky charm, dude. Not even my own..."

"Don't say that," he says, rifling through a stack of about fifty lottery scratchers. "You don't know. You never know. The universe is always conspiring. And the government. I could win the lottery. So could you. Blue cats. Easy number nine..."

I smile. I see Esteban, the crew boss, signaling me outside.

As I walk out of the 7-Eleven, one of the black guys is mumbling something, and then he suddenly keels over and starts seizing.

Seizures are far more terrifying to witness than they are to have, actually. Luckily, it has been a few years since I've had a bad one.

It was the second morning since I'd been out of the psych ward. My phone rang, and it was my mother calling from the Philippines, where she was doing business. I looked at my clock. It wasn't morning. It was actually two-thirty in the afternoon. And it was probably the fourth day since they had changed my seizure meds in the nut ward.

"Why are you still in bed?" she asked.

I had no idea. Actually I had no idea about anything.

"What medications are you on, sweetie?" she asked.

"Hmmmm...What? I don't knowwww," I trailed off.

"Okay...baby. You sound sleepy. Are you okay?"

A long silence. "Huh?...I'm sorry. What did you say?"

She got off the phone, alarmed, and called my father, who immediately called me.

"Ames, what did you take last night?" he demanded.

"Nothing...Just the regular stuff," I answered softly.

"Uh-huh...Call 911. You're gonna die!!"

"I can't find the phone," I said spacily, unaware that I was actually holding it. "And I'm naked."

"Put a fucking robe on and go knock on your neighbor's door. I'll stay on the phone with you."

"Okay," I said.

The last thing I remember was knocking on my neighbor's door. When I came to, I was in the ER—for the third time in a month. I quickly recognized my classic post-seizure headache—only this time there was a lot of pain concentrated in one specific spot on the back of my head. I touched it with my hand, and it felt wet and sticky. I probed around a bit more with my fingers and I felt knots: a few hard knots in a row.

"Please don't touch your stitches," the nurse said.

*Stitches?*

"Where am I?" I asked her.

"You're in the ER."

Turned out my neighbor hadn't been home, and as I was walking back to my apartment, I had a massive seizure, fell backward, and split my head open. I dropped out of the conversation with my dad midsentence, and he figured something horrible had happened and called 911 from Oregon.

My father was still on the phone when the paramedics arrived. They told him that I'd lost a lot of blood but that I probably wouldn't need a blood transfusion. My father asked them if I was conscious, and they said yes. Well, my eyes might have been open, but I certainly wasn't home. I don't remember a single moment of this. My landlord saw them carrying me out on a stretcher, blood pouring down my face.

I was so disoriented in the ER and in so much pain that I just started freaking out. After a few threats of sedation or restraint, I calmed down and was taken upstairs to another floor of the hospital to my own room. I kept screaming about the pain, so they shot me full of morphine, and I drifted off into my own private Idaho.

I don't like morphine. All it did was make me sleep (a lot) and have me hallucinating that the security guard had put my "valuables" in the hospital safe. That was it. Boring. It didn't make me crafty or horny, and I certainly didn't feel that awesome warm cocoon of happy that junkies die for. Yeah, I will never be a heroin addict.

I had a pretty severe concussion from the fall, and it made me incredibly stupid for a while, but everybody agreed it was "probably temporary." Right. "Probably temporary" didn't change the fact that I didn't know who the president was, couldn't spell, and could barely count. I constantly repeated myself, and my short-term memory was nonexistent. I also had a shaved spot on my head from where they had stitched my scalp closed. The rest of my hair was in bloody dreadlocks, making me look like a devout Rastafarian with a head wound. They told me they couldn't do an EEG until the "hair doctor," an old Jewish man from Beverly Hills who makes room calls, came and combed out the bloody rat's nest. And because I had a "fall," I was on "fall alert," which meant that every time I got out of bed to pee or brush my teeth, this incredibly annoying alarm went off and a nurse rushed into my room to make sure that I hadn't just collapsed into a pile by the side of the bed.

"I'm not ninety-six years old. I didn't have a 'fall.' I had a fucking 'seizure.' Big difference. Can't you turn that damn thing off?"

"I know it's a bit bothersome, but it is hospital policy," the overly chipper nurse said. "Sorry!"

The doctor overseeing my case was actually a nephrologist (kidney doc) by trade. He had a very dry manner and didn't seem to like me at all. He sent a neurologist in to see me during the early days of my recovery. I don't remember much of that meeting except that she had a strange accent and absolutely no sense of humor. The next time I saw my treating nephrologist, he said, "I have to find you another neurologist because you scared off the first one."

"What do you mean? What did I say?" I asked, perplexed.

"Well, I don't know. I wasn't in the room," he answered.

I couldn't believe it. Neurologists deal with people with fucked-up brains for a living. You'd think she'd be used to it. Plus, I just had a seizure, a concussion, and a bunch of morphine. What did she expect?

Two days later, in walked neurologist number two.

"I guess I scared the first doctor away," I said to her. "You're up."

"Yeah, well, I always get the rejects," she quipped back, not missing a beat.

She and I would get along just fine.

The old me would have been freaking out about my new bald patch and the strange shag haircut given to me by the ER. But I had a bigger concern now: I was stupid. When I wasn't busy being puzzled and awed by Court TV, I was asking the same question nine times in a row.

On the upside, I was grateful I hadn't bled into my brain, fractured my skull, or broken my neck. I could have easily ended up drooling while wheeling myself around in a chair. My priorities had changed in a flash. The week prior, I had been praying that some boy I liked would text me, and this week, I just wanted to be able to spell my name again.

The phone rang. It was my father. He called every day.

"The fact that you can surround the problem—that you know you can't remember stuff or that you're repeating yourself—is a good sign," he said. "It would be a bad sign if you didn't realize you were doing this stuff."

"Oh...so the fact that I *know* I'm brain-damaged makes it better? It makes it worse. I'd rather *not know*. If I didn't know, I wouldn't care."

"It means it's temporary, Ames. It's not brain damage. It's a concussion."

He then read me the description of *concussion* from the Internet—periodically interrupted by me saying, "Totally!" "Yeah!" and "Exactly!"

Not one person came to visit me during my stay. Every night, I got down on my knees (once I persuaded the nurses to turn off that stupid "fall alarm") and prayed.

I didn't really believe in God, but I had never felt this lost or alone in my life. If there was a time to find this fucking "connection" they spoke of in AA, it was now. Knees on a cold floor, ass hanging out of a green gown, IVs everywhere, I looked for "God"—whoever or whatever that was—in a way I never had before. "It's just you and me, dude," I said to the ceiling. "Be with me. Help me through this. Please don't let me be brain-damaged." I took a deep breath and bowed my head to clasped hands.

Every day, my nephrologist doctor would come into my room and ask me to spell "world" backward or count back from one hundred in threes, which, to be fair, is kind of difficult normally. I'd start and then...nothing. Just a terrifying void. My mind was literally blank.

The hospital kept me for eight days and then sent me home. Whereas before, nothing had been enough, now, everything was bountiful. When you could have ended up dead or retarded, the fact that you are walking while eating a muffin on a beautiful sunny day with a head (mostly) full of hair is a miracle. I hoped but seriously doubted that this blissful state of gratitude would last.

Because of my seizure, my driver's license was revoked for a full year. My father suggested I come up to Oregon for a few weeks to chill out and recover and take a break from bumming rides from friends or cabbing it everywhere. I agreed.

My dad lives in Ashland, where they hold the annual Shakespeare Festival. It's a small town, about thirty minutes from Medford, Oregon, populated mostly by hippies, ex-L.A. industry types, and hippies.

While I was there, I woke up at seven thirty every morning to go have coffee at this tiny local café. I ordered my iced soy latte and overheard the baristas talk about how certain shoes had "some leather" and that "wasn't cool." I rolled my eyes, brazenly pushing my fox fur coat out of the way to dig into my leather purse and pay for my overpriced organic locally grown whatever.

My father had printed out a list of all the AA meetings in Ashland, and every morning at nine a.m., I went to the same one. Ashland is a small place, and the AA community there is seriously tiny. This particular meeting had between eight and fifteen people and was held in a toasty church library. I'd been there years before, when I'd come up to visit after another brutal relapse. Hmm . . . back again years later, and still a newcomer. Awesome.

These meetings were very different from the hip/slick/cool L.A. ones. They were populated by crunchy New Agers and weird dudes with stupid crocheted hats. There were lots of lesbians—or maybe all the women just looked like lesbians. All of the women had weird names like Aries and Sunshine and Cookie, and nobody shaved.

Ashland was not a place where I blended in. With my heavy black eyeliner, fur coats, sarcasm, and chain-smoking, I was a far cry from the local chakra-worshipping, purple-wearing vegans. Crystal shops and acupuncture clinics, bead stores and bad art galleries populated the tiny streets of the main square. I hated it. I went to the local tennis club every day and tried to put some muscle on my emaciated frame. A friend of my father's who had known me from previous visits saw me and said, "Eat a fucking sandwich, will ya?" I was not amused. Interesting how, when you're fat, nobody says, "Hey, you might cool it on the chow." But when you're skinny, everybody feels completely free to jump in to tell you to eat up.

I went to the local co-op—the health food store—to pick up some snacks, and I saw a woman from the meeting. She was eating kale and tofu and drinking kombucha. Perfect. She bowed her head over her praying hands and whispered, "My blessings to you." I smiled back stiffly.

My father and I are very close, but we are similar—probably too similar. Also, when I fall apart, he alternates between unfaltering "You will get through this" support and angry "Knock off this bullshit, and get it together already" frustration.

One night we were watching *Factotum*, the semi-autobiographical movie about the famous alcoholic, womanizing author and poet Charles Bukowski, and we got into a seething debate about what differentiates art from personal expression. It's a typical family argument—at least in my family.

"You aren't expressing shit, Ames. And you certainly aren't making any art. You're just in reaction to everything. You think you're a fucking social revolutionary because you say shocking things. You're not espousing any tenets. You just say whatever you feel like saying at the moment. That doesn't make you revolutionary. It just makes you inappropriate and undisciplined."

"Wow! Harsh! Well, I think 'speaking your truth' *is* revolutionary."

"What is your truth, Ames? Just anything outrageous? Shocking everybody?"

"I think that saying the thing that everybody is thinking and nobody dares say is revolutionary," I said. "I don't edit myself for fear of what other people may think. That takes courage. You know, George Orwell said, 'In a time of universal deceit, telling the truth is a revolutionary act.'"

"Uh-huh. But you don't even write anything *down*, Ames. You just lose a lot of friends. You fucking burn bridges while you're still on them! And AA is not a stage for you to do your act. You even told me that they think you're fucking crazy."

"I don't deny that I have an impulse control problem. Cut me some slack, will you? I just cracked my head open, and I'm newly sober again."

My composure was starting to go. My eyes began to well up. I was going to lose it, and it was not going to be pretty. I knew there was truth to what he was saying. His delivery, however, left something to be desired. No surprise. We always served it up to each other with savage directness.

I began to walk out of the room.

"If you're going to bed, say good night," he said.

"Good night," I grumbled. I stomped into my room and slammed the door and began hysterically crying. Thirty-seven years old, going on twelve. Pathetic.

On the drive to my morning meeting, I broke the uncomfortable silence between us.

"Look, I don't know what it's like to be you, Papa. And you don't know what it's like to be me. And you're doing the best that you can. And I'm certainly doing the best that I can. And I'm going to have compassion for you. And it'd be great if you had compassion for me. And know that I love you, okay?"

"And I love you," my father said back.

"Aren't you amazed that I didn't yell at you last night?" I asked.

"What? You want the Nobel Peace Prize for not saying 'fuck you' to your father?"

# CHAPTER TWENTY

"D o you know what your body would be like if you worked out?" Elizabeth, my new sober living roommate, says to me one morning.

"That sounds like a veiled compliment if I've ever heard one."

She's naked on her bed, in some weird acrobatic pose, putting lotion all over her body. She stops and looks over at me, examining me.

"You're actually really pretty. You just need a makeover and new clothes. Let's go shopping!"

"You just don't get my homeless rocker look."

"Oh, I get it. But you just look like you've been heartbroken your whole life."

"Well... that's not entirely untrue."

Elizabeth and I get along fine. I make fun of her, and she laughs. At night, she reads aloud from that stupid book *The Rules*, her paperback bible.

"Dude, I can't hear that shit. Please," I beg her.

"'Rule number three: Don't stare at men or talk too much. Don't feel you have to be entertaining or have interesting conversation all the time. On the date itself, be quiet and reserved.'"

"So basically I should have a personality transplant."

She laughs.

"I have to go to sleep," I tell her. "I work early tomorrow. Some of us need to make money. And, oh, yeah... if you open that book again tonight, I will beat you with it."

\*    \*    \*

I go back to see Dr. Fedoseev, the rude Russian psychiatrist. I bring a Russian-speaking friend from AA, hoping that her ability to wax poetic in the native tongue will buy me some bonus points—as my vague resemblance to an eighties Soviet prostitute wasn't cutting it.

The office is manned by curt, doughy, middle-aged women wearing too much makeup. I scan the selection of the local Russki papers that might as well be hieroglyphics to me. An extremely depressed black guy in a hoodie, clutching his shoes to his chest, sits down next to me.

They call my name, and my friend and I go into Mrs. Putin's office.

"Which one of you is Amy?" she asks.

"I am," I say, surprised.

"Well, how would I know? You haven't been in since last June."

This is going to go well. I shoot a sideways glance to my friend, and she begins to speak to the good doctor in Russian. The following is all translated.

"I'm here because you weren't very nice to my friend the last time."

"I won't be nice to her this time. She is here for more drugs."

"She's here for Prozac."

"I know exactly who she is and what she's been up to, drinking and all that."

"You have no idea who she is."

"I don't need more alcoholics in my office."

"Let's go," my friend says to me. "She isn't going to be nice to you or helpful. She says she doesn't need more alcoholic patients."

My mouth drops open, and before I can explain again that I am almost two years sober and that I just left an AA meeting, where I am the goddamn motherfucking secretary, all that comes out of my mouth is a soft, almost whispered "You fucking cunt."

My friend takes off her sunglasses, and, in Russian, tells her that doctors should work not just with their heads but also with their hearts. And that she is a heartless monster. The doctor looks back at her in quiet shame. I am already out the door and in the parking lot, chain-smoking and pacing furiously.

I am PMSing, so I am already particularly agitated. Thanks to hormones I'm sporting tits that rival Pamela Anderson's and the acne of a sixteen-year-old who works over a fryer. Coming up against this discrimination—from a doctor, no less—ignites a rage in me that I am scared I might not be able to contain.

As I smoke-pace, pace-smoke, I am so angry, I am almost crying. It has been years since I'd been accused of using when I was clean. My parents had always been extremely supportive of my recovery. They of course weren't happy about my addiction and multiple relapses, but I never felt like they were judging me. It was more that they felt lost, helpless to help me.

Later, I call my current sponsor, Jay W., to complain, and I get my ass handed to me for my lack of "restraint of pen and tongue."

"You might be the only version of the Big Book she ever comes across. I don't think calling her a 'fucking cunt' is going to change her mind or her behavior."

Boom. You can hear the cloak of shame fall over me.

"And maybe, just maybe, this was a blessing, because she would not be able to give you the kind of care you need or want."

Double punch to the gut. I drop.

Granted, I probably wasn't the epitome of ladylike recovery. But what does this say about the medical community and their grossly prejudicial view of alcoholics? It's not like I went in there shit-faced and demanded a bunch of Class 2 drugs. And I get that she's Russian, and alcoholics are more widespread in her community than borscht or matryoshka dolls. Even though they have begun teaching about addiction and alcoholism as a "disease" in medical schools, there still exists the social stigma of it being some sort of degeneracy, with recovery as the exception and not the rule.

This visit was a harsh reminder of how the public still sees alcoholics. I forget sometimes, because in the program, there can be a weird type of reverse pride, a perverse hubris that comes with who had the lowest bottom and then rose, phoenix-like, from the ashes. I, myself, am guilty of this, but I think, for many of us, it is actually a way to reframe the shame. If we can't laugh at or revel in the degradation, how can we get past it?

I hadn't experienced much outright "prejudice" like this before. Writing for *The Fix*, being a voice of addiction for *Huff Post Live*, being "out" with my alcoholism, drug abuse, and sex addiction, being surrounded by "program people"... I suddenly realized that I had been living in a bubble wherein I was out of touch with what much of the "real world" still thinks about alcoholics and addicts, and why anonymity is still crucial for some people.

I was referred to another psychiatrist, also Russian, and when I explained the prior situation, she asked, "Why you didn't get along?"

"She didn't want any more alcoholic patients," I explained.

"How long are you sober?" she inquired.

"Over two years," I said.

"Yes, well, I'm not taking any more patients right now, I'm sorry."

Uh-huh. And the hunt for a doctor with a heart goes on...


I didn't think the Xander thing could turn out to be worse, but surprise, surprise. Not only is he thirty years old and newly sober, he's also a "burner" (Burning Man enthusiast), a singer-songwriter, and—wait for it—polyamorous. As he explains it to me, he doesn't believe monogamy is the natural way of things. He doesn't find it conducive to most people's "authentic and full expression of themselves," whatever the fuck that means. He assures me that he "loves all women the same... it's like living in a flower garden."

"That's the gayest thing I've ever heard."

"When you can be complete without a relationship, then you can be in a relationship with everybody."

In my head, I wave all of this off. This would be a fuck. Nothing more. We'd get this out of our system and be done with it. I sure wasn't interested in all his hippie Osho bullshit.

I notice a silver medallion hanging on a piece of twine around his neck.

"What's that necklace? Is that a quarter?" I ask him.

"Yes. It's a reminder for me to embrace change."

"Ahh," I say, trying hard not to visibly die laughing. Yeah...this will never work.

Xander invites me to hear him perform at a tiny dive bar in Venice. He sits down at the piano and proceeds to mellifluously belt out sweet, passionate songs about love. I realize then that I'm screwed. I'm going to like him, maybe even love him. And I'm going to get hurt.

Afterward we go and play Cards Against Humanity at the home of a mutual friend from the program. When the host goes up to bed, Xander and I start making out on the couch. He goes to get a drink of water, and when he returns, I'm naked.

"Why are you naked?" he asks.

"I thought we were gonna fuck."

"I like to take things slow...build a connection."

"You just wanna make out for hours? What are we, fifteen and gonna share a milk shake after? Come on..."

"Put your clothes back on. You're not in charge here."

A week later, we have our first official "date" at an outdoor restaurant in Echo Park. He's wearing another stupid necklace. It's a circle sitting atop a cross that looks almost like the symbol for woman.

"Is that because you're *really* into women?" I snort.

"It's a rosary ring. My grandmother gave it to me."

God, I'm an asshole.

We talk and laugh. He brushes my long rocker bangs out of my face.

"Let me see you," he says, holding eye contact for a weirdly long time. I feel wildly uncomfortable.

"You love to be looked at, but you hate to be seen," he says.

"Guru Xander," I mock, but he's absolutely right.

# CHAPTER TWENTY-ONE

_A_ new girl moves into the sober living. Her name is Melinda. She's in her early twenties, a junkie, sweet but angry. She has shiny long brown hair and a tiny Yorkshire terrier named Rodney that doesn't shut the fuck up. She plays music I've never heard. Loudly.

Melinda has a huge scar on her neck from where she nodded off onto a candle when she was shooting dope a few years ago. But did that get her sober? Of course not.

One night, I hear Melinda weeping through the wall. I get up and knock softly on her door.

"Come in," she sniffles.

"You okay, girl? I can hear you crying."

She starts sobbing. She tells me her dad died a few months prior.

"I miss him so much. I wish he could have seen me get clean. It hurts so bad. I just wanna get high."

"I get it," I say. I stroke her hair. "It's just going to take time. It gets easier, I promise."

I say that because it seems like what I should say, because I want to comfort her. I have no idea what to say about her dad. Both of my parents are still alive to witness my dramatic tumbles to the bottom and glorious triumphant returns...only to watch me tumble down again. I don't know how they continue to believe in me, long after I've stopped believing in myself. It must be some delusional part of parenting.

My mother has been a recovered alcoholic for more than thirty-five years, transforming herself from fall-down drunk to international textile designer. It's possible that's why she had no doubt that I could and would do the same.

I think my father's faith sprung from a different source. Two sources, to be precise. One was pure ego. I was *his* daughter so I *had* to be okay. Eventually. The second was writer's denial. What I was going through was so ridiculously cliché, it couldn't possibly be real.

I'm so poor at this point that the girls have started a donation jar for me in the bathroom. I'm the only Jew in the house, and I get lovingly ribbed for it. So, one morning, I go into the bathroom that three or four of us share, and there's a mason jar with masking tape on the front. On the tape is scrawled "Jew Jar." I'm not offended. On the contrary, I think it's hilarious—and generous. Occasionally, I fish a few dollars out of there and stuff them into my pockets. I'm barely surviving on some freelance writing gigs. I'd probably make more selling oranges and tube socks on a street median, but at least I'm writing and avoiding what I call a "real job."

To increase my cash flow, I start moonlighting for my old boss, Siri. Siri has a fashion line, but she's like an evolved fashionista—cool and hip but all about love, spirituality, and Kundalini yoga. She's tall and lean—kind of like an adolescent boy pollinated with a supermodel, topped off with a dirty blond shag circa 1978 Rod Stewart.

Back when I was twenty-six and just out of my first rehab, I managed to stay clean for almost a year. Then I thought, "Well, I'm a drug addict, but not an alcoholic"—a mistake I'd come to find out that many people make. Thinking that speed, specifically, was my problem, I tried some "controlled drinking." That experiment turned into a three-week blackout, with multiple close friends telling me afterward that I "bug out" when I drink. I'm not exactly sure what "bug out" meant, but it did not seem positive.

As I've said before, I was never a big fan of alcohol. It immediately makes me into a violent, crazy person, and these three weeks were no exception. Quickly realizing that drinking was off the table, I got back on the wagon—and stayed there for almost seven years. During that time, I was repping a small clothing line designed by an outrageous British club queen whom I'd met at sober living. The Brit would design the stuff, and I'd shop it around to stores trying to get them to buy it. So, one day, I brought the collection into a cool boutique on Melrose. Siri owned the place. We instantly connected, downing espressos and laughing and chatting for hours. A year or so later Siri and I lost touch when I moved to the U.K. briefly to continue my escapades in the fashion industry.

I'd been in and out of various forms of therapy since I was fifteen, but it was in London where I first landed in "analysis." I thought that was for rich, neurotic Jewish New Yorkers, but evidently, I was mistaken.

My analyst was a proper English gentleman—a doctor and a professor.

"I don't have your mobile number or pager," I told him.

"That's only for psychiatric patients," he answered.

"I don't have your home number," I continued.

"That's because you don't live with me."

I was irritated by his witty comebacks.

"Analysis is different here in England than it is in the States," he continued.

"Yeah, I can see that," I answered.

In the six months I lived in London, I constantly heard: "It's not the States...blah, blah, blah" or "This is England. We do things differently here." Well, if I'd thought England would be an exact replica of the U.S., I wouldn't have come, now would I? What did they think I came for? The glorious weather? The tan, buff bodies? The gleaming dental work? Please.

Professor Gibson told me that I was "treatable," but that I was a very complicated case: the eating disorders, the body dysmorphia, the drug addiction, the depression, the sexual dysfunction...all of these were symptomatic of a deep childhood wound. It was going be a long, hard, painful road.

Ugh. His prognosis alone made me feel totally exhausted. I'm an addict. I like quick fixes. I don't go for long, painful roads. And really, it couldn't be that serious, could it? I mean, I knew I was depressed. Okay,

I was more than depressed. And I felt terribly ashamed about it. I mean, what was so fucking stressful and terrible about being me?

The truth is that I had always sensed that something was wrong with me. I couldn't pin it down, but I just felt different from other people, and not in a good way. Objectively, I had as much as—if not more than—other people around me. I had parents who loved me. I was well educated. I was attractive and healthy. I wanted for nothing. Still, for whatever reason, I just couldn't pull off "happy."

I tried to explain it to myself. It was as if I was haunted by some deep existential sadness. It would come out of nowhere and knock me on my ass, leaving me bedbound and sobbing for days at a time. It felt like my wiring was off or there was some horrible chasm in me. Drugs numbed it all and provided a much-needed artificial wholeness—until they didn't.

It didn't help matters that I was still reeling from having been dumped seven months prior. I'd fallen in love for the first time—in my thirties—with a newly discharged marine. He had plenty of his own demons to grapple with, and after six months of a long-distance whatever, he ended it. It was my first real heartbreak, and I was already so emotionally fragile that I just collapsed under the weight of it.

"My roommate says I'm having a nervous breakdown," I announced to the professor. I was looking for confirmation from him. For some reason, I thought that getting validation of the gravity of my situation would make me feel vindicated; see that I wasn't just being my usual tantrum-throwing, melodramatic self but that I was actually losing my mind.

"Again, this is a just a label...but yes, you are having a depressive collapse."

"Do I need to be put into a hospital?"

"No, not at this moment. You have not had a psychotic break. You are still somewhat functional."

"Functional?!" I yelled, through a face full of tears. "I fucking go to bed at four o'clock in the afternoon, and when I'm awake, I'm writing out my goddamn will. How is that functional? Because I'm not wearing my pants on my head?!"

For the next week, whenever he came to retrieve me from the waiting room, I'd be sobbing.

"How are you?" he'd always ask in his crisp British accent as he led me into his office.

"Feeling good," I'd say, giving him a sarcastic thumbs-up.

At one point, I'd been wearing the same clothes for about two weeks. I was scared to change clothes and too distracted to read or watch TV. I couldn't be bothered to shower. Between analysis sessions, I would just cry and sleep.

On the phone, my father told me that all of his heroes had had nervous breakdowns.

"You're one of the most courageous people I know," he said to me, "because you're facing your shit."

"No," I told him. "I'm just desperate."

"Ames, sometimes the bravest people are the desperate ones."

Some people can just drive down the road of life, swerving around the boulders in the road. But for others—like me—the boulder is too big. We have to stop the car, get out, and move the boulder out of the way before we can carry on.

One day, however, I just cracked. I knew it was coming. I kept warning Professor Gibson that I was going to do "something stupid"—that I was going to hurt myself. And then, that day came. I even called him to cancel my appointment ahead of time.

"I'm sorry to inform you that I will not be coming in today, because I am going to kill myself," I said matter-of-factly into his answering machine.

Life, you win. I was tapping out. I was tired of hurting, tired of temporarily propping myself up on false hopes that it would get better. I wanted out. In retrospect, I didn't really want to die. I just didn't want to suffer anymore. I suspect that's how many people who attempt suicide feel. Death seems like the only way to make the hurt stop.

I grabbed a box cutter that was lying on the table and took two swipes at my left wrist. The blood quickly started to flow, and I smeared it all over my face. And then, throwing away seven years of sobriety, I popped open a bottle of red wine and guzzled down three-quarters of it. Why the fuck not, right? I was on my way out.

I called my mother and father to say good-bye.

"I love you, but I can't do this anymore. I'm sorry."

I hung up before they could try to talk me out of it. With a decent buzz on and before I could change my mind, I took the box cutter with a bit more force to the right wrist. I looked at it. I saw capillaries and veins peeking out of the sliced flesh, and I started screaming.

Blood started streaming down both my arms. I was very drunk and felt mentally unhinged in a way I never had before. Absolutely fucking nuts. Before I knew it, not one but two sets of policemen and paramedics arrived, and I was taken to the hospital.

I was led into a small, barren room where I was examined and then sewn up. The solemnity of the hospital sobered me up quickly.

"You're very lucky," said the doctor, a jaded, pasty, thin-lipped woman.

"Am I?"

"You missed severing this major nerve here—the one that controls your pinky finger—by millimeters."

"That's good" was all I could muster. I felt numb.

"I'm giving you a tetanus shot...God only knows how dirty the knife was."

"It was a box cutter."

"Even better, except you're not a box."

I looked down at my now embroidered wrists. My buzz was wearing off.

"Have your local doctor take out the stitches in ten to fourteen days. Keep the incisions clean. Do not get your stitches wet."

"How do I bathe?"

"You wrap them in Saran Wrap and you have somebody help you. Baths are best for now."

"Okay."

"You're young, pretty, and seem smart—aside from doing this stupid maneuver. Life can't be that bad. This is a tad dramatic, no?"

I was silent.

They released me. I couldn't believe it. I had tried to kill myself, but in the U.K., there was no mandatory seventy-two-hour hold. And unlike doctors in the U.S., they didn't feel bad for me, weren't interested in analyzing how I felt. Honestly, they just made me feel like an asshole for what I'd done. Welcome to the NHS.

The next morning, I felt a weird sense of relief. It was like I had just let out a primal scream of such proportions that my angst had been lessened considerably but the world was left deafened and stunned.

What had actually changed? Nothing. Nothing at all. The feelings and circumstances that had driven me to slit my wrists were the same, only now instead of everybody's concern or sympathy, I had their anger.

My father said to me, "How the fuck do you think people are going to react? You are something beautiful and special in their lives, and you took a fucking box cutter to it, and tried to take it away."

After my suicide attempt, I moved back to Los Angeles, into a sweet, overpriced deco apartment. I contacted Siri, and she offered me a job working as a salesgirl at her boutique while doing PR for her line. I took it. I could sit around her shop during the day and send emails to fashion editors and store managers on my days off. Seemed low stress enough.

I *intended* to stay sober, but, of course, that plan went quickly awry. One night, Siri and I were hanging out downtown at the Standard Hotel. A super-handsome Cuban surfer started talking to me. He lit up a huge joint right at the bar.

"I'm a big... 'marijuana enthusiast,'" he said.

"So you're a snobby stoner."

He grinned. "Wanna hit?"

"No... I prefer meth, but these days I prefer nothing. I'm sober."

Next thing I knew, we were making out, and he shotgunned me a mouthful of pot smoke. For the first time in seven years, I was *high*. Really fucking high. And it felt amazing. Yes, that's right. One dose was all it took to awaken the dragon of addiction from its deep sleep. I didn't know it then, but I was fucked.

*I'm okay smoking pot,* I thought. After all, I hate pot. I'm not going to get addicted to something I hate, right? And pot's a fucking joke. Nobody goes to rehab for pot. I mean, come on...What's "hitting bottom" on pot look like? Eating too many Chalupa Supremes and losing your day to binge-watching *South Park*? Bitch, please.

Before long, I was smoking pot all day, every day, and still hating it. But hating it didn't stop me. See, when you're an addict, you want to feel "different." You don't really care whether it's shitty-different. And sure, occasionally, I'd have a laughing fit or one of those weird profound insights about how the universe worked. But, in general, pot made me anxious and paranoid and led me to overthink the things I naturally already overthought.

However, as long as I'd opened the pot portal and was no longer "sober," I decided to add drinking to the mix. *I can drink,* I lied to myself. At first, it was just beer and wine. I've never been a good drinker. I always got sloppy and obnoxious. Alcohol removes the very few inhibitions I do have, which is not a good thing. It also opens up some weird unfillable vortex in me where I. Just. Can't. Get. Enough. This meant that when I wasn't drinking, I was thinking about drinking. It was a short hop from there to drinking in the morning. The truth is, being drunk in the morning is the best. You feel like you have a secret or a head start on the rest of the world. Unfortunately, that "secret" is just that you're an alcoholic and the head start is on your cirrhotic liver.

Of course, it wasn't long before I got fired. I was "disrespectful." I had a "substance abuse problem." The list went on and on, and I'd admit it was a stunningly accurate description of me. But I still felt rejected by Siri for being canned. And without the structure and discipline of a daily job, I felt out of control. It was a bad combo. But it was the perfect combo for me to get and stay loaded.

I pleaded with Siri to take me back. She refused, but, to her credit, she did offer to take me to rehab.

"I don't need treatment!" I snarled to myself as I pounded a bunch of sickly sweet bottled vodka drinks and went for a drive. I was speeding, and in my drunkenness, I blew a red light. Immediately, I saw the flashing lights and heard the siren of a cop car. Perfect.

I pulled over and quickly tucked the empty booze bottles behind the front seat.

One of the cops took my license and registration and went back to his car to run it. I stuck a mint in my mouth and lit a cigarette to disguise my boozy breath.

Suddenly I got the idea that I should plead for mercy and I jumped out of my car.

"Please...I just got fired on Sunday," I said. "My life is coming apart. Please don't give me a ticket."

"Get back in your car, ma'am. Don't leave your vehicle."

I went back to my car and sat nervously in the front seat, smoking. I saw one officer swagger back to the driver's side.

"Now, listen...I don't usually give tickets, but you deserve one. I'm going to let you off, but don't think that you can get off in general by being cute."

"No, sir," I say, all tight T-shirt and bedroom eyes. "Thank you."

"Where are you going now?"

"Home, sir. I'm going home."

"Good. Go straight home. Have a good night."

I drove off. Suckers. I went straight to a bar, drinking one vodka after another until I ended up at a club on Hollywood Boulevard with a bunch of guys who sold jewelry to Siri's shop. One was a French guy I'd fooled around with a couple of times. He'd always been too fucked up on coke to get it up.

Even drunk, it suddenly occurred to me that I was wearing my scary granny panties underneath my seventies wrap skirt. Hmmm. Well, better to have on no underwear than ones that make you close to unfuckable! So off they came, and I jaunted inside.

I started talking to a very good-looking guy who had the hiccups. He was sporting a porn-stache, and he had thick, dark hair and Eurasian eyes. I noticed a gun on him, but I knew the jewelry guys were all Highland Park gangsters dabbling in fashion, so I thought nothing of it.

"I can cure your hiccups," I slurred. I proceeded to try to impress him with my father's "knife in the glass" trick from my childhood. You put a knife, blade up, in a glass of water and make the person drink the water without stopping, while the tip of the blade is pressed against their forehead. It immediately stops their hiccups…basically because, if they hiccup while drinking, they'll spear themselves in the brain. The guy, whose name turned out to be Riley, only had a huge hunting knife on him, so that's what we used. It worked like a charm—cured his hiccups and made me seem like some fucking magical siren. Next thing I knew, we were off to my house.

We walked in the door, and I tossed my purse on the couch.

"You're pretty fucked up, huh?" he said.

"Yeah, I got fired recently. Drowning my sorrows and all that shit."

"Gotcha."

"What do you do?" I ask.

"I'm a cop."

"Ohhh. That's why you have the big knife and the gun. I get it now!"

I didn't tell him about my drunk driving incident earlier, but I did wonder about the cop theme of the day.

"Let's fuck," I said. "I've always wanted to fuck a cop," I lied.

But I was so fucking wasted that I just started throwing up and didn't stop. He ended up rubbing my back the whole night and holding my hair out of my face while I elegantly dry-heaved. In the morning, when I woke up, he was gone, but he left a note with his phone number and a funny cartoon drawing of a bunny rabbit with X's as eyes, a bottle by his side, and drunken swirls above his head.

I threw up for another twelve hours—just green bile at this point. I couldn't even keep water down. I started to panic. Maybe I had alcohol poisoning. I called 911. The medics came, and they wanted to take me to the hospital. I was way too coherent to have alcohol poisoning, I decided. Plus, I could already see the night ahead of me: four hours waiting in emergency just to be given an electrolyte drink and sent on my way. No, thank you. I refused transport.

I noticed that something stank.

"What is that smell?" I asked them.

"I think that's your trash, ma'am."

"Ewww. Can you guys take that out for me? I'm going to try to sleep this off."

They were stunned by my request but grabbed my trash and walked out the door with it anyway.

As my addiction roared out of control again, my parents began, understandably, freaking out.

"What triggered this, Ames?" my father asked.

"I got fired."

"Plenty of people get fired and don't go on a drinking binge."

"I don't know what to tell you. I'm nuts. Is that news to you?"

"I've never bought into that theory. I think you like playing at the edges."

"You think I like playing at the edges? It's not a choice!"

"You like to see how far you can go and see if you can bounce back."

My mom, however, had a different take. "Honey, you've got a demon inside you that would happily see you dead. It's a side of you that wants to sabotage everything."

My parents don't talk much. They divorced when I was a baby. They'll confer if I'm really going off the rails or shoot each other an email if something terrific happens, but, in general, they're incommunicado. While my mother was lining up readings with Santa Fe psychics, my father was researching Jewish exorcisms in Oregon. I was in L.A., smoking too much pot and drinking beer for breakfast.

Two days later, I called Riley the cop, and I went over to his house to fuck him under the pretense of "using his Jacuzzi." I wasn't as drunk this time, so maybe I could find out a little bit about him and not puke all over myself before we got naked. Turned out he was half Korean and half Argentinian and a serious surfer. He had a huge dick and a very beautiful, muscular body, covered in tattoos. However, he was also crazy and a serious drinker. He confessed that he *loved* to go to punk concerts, pour Everclear all over his chest, and then light himself on fire... when he wasn't on duty, of course.

Riley and I started hanging out and fucking occasionally. He was sexy, but quiet and pretty emotionally unavailable. Honestly, I don't know if he was stupid or just shy, but I found him a bit boring when he wasn't naked. However, since I was driving blasted all the time, it was great to have a cop to follow me home.

By this point, I was pretty much surrounded by other alcoholics, so nobody gave a shit about my drinking. But then, one night, somebody offered me coke. I hadn't done coke in years. My head told me, *You can do coke. Meth was your problem.* And before I knew it, I was doing coke all the time.

One night, I met Riley at a trendy little wine bar on Cahuenga.

"Hi." I smiled.

"You're high," he said, accusingly.

"What?"

"Don't, Amy. I'm a cop. It's my job to know these things."

"Okay, I did a little blow. Whatever. You're an alcoholic. Same difference."

"It's not the same. Coke is illegal."

"So fucking stupid."

"I'm sorry. I can't hang out with somebody who's doing illegal drugs."

And that was the end of the cop, but not the end of the coke. In fact, the coke quickly became a huge problem—dwarfing the booze—and about eight months later, I took Siri up on her offer to take me to what would be the second of my six trips to rehab.

# CHAPTER TWENTY-TWO

The Xander thing is passionate but very volatile. He continues to date other women, whom he encourages me to meet. That's the poly thing: everybody knows and loves each other and "gives their permission and blessing" to fuck other people or whatever.

"Wanna have a sleepover tomorrow night?" I ask him.

"I have a date."

"Oh. What about the night after?"

"I have another date."

I start bawling. I can't do this. He had given me books to read: Anthony De Mello's *The Way to Love*, about how to love without attachment, and *The Ethical Slut*, a...umm...*Practical Guide to Polyamory, Open Relationships & Other Adventures*. I was really trying to get on board with the polyamory thing, but I am super jealous by nature and highly monogamous at heart. If you really love somebody, why would you want to be with anybody else?

Xander keeps trying to explain his point of view: "If you want to date or have sex with somebody, I'm happy for you. I'm happy that you're happy."

"Yeah...I don't get it. I'm sorry. Maybe I'm not evolved enough, but the thought of you fucking somebody else makes me homicidal."

"What I feel is called compersion. It's the opposite of jealousy. It's the good feelings I get when you're enjoying somebody else."

"Bullshit! Bullshit dressed up in some über-spiritual millennial version of free love. If you're seeing a bunch of girls, and one dumps you, who cares? You've got four more in rotation. It's like insurance."

"I'm actually turned on by the idea of you being with another man."

"Oh . . . so you're into cuckoldry."

"Yeah. I'd *love* to see you fuck my friend."

"Are you serious? *You* haven't even fucked me yet. So while your friend fucks me, what are you doing? Braiding my hair and reading me a sonnet?"

Though Xander won't fuck me yet, he and I go and lie in the park and look at the stars and make out for hours. It is beyond frustrating.

"Oh, my God, why won't you just fuck me?!" I finally ask.

"If we have sex, it will be because it feels like the right time. Right now, you feel . . . I don't know . . . rapey. It feels like you and your ego just wanting to get off. It doesn't feel like it's about you and me, and it should be. It should be about our spirits connecting."

"Jesus Christ . . ."

"It's funny. You were married, but you know shit about real intimacy."

Every time Xander has a "date," I go on Tinder and fuck somebody. For whatever reason, this does not fit into his compersion bullshit. He is not turned on by it. He gets angry. And instead of feeling jealous, he's disgusted at my reactivity.

"You're fucking *at* me," he says.

*Damn right, bitch.* My revenge fucking makes me feel better. I'm evening the score a little bit, and putting some distance between myself and my feelings toward him.

Tonight he has a date with a fire-eating burlesque dancer whom he met at one of his Burning Man "day parties." Her name is Aria or Gemini or something ridiculous. When she isn't performing, she's studying Reiki and Tantra. You get the picture.

I log onto Tinder and start chatting with a twenty-eight-year-old kid with a man bun and a scraggly beard. His name escapes me and couldn't have been less important. Turns out that he, too, is struggling in a relationship with somebody who wants to be "open."

I drive forty-five minutes to his loft in a scary, deserted part of downtown. He's young and skinny, a vegetarian who takes a lot of psychedelics and smokes American Spirits. He photographs "botanical life" for a living.

We sit on the concrete floor of his loft at two in the morning and talk about polyamory. I know that the millennials' Burning Man circle is small, and I have a flash of fear that he might know Xander from the circuit.

Burning Man is a multimillion-dollar industry now. When I was twenty-four in San Francisco, I answered an ad for a job "developing an art festival." I went to a cocktail party in Marin where a few guys were talking about an event in the desert with music and huge art installations. They were going to call it "Burning Man." Stupidest idea ever, I thought. Who's going to trek out to the middle of nowhere to take drugs, dance, and see some temporary oversize sculpture made out of car parts or whatever? I idiotically turned the job down. So no, don't be asking me for stock tips.

"Do you know Xander? He plays piano and sings. Shorter Italian guy." I need to cover my bases here.

"No . . . doesn't ring a bell. Sorry," Man Bun says. I'm relieved, and we fuck. In the morning, I wake up to a slew of messages from Xander. His date was a bust. How was my night? He woke up with me very much on his mind.

I smoke one of Man Bun's cigarettes and drink a glass of tap water.

"Hey, wait," he calls from the bedroom. "Did this guy you're seeing used to have a girlfriend named Jasmine?"

"Uhh, yeah," I say, trying to sound casual. My heart races, and I tremble tying my shoelaces.

"Yeah, then I do know him. Jasmine has a tattoo of a fairy on her inner thigh. My girl and I had a threesome with her a few years back." He laughs. "Small world, huh?"

I don't answer. I'm already out the door.

After four months of being on and off with Xander, I am done. He did eventually fuck me. The first time, it was on the porch of the sober living, right in the view of the video surveillance camera. Mariana never said a thing.

"This isn't going to work," I told him. "You're never going to give me what I want, and I feel like I'm falling in love with you."

"You're not supposed to fall in love. You're supposed to rise in love."

"Dude..."

"It is my role as a man to inspire the goddess within."

"I don't even know what that means."

"A true goddess knows the power of submission and vulnerability."

"You're a pretentious dickhead. That's what my true goddess has to say to you."

"It's okay if you need to take space. I will love you at a distance that you're comfortable with."

"Oh, fuck you. You were always at 'a distance' thanks to all your poly bullshit."

"I understand you're angry. We had soul contracts we needed to complete. I don't regret our connection."

"Seriously, Xander...Go. Fuck. Yourself."

I block him on my phone and Facebook and retreat back to Tinder to lick my wounds. Xander was all tenderness and sensuality without the sex. Tinder is all sex without the tenderness. It's an abrupt change.

A younger guy, early thirties like Xander, hits me up. Joe is cute in a sort of "I'm Italian and used to be a boxer and somebody fucked up my face" kind of way. He's also sober—almost seven years. I hope—in vain—that this means he won't be a total asshole.

There's a thing I've noticed about a lot of sober guys. They'll have integrity in every area of their life—except for love/sex/romance. They'll spout magical wise words from the podium at meetings but treat women like absolute trash. I get that it's AA and not SLAA or SAA, but we're supposed to apply these principles in *all* of our affairs—including the ones that involve pussy. Maybe sex and love is the one area of their life where they can still be degenerate douchebags without losing their precious sobriety. But it still sickens me. I tell myself that when I have a good chunk of recovery, I won't still be on Tinder, sport-fucking and having soulless connections with strangers.

Some of Joe's early messages on Tinder set off red flags so I unmatch him. Twenty minutes later, I get a Facebook message from him. Despite not knowing my last name, he was able to find me thanks to our nine hundred mutual friends in AA.

"You could've had the decency to tell me why you were going to unmatch me. That isn't very sober behavior. You don't know me."

His persistence to find me is intriguing. I choose to think of it as borne of interest in me, not just his rage at my rejecting him. I give him my phone number, and we began texting. It gets weird, fast. Too weird, even for me.

Joe will not talk to me on the phone. He will only text. I was to be obedient and text back, "yes sir" or "yes daddy." I get that this is just a role-play thing, but honestly, I think that stuff is super stupid. However, wanting to fuck, I think, *I can do this for a bit. Surely, this is not his only mode of communication or connection.*

He gives me the plan. He'll meet me outside my sober living, on the corner, ten thirty p.m. He'll be in the backseat of a silver Porsche SUV. I am not to speak. I am not to wear underwear. I am not to wear any makeup. When it is over, I am to get out of the vehicle, and only then am I allowed to speak, and only to say "Thank you" and "Good night." My heart is pounding furiously. Am I turned on? Terrified? I can't tell.

I slide into the backseat of his car. He is very aggressive. He pulls off my sweatpants. He doesn't kiss me. He finger bangs me pretty violently and then makes me do things to him. It feels super impersonal and objectifying, but I tell myself not to be a pussy. When it is over he says, "You can speak now."

"Oh, okay. Oh, my God, I'm so thirsty," I say, reaching for a water bottle on the floor of his backseat.

"Holy shit, your voice is deep. You sure you're a woman?"

"Really? You basically just lost your class ring inside my vagina, so if you can't tell…"

"I know. I'm just kidding."

Hilarious.

Mariana, the house manager, has a baby: a perfect towheaded daughter named Lily. With a full-time job, an asshole of a baby daddy, and a house full of junkies, caring for her new kid is overwhelming for her, to say the least. Luckily, she has a house full of quasi-qualified women (some who are moms) to lean on, right?

One night, after one a.m., I hear her waking up the various mothers in the sober living.

"I'm so tired, and Lily won't stop crying," I hear her say.

The various and sundry sober mommies try their well-worn tricks. But Lily still will not stop wailing.

At the end of her tether, Mariana walks into my room.

"You're up!" she says in her clipped British accent.

"Whoa, whoa, whoa. I'm not very maternal, and I've never had a baby. And I don't want one."

"Just try *something*... anything. I'm exhausted, and nothing is working."

"I really think—" and with that, Mariana thrusts two-month-old Lily into my arms.

*Fuck.* I hold her up by the armpits at arm's length. This thing is wriggling like crazy, tiny knit-bootied feet windmilling in the air.

I sling her over my shoulder like a sack of potatoes and start pacing the hallway of the house. I remember my mom used to say she would lull me to sleep with what in Spanish is called a *ru ru*, a loop of "ch-ch-chuh, ch-ch-chuh." Having no clue of what else to do, I give it a shot. "Ch-ch-chuh, ch-ch-chuh. Ch-ch-chuh, ch-ch-chuh." *This is totally dumb,* I think to myself. But I keep going. "Ch-ch-chuh, ch-ch-chuh. Ch-ch-chuh, ch-ch-chuh." And within three minutes, Lily passes out, drooling on my shoulder. I can't help but smile. It feels nice.

Mariana is shocked, and all the "professional" moms are clearly annoyed. That's right, bitches—*I* am the baby whisperer!

Before long, I am Lily's nanny, rocking her to sleep on the porch swing or walking around the neighborhood in a ripped-up Van Halen tee with her strapped to my chest like a suicide bomber. It is evident to everybody that, despite my lack of previous baby experience, Lily and I have a special connection. Soon I am pushing her in a carriage and then in a toy car. I spend a lot of time with Lily that first year, singing Elvis Costello to her, changing her diapers, reading to her. I also watch a fuck-ton of *Sesame Street*.

One day, Lily and I are in the living room playing and Lily begins hysterically laughing. Mariana comes gliding in on her long gazelle legs.

"What is *so* funny?"

"We're playing bar. Watch." Then in my best redneck voice, I say to Lily, "What can I get you, little lady?...Oh, a scotch on the rocks? Comin' right up!" And with that, I take a smooth stone out of the coffee table pit and slap it on the top. Lily lets out a yelp of pleasure and delight.

"Oh, my God," Mariana says.

"You want some nachos with that? No problem!" I slap another stone on the table.

Another peal of laughter from Lily.

"You are too much," she says, shaking her head. "So you're preparing my kid to be an alcoholic?"

"I was thinking more barfly, but hey, she does have the genetics..."

"I know, right?" Mariana grimaces.

Mariana looks over and sees Lily trying to get my attention. "Looks like your customer is...uh...thirsty again," she says to me.

"Oh, I'm sorry, little lady! Another drink?"

Mariana's trust shows me that I can be reliable, responsible, trust-worthy. And Lily's love for me shows me that I do have a maternal side. I can be nurturing, a caretaker, and—dare I say—selfless. Hey, maybe the stuff I stuck on that vision board wasn't as delusional as I thought.

Elizabeth, my new Glamazon roommate at the sober living, spends her days working out, getting her face injected, and having long lunches with Arab men at the Beverly Hills Hotel.

She's dating a new Persian guy. He's completely out of his mind. He sends her videos of himself telling her how much he loves her—multiple times a day. It's more stalkerish than romantic. He drives a yellow Lamborghini, so I call him Bananamobile. He bought her a silver ring from Tiffany, but she is unimpressed.

"I looked it up online, and it was only a hundred and twenty-five dollars," she says, doing her best at making a pouty face, which is hard with all her Botox.

"Oh, my God, that is horrible," I say. "Are you okay?"

She laughs. "You think I'm a terrible person, don't you?"

"Not terrible, just shallow. You're still young. I was married, and I got lots of super-expensive presents and spoiler alert! They did not make me feel loved. Not to put it too poetically, but you're searching for something that doesn't come in a small gift box."

"You're really smart, huh?"

"Obviously not, because I'm in sober living at forty-three."

"You're forty-three?! OMG! You look so much younger."

"It's the acne."

"You're funny."

"Speaking of age, Elizabeth...you're too young to shoot all that shit into your face. You don't need it yet. And it makes you look..."

"What?"

"I hate to say it, but...unnatural."

"Good. Who wants to be natural? Gross."

"You wanna look like a doll?" I ask.

"Totally."

"Okay then...carry on," I say with a wave of my hand.

I have an appointment to get a Pap smear. MediCal has sent me to a new clinic in downtown, but I can't find the building. I keep driving by the address, but I don't see anything vaguely medical. I decide to park nearby and walk.

Number 6212. This *is* it. But all I see is a "Swap Meet Mall." I peer inside. It's a long corridor off the sidewalk with different stalls: El Salvadorean food, Hello Kitty leggings, cheap iPhone accessories, four-packs of socks. I walk back outside and look up. There is a small hand-painted sign, "Clinica Medica," with an arrow pointing to the second floor. Are you fucking serious?

As usual, I'm the only white person in the waiting room. A young black kid bounces a ball against the peeling wall. A girl who can't be more than seventeen waddles in, pregnant, bursting at the seams. Another young Hispanic girl is rocking a screaming baby in her arms. I feel thin, snobby, and barren.

"DRESNER!" I'm called in after a relatively short forty-five minutes. The nurse weighs me and gives me a paper gown. Eventually, the doctor comes in. She has what looks to be the remnants of a black eye. I pretend not to notice.

"Are you sexually active?"

"Yes."

"Are you in a relationship?"

"What's that?"

"Do you have multiple partners?"

"Yes."

"Do you use birth control?"

"No."

"You're not worried about getting pregnant?"

"I'm old."

"What about STDs?"

"So far so good."

"I'm going to test you for all STDs."

"Knock yourself out."

A nurse comes in to take my blood. I have *huge* veins. I'm very vascular. I wasn't a good junkie, but I was an easy junkie.

"Oh good; you have nice veins," she says.

"Yeah. Even Ray Charles could be my phlebotomist."

I'm told to call in two weeks for my results.

\*     \*     \*

I call back a few weeks later. I'm terrified that I have some virulent form of something as I've been fucking a lot of people I know very little, all unprotected.

"Last name?" the nurse says in a light Hispanic accent.

"Dresner."

"Date of birth?"

"Eleven six, sixty-nine."

"You're clean. Negative for everything."

"Are you sure? Can you check again? Last name is Dresner. D...R... E..."

"Amy, right?"

"Yes."

"Yeah, I'm looking at your chart right here, miss. Nothing."

"Wow...awesome." What I wanted to tell her is: "That, right there, is a water-into-wine-style miracle, lady! I mean, talk about beating the odds."

I wish I could tell you that this clean bill of health made me start using condoms or be more discerning or less slutty. But that would be bullshit. It only served to reinforce my belief that I was special and that I would keep dodging any real physical repercussions of my sexual addiction. Think about it: you don't stop speeding because you *don't* get a ticket.

# CHAPTER TWENTY-THREE

Mariana, the house manager, is going to the south of France to visit her sick mother, and she's putting me in charge of the sober living. I'm the oldest, and I've been there the longest. She'll throw me a few hundred dollars. How hard can it be, right?

I'm allowed to stay in Mariana's room while she's away. It has a huge bed, a new AC system, and its own adjoining bathroom. I'm also to take care of her plants.

"It's easy. You just water them every few days."

"Got it," I lie.

"And the door camera is broken . . . but the girls don't know that."

"Right."

"So make sure they all sign out and are home by curfew."

The girls in the house are sweet. Most are young and new in sobriety. But running a women's sober living is not easy. It's like herding cats . . . if the cats were on heroin.

One night, I'm wedged on a bed between two of them, both in their twenties, as we binge-watch *Mr. Robot*. They both text incessantly—when they aren't laughing about how their moms freaked out when they turned forty.

"My dad put tombstones in the front yard," one young junkie girl says, laughing. *Oh, isn't that hilaaaarious,* I think.

Within the first four days, it looks like I've definitely killed Mariana's plants. They don't seem to like my chronic vaping. I quickly hatch a plan to replace the plants if they commit suicide before she gets back.

It's nice—and dare I say shocking—to be considered trustworthy and responsible enough to be handling somebody else's money, credit cards, mail, and home. But it's strange when, just the week before, you were one of the girls in the house that the other girls confided in, making pacts of "Don't tell the manager" with. And then suddenly, you are the fucking manager.

They think that because I crash early (with an eight thirty a.m. start time moonlighting for an advice columnist) that I won't know if they blow curfew. But I do. When one girl is a bit late, I just pull her aside and say, "Listen. I've been a wildcat since I lived here, and I have never blown curfew. Not once. So you have no excuse not to be back on time. Don't make me police you. I'm too old for this shit, and so are you."

I only have a measly two years and change sober now, compared with Mariana, who has over a decade in recovery and a black belt in Al-Anon (the twelve-step program for friends and families of addicts/alcoholics). In addition, she's a lady and a mother, and, well, let's just say we have different approaches. Hers is more "Hey, are you coming to the meeting? It's time," delivered with a posh British accent and a smile. Mine is more Gunnery Sergeant Hartman: "Let's go, assholes. Meeting time!" or "Nobody's getting loaded on my watch!" Mariana is also maternal and concerned: "I'm worried about you. We need to talk." I'm more "Hey, if you need to talk, I'm here. If not, journal or cut yourself. And Tinder worked wonders for me." And because I've been there so many times, on that terrifying roller coaster of early sobriety, they take to me and weepingly confess their boy dilemmas or thoughts of relapse. No good deed goes unpunished, I guess.

It's eleven thirty at night, and I hear a soft knock on my door. It's one of the girls. She's crying, of course.

"Come in, mama. What's up?"

"Well, you know I had seven months and relapsed."

"Yeah."

"Well, because it was over a dude, my sponsor says I can't date for at least six months; maybe a year. What the fuck? I mean, that's so unfair."

Ahh, yes, sponsors. They're trying to help, but sometimes it can feel like you've unwittingly become a citizen of their own personal police state. One of my most memorable sponsors crossed my path back in 2006, after I fell off the wagon with Ativan, ended up in the psych ward, and then promptly cracked my head open. She was a militant black lesbian with an old-school fade who worked with a lot of the chronic relapsers in AA. This woman was so fucking program that she had changed her name to DAJARIE—an acronym for "Denial Ain't Just a River in Egypt." She'd been through it all: molested at a young age only to become a homeless junkie and prostitute. When I met her, she had over two decades of sobriety and thirty sponsees, 98 percent of whom were rich white women. And despite calling each of us "baby," she was...terrifying.

"Baby, you only going to go to women's meetings or gay meetings from now on."

"How am I going to get laid going to women's meetings or gay meetings?" I whined.

"You not. You gonna concentrate on recovery."

"Well, that sounds fucking boring."

Still, I was so desperate that I complied. I was unemployed and a mess and I went wherever she told me. During the week, we attended these rich white women meetings in Brentwood or Beverly Hills. I loathed these meetings. They were filled with "mature" women with overly taut faces and expensive handbags, who complained about their gardeners. I did my best to shock and horrify them, and I was wildly successful. Part of this was due to my concussion. At the best of times, I'm emotionally volatile, but at fifty-something days sober with a brain injury, I was fucking feral. Since whacking my head, I felt different. I'd always been bold and irreverent, but I'd become freer and almost fearless. On the downside, my social cuing seemed to be off. I'd say something, laugh maniacally, and notice that the whole room had gone silent. Or I'd think of something, and before I could filter which part would be appropriate to say aloud, it was out of my mouth. I could feel that I had less impulse control than ever, but there didn't seem to be much I could do about it. I tried to pretend it was intentional—part of my shtick—and that I didn't give a shit, but in actuality, I was mortified. I was also experiencing brief bouts of mania that felt like good crack laced with religious fervor. Unfortunately, these were always followed by crushing migraines and paranoid, gut-wrenching lows. And then the inevitable: narcolepsy.

The doctors had assured me that this was all "temporary," but this particular "temporary" had lasted almost a year, and I'd managed to do some pretty impressive damage during that time. The thing is, nobody cares whether you're an asshole because you have a concussion. They just care that you're an asshole.

Dajarie made it mandatory that all her sponsees went to "Women's Self-Acceptance," an all-women's meeting in Crenshaw on Saturdays. It was held in a tiny, shitty house deep in the hood. There was a podium with the word "HOPE" on it and a big bouquet of white flowers. It always felt more funereal than AA to me. This particular meeting was 99 percent black lesbian. All the women looked like men who looked like women. They all had names like Tyler or Jeri and bore a striking resemblance to Ice-T. I felt very intimidated, despite their warm welcomes. I was one of maybe two white girls and definitely the only straight one. I sat in the far back, in the corner, my leg bouncing nervously.

Dajarie came over to me.

"Why you sittin' in the back, sugarplum?"

"Because I'm scared."

"Well, be scared in the front."

Fuck. I moved to the front, all long bangs and sad dog eyes, scratching where the stitches had been on my head.

Black lesbians get very involved in their meetings. There were lots of random shoutings of "That's right!" "Get it, girl!" and "God is good!" It felt like what I'd imagine a revival church would be like, but I'm a Jew, so what the hell do I know.

An enormous black woman with a shaved head came up to the podium to share. "I like them hard chairs," she opened with. "They remind me of prison."

Okaaay...

\*　　　\*　　　\*

One day, I was at one of those horrible Brentwood bitch meetings, and in walked a cute dark-haired guy with glasses and tattoos.

"Excuse me, but this is an all-women's meeting," said one of the tight-faced housewives.

"I am a woman," she answered, taking a seat.

Huh? Turned out her name was Lori, and she was a butch dyke who had recently gotten out of prison. She had a flat chest from a double mastectomy due to breast cancer and was two years clean from a really, really bad heroin habit. Cancer and her heroin addiction coincided for a while. In fact, back when she was undergoing chemo, she shot dope into her chemo ports. Now, that's some junkie dedication.

Lori looked so much like a man that strangers she encountered called her "sir." When she walked out of a women's public restroom, other women would do a double take and check the "ladies" sign on the door. When she used to work out at Bally's, a security guard once came into the women's dressing room to remove her because somebody complained that there was a man in there.

I am not gay, but I was instantly and bizarrely infatuated with Lori. She wore these big Buddy Holly glasses that framed gray-blue eyes, and her face was covered in freckles. She was this amazing combination of all the best traits of a female best friend and all the machismo and chivalry of a man. She was like "guy lite." She could fix your car and then stay up all night with you eating ice cream and talking about feelings.

When you're newly sober, you are looking for any distractions from your feelings, and sex and romance are very effective ones. After years of numbing out with booze and drugs, suddenly experiencing my raw emotions, with nothing to take the edge off, felt uncomfortably intense. Granted, some people in early sobriety describe having what's called a "pink cloud," where they feel deliriously happy and optimistic. But I've never experienced this pink cloud—or had a pink anything, for that matter. For me, getting sober always feels like getting woken up military style: suddenly, at the crack of dawn, with rows of blinding fluorescent lights and a bugle blowing in your face.

As I said, Dajarie was only letting me go to women's meetings and gay meetings so I wouldn't fuck my way through this sobriety. Add to that that the majority of my sponsee sisters (my sponsor's other sponsees) were lesbians. This left me the lone straight girl in this sober gay family. I was the minority. And I felt like the outcast and the weirdo, and I desperately wanted to fit in. My romantic life with men had been a fucking train wreck so I thought, hey, maybe girls are the answer!

So I started watching *The L Word* religiously. I became convinced that Lori would fall in love with me. We'd move to San Francisco and get a house with dogs and wear backpacks or whatever lesbian couples do. I had it all planned out.

Dajarie was also Lori's sponsor. One night, after some intolerable sponsee dinner in the hood, I drove Lori home. I was wearing the most lesbo clothes I could find: a ripped-up, studded Iron Maiden T-shirt, a leather jacket, black jeans, and boots. When we got to her house, I turned off the car and looked at her.

"I have to tell you something," I confessed, shyly putting my face in my hands.

"Okay."

"I have a crush on you, and I'm not even gay," I said.

"Maybe it's because I look like a guy," she offered.

"I've had a dream about you every night since we met. It's kind of freaking me out. I don't want to be gay."

"Gay is not the worst thing in the world, Amy," she reassured me.

"I mean it would be better if you had a penis, but we can work around that," I said bluntly.

"That's very kind of you."

"I wanted to kiss you the other night, and I've even jacked off thinking about you."

"I think that's kind of hot," she said, with a half smile. "Listen, I . . . I . . . I'm flattered . . ."

"Flattered? Flattered?!" I said, astonished. "You should be fucking flattered. All the boys in AA wanna fuck me!" *Oh, lord, here I go...*

"Look, Amy...you're newly sober, and you just bumped your head. This is a very vulnerable time for you. And I don't jump into anything. My sobriety is everything. Let's just hang out and get to know each other."

"God, that sounds condescending."

"It's not meant to sound condescending. Your sobriety is the number one priority. You are attractive and funny and smart, but you're also a newcomer, and that's a sanctity I can't violate."

"Just you saying the word 'violate' turns me on," I said coyly.

"One day, when you tell your story, you can say that you bumped your head and when you woke up, you were a lesbian!"

I was silent.

"Come on," she said. "Smile...that was funny."

"I'm not a fucking lesbian. It's just you. You're a fluke."

As I drove home, it occurred to me that maybe lesbians have more willpower than men. Or...maybe I have less pull in the gay world? No guy in AA ever had so much respect for my vulnerability and sobriety that he wouldn't fuck me when I was a newcomer. Guys don't even have to like you to fuck you. You could have a wood eye or a peg leg, or be their best friend's girlfriend or be passed out, and they'd flip you over and stick it in.

I confessed my crush to one of my gay "sober sisters."

"She's a lesbian, Amy, not just a nice-smelling man with a better manicure. She's gay. It's different."

I tell Dajarie that I'm crushing out on Lori.

"Baby, you too ill to be involved with anybody—man or woman," she says without hesitation.

Lori and I agree to be "friends." There was an unspoken pact that conversation will be limited to topics with no romantic charge: sobriety, Tori Amos songs, burritos, whatever. We never speak about my "confession."

Lori didn't have a car. She was broke and lived in a small, shitty room she rented in some lady's house in the scariest part of Culver City. It's tough to land a job as an ex-con, so Lori, who was almost fifty, worked construction with a bunch of twenty-year-old Latino guys. Welcome to the freedom that is post-prison life.

I ended up chauffeuring her everywhere. I pretended that I was "being of service" as they say (and encourage) in AA, but I was really just desperate to be around her.

One day, she was in agony—having really bad chest pains.

"I'll take you to the ER."

"Just drop me off. I can take the bus home. I don't want to make you wait."

"Holy shit, your martyrdom is annoying," I snapped. "God forbid you should let anybody do anything for you."

"No... it's just that I like to do the giving," she said. "Because I like to be in control."

"You can receive and still be in control. I'm the queen of it. I actually teach a course," I cackled—my new scary head injury laugh.

I drove her back to her house, and we sat in the driveway chatting. She showed me photos from prison: one of her at fire camp (firefighting training in prison) and pictures of her twin sister, her old girlfriend, her best friend. One photo she quickly extracted from the pile and stuck in her pocket.

"What's that one?" I said.

"Nothing," she said.

"I want to see that one."

"It's nothing."

"Tell me why you don't want me to see it, and I'll stop pestering you."

"Because I don't."

"Fine."

As she was putting all the photos away, I caught a glimpse of the one she'd hidden. It was a picture of her—young, maybe early twenties, topless, on a horse. She had nice tits—nice tits that had been replaced by flat, aggressive scars.

She blurted out, "I don't mess around with straight girls. They don't know their sexual orientation. It's messy. I've been a lesbian my whole life. I had a girlfriend where I was her first lesbian relationship. Even after five years, she hadn't introduced me to her parents. She was afraid they'd disinherit her."

"I get it," I said, trying to end the conversation.

"Well, eventually you'll meet a nice guy..."

I stopped listening. Her voice trailed off as I stared at her freckles and her mouth that revealed her chipped teeth when she smiled.

A few days later, she took me by total surprise by walking into a meeting she never attended—one that I'd gone to expressly for that reason. I was shaken. I felt a physical lurching toward her. I looked longingly at her tan, muscular, hairless legs with their pretty swirling tribal tattoos. I played with my hair and posed my hands, trying to get her attention. Nothing. She was not even remotely interested in me, and I felt a deep rage rising.

Later that night I called Dajarie.

"I can't hang out with Lori. Honestly, I can't even see her at meetings," I admitted.

"I knew you would not be able to handle being Lori's friend. It's like trying to break up with somebody while still living with them."

"Can I skip all our regular meetings for a while, especially the Crenshaw one?"

"Okay, baby. But you need to tell Lori what's up and tell her no more contact."

I got Lori on the phone. "Listen...I'm, like, in love with you or something. I can't handle it. I can't hang out with you right now."

"What? I thought we were cool."

"No. I think you're fucking magical. You can fix cars, and you look like a dude, but you can talk about feelings and sad songs and stuff. It's rad."

"Well, women are really amazing, Amy. And there are plenty of us out here."

"No!" I scream into the phone—like a two-year-old. "I want you!"

"Well, having a relationship is not my priority right now. My recovery is. I don't want to end up losing my shit and living under a bush again. And...I don't think that's what our connection is about."

"How do you know?" I whined into the phone.

"I just know."

"But *how*?" I demanded. "Is it because I'm too crazy and broken?"

"Yeah, you are pretty crazy right now. I mean, there's some really cool stuff about you, but when you have these little tantrums, it's kind of scary..."

I broke into hysterical, heaving sobs. "You are withholding—just like every guy I've ever picked!"

"I'm not withholding. I have nothing to give."

"Same difference! That girl you were in love with for sixteen months... she crawls into your bed...you're a horny parolee...you haven't been with anybody for, what five years...and you do *nothing*. You don't even kiss her! What are you so afraid of?"

"She had a boyfriend," she said. "It would have been wrong."

"Wrong? *Wrong*? You shot heroin into your chemotherapy ports! You robbed houses and ended up in prison! Since when have you cared about 'wrong'?"

I lit a cigarette and changed ears. "I thought there was a charge between us," I continued. "It felt relationshippy."

"Haven't you had friendships with girls?" she asked. "They are kind of relationshippy."

"Yeah, I've had close girlfriends. I've even had girlfriends I made out with, and it didn't feel like this," I said.

"We will be friends down the road, Amy. You'll see. We will laugh about this one day."

I was silent.

"Hello...?" she said.

"Fuck. You," I said softly. And I hung up on her.

A month or so went by, and then Dajarie told me I needed to go back to the Crenshaw meeting.

"You can't avoid her forever, baby," she said.

I put on some jeans and tucked them into tall suede boots, threw on a crew-neck T-shirt that said "Perfect Angel" (yeah, right), a dark purple rabbit bomber jacket, and a long, thin scarf. I was dressing to impress Lori, going for seventies rock star. Unfortunately, by the time I pulled up at the meeting, I realized I looked more thirties aviator. Oh, well. I walked into the room, and I saw Lori in the far left, her arm draped over the back of an empty chair. I tried not to look at her.

After the meeting, I joined all the lesbians smoking and chatting out on the lawn. Lori shuffled over, little lesbian knapsack draped diagonally across her sunken chest, snaggle-toothed smile, aqua-blue soulful eyes darting nervously behind glasses that hid nothing.

"How are youuuu?" she asked, in the tone you might use on somebody developmentally disabled.

To my surprise and dismay, I just hauled off and punched her. Hard. In the shoulder. I was shocked. She looked mildly astonished and walked away. I started crying hysterically. Needless to say, we didn't speak for a while after that.

# CHAPTER TWENTY-FOUR

I tune my car radio to HOT 92.3. It's my favorite station these days: all late seventies jams. It reminds me of my days as a young'un, roller skating at Flippers, dreams and hopes still intact. I dance around badly in the driver's seat, sucking violently on my e-cig, driving down the quiet, empty, early morning streets of Hollywood.

One guy who winds up on my crew this morning is a young, black, aspiring R & B singer. While we're working, he sings the same two verses of his crappy song for four hours straight. He finally stops, but only because he passes out from exhaustion.

When he wakes up, he says, "Shit, maaaan. I forget how my song went now. How'd it go again? You remember, girl?"

"I don't, dude. Sorry."

Another new face is an Armenian security guard who got arrested for "disturbing the peace"—with his gun. I don't even wanna know.

There are only a few regulars. Everybody else I see sporadically or just once and then never again. One of the regulars is a tiny black woman who looks exactly like the comedian Katt Williams. She rides a bicycle and does not shut the fuck up. Another is an old Russian guy with surgical rods in his back. Obviously an alcoholic, he has had an astounding six DUIs and has that red bulbous W. C. Fields nose that only real hard-core drunks get. He is very quiet and works harder than anybody else on the crew, despite not being able to bend over.

A rabid old man passing us with a shopping cart mumbles something about the New Testament and Jack in the Box. I couldn't hear what he said so I stupidly say, "Excuse me?"

"You heard me!" he screams, and then starts spitting at me. "Evil bitch! Demon! Jesus said..."

I clutch my dustpan and broom and do a quick shuffle up the street, heart racing.

*PING!* A text from Linda. I look around and then slyly pull my phone out. She has sent me a picture of a purse. "Do you like this Givenchy Pandora handbag for me? It's on sale at the RealReal."

I quickly text back: "Sorry, I'm being spat at by a homeless lunatic while I sweep up trash. Can I look later or is it pressing?"

"Whore."

"Faggot."

I hear the crew boss whistle at me and then yell, *"Apaga ese pinche teléfono, guera!"*

"Okay okay!" I put my phone away.


It was the Fourth of July, 2009, and I'd later joke that I was still so torn up by the split between America and England that I just couldn't take it anymore. But, at the time, there was nothing funny or patriotic about it.

I was performing regularly as a comic and getting good reviews. I had a sponsor, four sponsees, a few years sober. But I still felt a deep despair. I had been insecure about the way I looked at twenty; and pushing forty at the time, I could only imagine how my slow physical decline would impact my already fragile self-esteem.

I hated myself and worried that my husband, Clay, hated me, too. No matter how hard I tried, I couldn't muster the kind of love for him that he felt for me. As the marriage went on, the disparity became obvious. There were other surprises, too. Being married didn't feel like security to me. It felt like prison.

The two of us waged a silent war. The territory was the marital bed.

He wanted to make love, and I wanted to get fucked. He wanted to connect, and I wanted to check out.

I remember the very first time I spent the night at Clay's, years before, when we were first dating. He turned to me in bed and said, "I'm really glad you're here."

"Me too," I answered. "Because you have central air." In my defense, it was a scalding L.A. summer, and I lived in a 1930s apartment with no AC. But it was a horrible thing to say. And, ultimately, this remark was a model for our marriage: he was in love, and I was in need. I did eventually grow to really love him, but by then, it was too late, and the damage had been done.

So Clay and I were fighting. Again. If you really want to hurt someone, just tell them the truth. No need to insult them. Just say that thing that they know but hide from themselves: the thing that they drink over, the thing that jolts them awake at three a.m., the thing that they look to disprove in every lover's eyes.

I don't remember exactly what he said, but I do remember the feeling, like my insides were breaking. It had all become clear. I was a fake. I was surrounded by sycophants. I was getting old. And my marriage was a fraud.

"I need to get loaded," I said vacantly.

"Get loaded! Do it! It will be easier to get rid of you," he snapped.

"Oh . . . you want to get rid of me? No fucking problem." He had just given me what I needed: an excuse.

I went into the kitchen to retrieve my epilepsy medication. I'd read somewhere that there was no antidote to a phenobarbital overdose. I had a full bottle in my hand. I thought of Marilyn Monroe, Judy Garland, and Elvis. Fuck it. I can go out like that.

I poured the phenobarbital onto the bed. I took off my wedding ring and tossed it on the bed. Then I shoveled a handful of white pills into my mouth.

"Don't do that," Clay said. "You're not going to die. You're just going to get really sick."

I paused. A mouthful of chalky pills. *Whatever*, I thought, and swallowed. I was immediately greeted by a sense of relief mixed with horror.

He called 911. I went into the kitchen and grabbed a steak knife to slit my wrists in front of him. Classic borderline move: you hurt me so now I'm going to hurt myself. This was my first knife incident. Evidently I have an unfortunate penchant for utensils when I'm upset.

"She's brandishing a knife!" he said into the phone.

*Brandishing?* Who says "brandishing"? Was this a production of *Hamlet*?

Knowing the cops were on their way, I bolted out of the apartment. At the elevator, I was nabbed by the EMT people. I slumped down the wall onto the floor, defeated—but by no means calm. An overdose of pheno gives you a drunklike high, and when I'm drunk, I'm angry, so I was very fucking angry.

A female EMT asked me what I took.

"Phenobarbital," I slurred.

She looked puzzled.

"If it's good enough for Judy Garland, it's good enough for meeeee!" I said, lying down on the gurney.

By this point, Clay was in the hallway, watching it all go down. As they wheeled me into the elevator, I gave him the finger and shouted a loud "Fuck youuuuu," just as the doors closed. Very dramatic exit.

In the ambulance, as the paramedic started an IV line, she said, "Why not just get a divorce, honey? I mean, you don't have to kill yourself."

"You don't understand," I murmured.

The thing was, I had married a parental figure to police and take care of me. My husband was my daddy, my mommy, and my therapist, all rolled into one. Who would I be without him . . . a feral, forty-one-year-old, mentally ill, broke divorcée? I'd sold my soul to the devil, and the devil's name was security.

Next thing I knew, I was in the ER, being forced to choke down liquid charcoal. I was blasted. The ER, however, is not the place to enjoy a buzz. As medical personnel worked to save me from a lethal overdose, I cracked Jew jokes and did bad impersonations of old Southern black men.

"I'm ready to go home. I'm feeling goooooooooood," I said brazenly.

"You aren't going anywhere, Ms. Dresner," a nurse admonished me.

"What?" I was puzzled.

"You tried to kill yourself. You are going to the psych ward for a seventy-two-hour hold."

"Oh, that." I flopped my hand with disdain. "That was just a little... woo... mistake."

"Yes... sometimes life can be confusing," she said, smiling softly.

I blacked out and woke up in the psych ward. Unfortunately, familiar digs. Clay came to visit. I'd been vomiting from the overdose, and my face was very swollen—my eyes just tiny slits. He brought me my wedding ring and a card. I wept in his arms. "I'm sorry," I said. Even I was tired of hearing me say it. The next day he jetted off on a business trip.

My sponsor made me reset my sober time. I'd had three and a half years sober, but she said I abused my medication and that I needed to identify again as a newcomer.

"It wasn't a relapse!" I protested.

"Did you take your medication as prescribed?"

"Is it really a relapse if you try to kill yourself, but just end up accidentally loaded instead? Isn't that just a shoddy suicide attempt or a faulty chemistry experiment?"

"Did you take your medication *as prescribed*?"

"No... I took all of it."

"There's your answer."

Goddammit.

At this point, Lori, my lesbian crush, was working for Clay, my husband. Weird, I know, but the recovery world is incestuously, claustrophobically small. Everybody dates everybody. Everybody sponsors everybody. Everybody works for everybody. I wouldn't exactly call it nepotism. It's more like "networking."

Clay told me that Lori got in a bad car accident. The doctor gave her pain pills, and, of course, she was shooting dope again in no time. One night, she shot a speedball and had a stroke. Almost died. I'm sure she'd heard about my latest debacle, so I called to check in.

"I was trying to die, and I only ended up getting high," I told her.

"I wasn't trying to die. I was just trying to get high," she told me.

"Maybe we need to swap recipes, then."

She laughed. "You're still funny…"

# CHAPTER TWENTY-FIVE

M y Russian friend who came with me to the cunty Russian psychi-atrist asks me to house-sit her place for two weeks while she goes back East for the holidays. I ask Mariana, the house manager, whether I can, and she says yes.

My friend has two super-annoying small dogs that need to be walked a couple of times a day. But after almost two years in a twin bed in a shared room in sober living, I get not just a queen bed, but a whole apartment to myself? I'll gladly pick up dog shit for that.

Her place is just a few blocks away from the sober living, but it feels like another world. It's so quiet inside, I can hear the skaters smoking blunts and doing tricks in a nearby alley.

Joe, the sober guy who insisted on silence as he aggressively fingered me in his Porsche, reappears. He starts calling me "slut" and "whore." It makes me really uncomfortable, but I don't want to seem like a prude. He orders me via text to go to a sex store and buy a huge black dildo—the biggest I can find. I don't even want to know where this is going. But, weirdly and mechanically, I obey, texting him pics of different ones—*This one? Maybe this one?*—as I lay them out on the floor of The Pleasure Chest.

"U r a good girl. A very good girl," he texts me.

I roll my eyes. This is fucking stupid. But I don't stop, and I don't have a good reason why. I'm lonely? Curious? Whatever my reason, it isn't a good one.

Despite having almost two years sober, I am still innately attracted to things that are bad for me. Whether my self-destructive inclination comes out of alcoholism, thrill-seeking, or is a symptom of my low self-esteem, I have no idea. Some people like to go wing-walking; I like to test my mortality and luck by shooting cocaine while having a seizure disorder or by barebacking promiscuous strangers. I am one sick motherfucker.

Joe wants me to dress like a seventeen-year-old trailer park whore: knee socks, high heels, girly underwear, and a ratty T-shirt. I send him a picture of my outfit for his approval. He is not pleased. First, the underwear aren't right. They're too sexy and hip; not juvenile and trashy enough. He finally agrees on a pair of baggy white mesh ones with pink hearts, and we move on to the socks. No, no...those aren't right. They are too wooly. I put on some different ones. No, no...those are too dark, and those are too patterned. *Jesus Christ,* I think, *this role-play stuff is a pain in the ass.* Maybe some people get turned on by the whole "ritual" of it, but I just wanted to get to the sex part.

It all feels demeaning and demoralizing to me, but even those feelings are preferable to being alone with the void that is me. I am coming up on the three-year anniversary of my domestic violence incident. I need distraction. "Just be with yourself," my friends advise. Honestly, I can't think of anything more hellish.

Like most addicts, I hate feelings. I know feelings are temporary, that they have a beginning, a middle, and an end. However, to an addict like me, they feel overwhelming, unbearable, and endless. Therein lies the violent urgency to fix or escape them. For example, if I'm hit with rage or sadness or desire, at the beginning, I think, "I can get through this." But as the feeling builds, moving toward the middle, I feel like a rat in a cage that's slowly heating up, and I start frantically looking for a way out. The way out can be handing somebody their ass in a vengeful text (that I'll have to make amends for) or masturbating over FaceTime for some freak from Tinder. It can be chain-smoking Marlboro Blacks while also chewing Nicorette as I feverishly troll eBay for the perfect vintage whatever. And sometimes just to make it to the end of a feeling, that magical place when you see that it doesn't actually last forever, I just make myself go to bed. I've been known to crash out for fourteen hours straight in the fetal position, hoping that when I wake up, I will have somehow rebooted.

I get a text from Joe with his instructions: "I'll come in @ 8:30. Leave the front door unlocked. U will be sitting on the edge of the bed. U will not speak. U will not look @ me. I'll take some photos 4 my own use. When I'm done, I'll leave."

"Ok," I text back.

"Ok what?" he demands.

"Ok daddy."

"That's right."

Joe shows up exactly on time. I'm sitting on the bed, precisely as he asked, and I'm so scared I'm shaking. He's wearing a hoodie over his head, partly covering his face, which I've only seen once in the dark backseat of his SUV. He doesn't kiss me. He roughly flips me over onto my stomach, rips off my underwear, and fucks me with the black dildo I bought. I can hear him breathing heavily. He's very aroused. I pretend to be. But I feel detached, shut down. I'm sort of hovering outside of myself, watching this whole bizarre scenario, wondering how I went from being a bejeweled CEO's wife to getting fucked with a black dildo by a stranger while dressed up as a seventeen-year-old white-trash prostitute. Was this my new sobriety—just exchanging one horrifying self-destructive behavior for another? While this guy is panting in my ear, shoving this black dildo into me, I hear my sponsor Jay's voice: "You put down a behavior when what it is doing *to* you is worse than what it is doing *for* you."

Joe finishes and leaves. I wash off the dildo and stuff it in the closet. I throw the torn underwear in the garbage. As much as I want to dress this up as "I am liberated" or "edgy" or "sex-positive," I know that I am out of control and deeply unhappy. I tell none of my friends about this latest incident, and I tell my friends everything.


There was a comic I'd been friends with for probably seven years. His name was Sully. He was big and kind of lunky, with a belly and a beard and sloe eyes. He looked like a lumberjack. A lot of hipsters do. And even though he'd been clean for a few years, he still had that slow, apathetic junkie drawl. There had always been an attraction between us, but I was married at the time, and he was having an on-again, off-again relationship with a crazy model. It was obvious that if we were ever single at the same time, we would at least fuck.

Once his relationship to Miss Cheekbones fell apart for the umpteenth time and I was divorced and sober again, he started calling me every day. He was funny and attentive, but he wanted me to video myself peeing and also call him daddy, and I thought that was fucking creepy. I did it, but I saw we had different kinks, and any long-term thing was ill fated.

He was in town from New York to see his family, and I had my friend's whole place to myself. He came over and we had sex. It was pretty good. He's dirty and uninhibited, but I felt some strange apathy in myself when we were in bed together, and I knew immediately I would never ever fall in love with him. But our long friendship was a good base. And we had the important commonalities of addiction and comedy. I should at least give it a go, right?

He was on his way over for the second time when Joe texted.

"I want 2 see u."

"I can't."

"20 min. I'll meet u anywhere u want."

"I can't. I'm sorry."

"You dare say no 2 me u slut?"

"I have somebody coming over."

"A guy?"

"Yes."

"I want 2 watch."

"No, that's weird."

"Do it! He'll never know. U can just prop up ur phone & FaceTime."

"No."

"Be a good girl & do this. Don't disobey me."

He hammers on, and I finally concede. I prop up my phone on the bedside table and aim the camera at the bed. Sully comes over, and we start fooling around. Somehow Joe gets disconnected, and keeps calling back again and again and again.

"Wow. Somebody is really trying to get ahold of you," Sully says.

"Don't worry about it. Ignore it," I say, kissing him.

Sully had been a homeless street junkie. He's no dummy. He quickly figures out what's going on.

"Are you filming us? Is somebody watching?"

"Uhhhh..."

"Amy!"

"I'm sorry. It's this weird guy, and he's so demanding and...I dunno... I thought it could be kind of hot."

"I just wished you'd asked me first."

"I know. It's shitty. I'm sorry. We've been friends a long time; I..."

"It's cool. Whatever..."

After he leaves, I call Joe. "What the fuck is wrong with you? You just kept calling and calling? He totally figured it out!"

"That was hot. I was getting really into it. Now you have to help me finish."

"What?"

"Go get that dildo and fuck yourself in the ass and touch yourself on FaceTime."

"That thing is huge. It will hurt."

"Do it!"

I go get the dildo and call him back on FaceTime. I touch my pussy and slowly push the dildo up my ass. It's extremely painful. I don't like this. It's complete vulnerability without a drop of intimacy or safety, and it leaves me feeling frightened and sick to my stomach.

I can hear him breathing into the phone and see a dark shadow of his hand moving as he jacks off. When he comes, he hangs up.

I just sit on the bed, silent. I hear a dog barking up the street. I hear the homeless guy who lives in the alley pushing a creaking shopping cart. I feel more dirty and alone than ever, and I don't like who I've become.

I realize that I need to stop making these grand pronouncements to people: "I've quit smoking!"; "I'm never going back on Tinder!"; "We're fucking over!" As true as those things might seem in the moment, these feelings can be as fleeting as your two-day attempt at veganism after watching one of those gnarly documentaries about factory farming. Before long, you're left all sheepish, saying, "Uh, yeah, actually, I'm smoking/Tindering/seeing him again."

Jay W., my sponsor, helpfully pointed out that I can't really be called insane, because insanity is doing the same thing over and over again and expecting different results. I do the same thing over and over again, knowing full well the result will be exactly the same. And I've realized that underneath all of this sexual acting out is my basic desire to be loved. When I say, "Don't you want to fuck me?" what I really mean is "Love me!"

I suddenly remember hearing this guy speak about shame and self-loathing at a Sex Addicts Anonymous meeting. I cried throughout his whole share. He seemed to have pretty good recovery. He was a comedy writer; a nerdy Jew with a kid. Harmless. I call him, a sex addict reaching out to another sex addict. It's what you're supposed to do.

"Hey, I just did something really degrading, and I just feel like I wanna hose off my soul. I feel really out of control and I'm scared."

"Are you physically hurt?" he asks.

"No, I mean my asshole hurts, but I'm sure it will be fine."

"You're okay. It's over now. It's done. You can't undo it."

"Right."

"It's what we do. You need to find compassion for yourself."

"Okay."

I have no idea how it happened, but he ends up masturbating with me on the phone, maybe aroused by the sordid details of what I'd just recounted. He seemed so nice—this sweet-faced Jew with a young kid. Later, I find out he lives with his girlfriend, and this is his MO. I'm not surprised. The rooms are full of sick people, exploiting each other at the behest of their "disease." Just when you think you've seen it all, the floor drops out and there's another basement, a whole other level of debauchery. I'm disgusted and appalled, but it is just what I need to be finally and irrevocably done with my sex addiction.

# CHAPTER TWENTY-SIX

I'm back in my room at sober living with my Glamazon roommate, Elizabeth. Though I enjoyed my freedom house-sitting over the holidays, I've never vaped so much or fucked so many losers in such a short amount of time. I'm sort of relieved to be contained again.

I'm unpacking my stuff and I notice that Bradley, the New York theatre actor (barf), has sent me another Facebook message: "Hey, thanks for your advice a few months back. Baby mama is doing much better. I gotta be honest. I have a talent crush on you."

"Oh, my God, this guy again?" I say aloud.

"What guy? Who?" Elizabeth asks nosily.

"Some actor in New York...I barely know him!"

"Let's see a picture."

I click on his profile.

"Wow...he's cute! Look at that cleft chin and those dimples," she coos.

"I don't know. Is he a...redhead? I don't mess with soulless gingers."

"He's a hottie. At least talk to him!"

"Fiiiine."

I start messaging with Bradley on Facebook. This guy is *not* my type. No visible tattoos. No drug problem. In fact, he's never even *done* any hard drugs, but brags that he's smoked weed a whopping four times. He stubbornly claims to be "blond," but I maintain that he's straight-up ginger. He's an Ivy-educated, German-Irish quasi-country boy from Virginia. "Half white, half trash," he calls himself. He's done pretty well in

New York, appearing on Broadway, done a bunch of TV shows and movies, headlines at several comedy clubs.

It's very clear that I'm way too fucked up for him. And I tell him that.

"I'm not worried," he messages back.

Well, I am. At this point, I don't trust men or love or any of that stuff.

"Would you go on a date with me? I'm coming to L.A. soon."

"I'll think about it," I say coolly. "Have you actually *read* my stuff?"

"Yeah, I love it."

"It's not fictional, you know. I did all that shit. Like, *all* of it."

"I get it, Amy."

"So why are you pursuing this?"

"At the risk of sounding cheesy, I'm going to use a line from *Avatar*..."

"Go for it. I never saw the movie."

"'I see you.'"

Fuck this guy. I know how this is going to end, and I'm not up for it.

Ivy-actor-comedian boy is very persistent. Turns out he got a degree in aerospace engineering, which means he's simultaneously a rocket scientist and a disappointment to his parents. He was also a yoga teacher who studied tantra and all kinds of esoteric shit. Hey, at least he's not a boring fuckboy. I cave and message him my number.

He texts me right away. Within hours, I'm blasting him with naked selfies—because I'm an idiot. I have an arsenal from my two years as a Tinderella. I might be a criminal ex-junkie living in a halfway house in my forties, but I've got abs that rival those of a twenty-year-old Olympic track star with a crack habit. Gotta lead with your strong suit.

"Did u just take this?" he texts.

"Yes, weirdo," I lie.

"How do I know that this isn't from a bank of nudies u have on ur cell?"

"What do you want me to do? Hold up today's newspaper like some kidnap victim?"

"Write my name."

"Yeah, I'm not doing that."

Amazingly, the next day I find myself scrawling his name in eyeliner on my stomach. Jesus, this is a lot of work just to snare a ginger.

After a week into our texting, he confesses that he's "terrified of relationships and marriage." Umm, calm down. We haven't even spoken on the phone yet, dude. And truth be told, though I respect his honesty, I really can't handle another emotionally unavailable asshole.

Late one Saturday night, he lands in Los Angeles and actually calls me like a gentleman.

"Come down to my hotel by LAX."

Well, maybe not that much of a gentleman.

"It's one thirty in the morning," I tell him.

"We'll just hang out in bathrobes, order room service, and talk like adults."

"Yeah, right. Look, I *like* you. I don't want to fuck you right away. I always do that, and it never works out. Plus, it's way past curfew."

"I like you, too. That's why we need to see if we have chemistry. Because if we have physical chemistry, we are in trouble. But if we don't, we can be friends, you know? And I'm not going to think less of you if you fuck me the first night."

"All guys say that."

I do not go down there that night, but I agree to meet and pick him up the next day, outside some weird Esalen-type self-help seminar he's doing in Culver City.

I pull up to the front of the building, and he waves me over. He throws his camouflage backpack into the backseat and jumps in the front passenger seat.

"Hey!" he says.

"This is so weird!" is all I can manage.

"Why?" He smiles.

He is gorgeous. He's so charismatic that he fucking glows. His smile is blinding.

My Vicks vapor stick is in the car console. Thanks to years of snorting anything that can fit into a nostril, I'm continually congested. I'm addicted to Afrin and anything that will let me breathe freely, if just for a moment. Bradley nonchalantly grabs my Vicks stick and sticks it up his nose and inhales. There's a boorishness and a level of presumption to this that I find oddly endearing.

We land at his L.A. crash pad, a place he stays when his good friend and fellow bicoastal actor is not in town. We sit on the couch, watching a movie and chatting about life. After my Xander fiasco, I try to hold back so I don't come off as "rapey" or aggressive. But, as with any new behavior I try, I tend to swing too much the other way. I look down and notice I'm still wearing my winter jacket—a vintage seventies leather bomber with a fur-trimmed hood. It is zipped completely up to the top and my arms are crossed tightly over my chest. Wow. I must be petrified.

It isn't just my past romantic disasters that make me scared. Whenever you meet somebody for the first time, it's always nerve-wracking. I mean, does he think I'm hot in person? Everybody puts their most flattering photos on Facebook. Do I look like my photos? He's sitting to my right, getting a profile view. I gotta be honest, my profile is pretty Jewy. Maybe he thinks I look too much like an ex-junkie. Maybe he thinks he's too good for me. Maybe he thinks—

Suddenly, Bradley's mouth comes crashing down on mine. The chemistry between us is heady. As soon as his tongue goes into my mouth, I can almost feel my eyes roll back into my head. All of my mental chatter stops. I forget my pledge not to fuck him and, next thing you know, we are lying naked in his bed, freshly fucked. Oops.

"You're so funny," he says, running his finger down the bridge of my nose and touching my lips. "You're like part porn star and part little girl, with Elaine Stritch's voice and perfect Christmas Barbie hair stapled to your head."

"Who's Elaine Stritch?" I ask, at the cost of sounding uncultured.

"Oh, my God—only one of the most famous Broadway actresses of all time..."

We stay up till four in the morning talking about everything: past relationships, personal growth, spirituality, addiction, stand-up. Before we finally fall asleep, I warn him that I snore.

"It's really bad," I say. "Like if a chainsaw and a rhino had a colicky baby."

"I like white noise," he assures me. He cradles me in his arms and holds me all night.

I immediately feel like this is my person. I know that sounds stupid and trite and maybe like I'm just grasping for yet another guy, but he is the whole package: smart, funny, handsome, deep, a good fuck, likes Jews. *I've been waiting for you*, I want to whisper. But then I remember what he said: "I'm terrified of relationships and marriage." Yeah, let's not get too excited here. Lady Luck hasn't been too keen on us lately. And if Tinder taught me anything, it's that it's easy to get laid and hard to find love. Sex is just sex. It doesn't mean they love you, even if they spoon you after.

Don't get me wrong, I love those stories of people who are like, "we met and we just knew, and we've been together every day since." It's just never been my experience. My experience is that people are confused and terrified, and even if they want to be with you, they still have to cross their own vast field of land mines around trust and intimacy.

# CHAPTER TWENTY-SEVEN

Bradley is in L.A. for the next week, staying at his crash pad, doing stand-up, going to auditions. He calls me every single day, and we have two more fantastic sleepovers. I even spend the last night with him, agreeing, like a sucker, to drive him to the airport the next morning.

"My friend, who I share this place with, is super anal. I can't leave any trash," he says.

So we go through the apartment, dumping wastebaskets, sweeping off counters, filling up a giant black Hefty bag of trash which, of course, ends up in the trunk of my car.

At the airport, I get a tight hug and quick peck on the lips. I try not to overanalyze it.

Once he's on the plane, I get a text: "You're a true gift in my life."

*I drove you to the airport and I have your trash in my trunk. You bet your sweet ass, I'm a fucking gift*, I think.

But I decide not to be an asshole and just text back, "Awww, thanks. You're sweet. Xoxo."

A couple days go by and nothing. Once Bradley is back in Manhattan, it's a little out of sight, out of mind. Maybe he has a girlfriend there. Maybe he has a boyfriend there. Wouldn't be the first time...

I finally text, "Hey, what's up?"

A day or so later I get back a "Hiiiiiii."

I can't help but answer: "Takes you 2 days to come up with that clever response?"

He texts back, "Here we go..."

There are a few more of these super-delayed text responses, and I finally just think, *No. I'm not putting myself through this again.*

I decide to drop the hammer via SMS: "This is not what I'm looking for. You're great but I think we want different things. Be well."

This prompts a flurry of phone calls from him, telling me about how "real" our connection is, but how he doesn't want to have a long-distance relationship, because they don't work, blah, blah, blah.

"I don't want a girlfriend right now. I'm focusing on my career," he says over the phone.

"Because it's impossible to have both. I get ya ..."

"Very funny. Okay, here's the truth: I don't want to have to take responsibility for another person, and that's what a relationship is."

"Wow ... that's romantic."

"It's just where I'm at."

"I get it. And I think that's lame and infantile, and that's where I'm at."

I stop calling him, and I delete his number. I don't quite have the balls to block his number, but I'm tempted to. He keeps calling me from New York, about once a week. I tell myself not to pick up when I see the 917 area code, but I always do. I don't say much. I'm pretty shut down because I don't think this thing has legs anymore. He chatters away, always sounding like he's a little out of breath—stressed, rushing around crowded Manhattan to auditions or gigs. I, on the other hand, am in L.A., stuck in a small shared room in sober living, leading a life that feels slow and uneventful.

This bullshit goes on for months. When he is in town, I'll get an "I'm here!" text. I want to blow him off, but he's charming and I do like him. But when he leaves, it's like he puts me in a little box on some shelf in the back of his head, compartmentalizing our time together and going on with his life in New York. He's like a dog. Wherever he is, that's where he is. Not in the future, not in the past. Just totally in the present.

Most of my friends tell me to dump him: *Don't waste your time. You deserve better. Fuck that guy.* Two people tell me to carry on. Only two. One is Elizabeth, who's convinced that Bradley and I are going to end up living together. She tries to school me in some weird manipulative withholding thing she does.

"You give, and then you pull back suddenly. Then you give again. Be really sweet and then pull back again and ignore them. It makes them obsessed!" she says gleefully.

"That's called intermittent reinforcement: give, withdraw, repeat. It's actually how and why people get addicted to gambling."

"You're so smart. I wish I was smart like you." She sighs.

The other person who tells me to hang in is transgender comic Ian Harvie, whom I used to tour with back when I did stand-up. He just looks at me and says, "Love is messy. Let it be messy."

As an addict, I'm not good at being patient or tolerating ambiguity. Bradley is making me do both. This is rough for me. I want what I want now. And I need to know what's going to happen. I don't like not knowing. It gives me anxiety. It opens a space in my head of "what if?" which is filled with extremes—only ridiculous fame, love, and fortune *or* homelessness, heartbreak, and tragic death. There's never anything in the middle, and that middle, that in-between part, is where normal life happens.

Because of this orientation, it is a real struggle for me to do nothing. I get that doing nothing is an action in itself. However, as an addict, my instinct is to always do *something*, even if it's to sabotage, because then at least, I know how it will end. Badly might not be ideal, but at least it's definite.

I've gotten pretty good at holding off on my impulses, but one day, on the phone, I blurt it out: "I love you, and I have for a while." An awkward beat follows.

"Love is gay," he says, his attempt at a little comic relief.

"Not exactly the response I was hoping for," I say.

"Look, I've said 'I love you' to way too many people who have completely vanished from my life," he tells me. "Romance is just something that Hallmark and Hollywood created so they can push product."

"I'm not talking about romance. I'm talking about love. Like what your parents have. How long have they been married?"

"Fifty years."

"That's fucking love. Love is commitment. Love is doing it when it's hard, not just when it's easy."

"Then why are you divorced?"

Ouch.

"It wasn't a good match. It wasn't right. And I wasn't ready."

"And . . . you tried to stab him."

"Oh, my God! I didn't try to stab him, I just . . . *waved* a knife—"

"I know, I know . . . calm down, Benihana!"

I laugh with my signature snort. He's derailed the conversation with his humor. And then he drops an emotional grenade.

"I think my parents are resigning themselves to the fact that I might very well die alone," he says.

I don't answer.

"Helloooo?" he asks.

"I heard you. You know . . . there is nothing cool or badass about never having been married or engaged or about being anti-relationship. It just makes you seem . . . like a frightened, pathetic little boy."

It is his turn to not answer. Eventually, he does.

"You're probably right."

A week later I'm complaining to my Vietnamese manicurist, David. He, as usual, has a mouthful of relationship advice for me.

"You whole package, but you not man. Let man be man."

"David, what does that even mean? And don't make my nails so pointy. You're making me look like Nosferatu."

"See! You bossy bitch."

"Oh, my God . . ."

Suddenly my phone dings as a text message comes in.

"That him. I tell you."

I eagerly look at my phone. But it's not Bradley, it's my ex-husband asking if it's true that I recently got kicked out of the Rainbow meeting for being loaded.

I make the mistake of responding. "No. I don't know what you're talking about. I'm the secretary of that meeting on Thursdays."

And now it's off to the races. Among Clay's gems are things like:

"Do your thing for the time you have left." "I'm just glad I survived you." "You're still an embarrassment to me." And my favorite, "I'd just assume you die." He also makes a point of telling me that he's remarried and how "awesome" it is.

This time, I try to explain how much guilt and shame I have around my behavior toward him and how much I've changed.

"How are you different? That's a joke. You are more fucked up than ever from what I hear."

Jesus, he's still so fucking angry. My shaking hands belie the calm formality of my next text. "I'd like the opportunity to make amends to you."

"It's been over three years. You're not capable so I won't waste my time."

Okay then.

I see another ominous gray bubble on my screen meaning he's in the process of typing more. He obviously still hates me, and I can't change that. How do you prove to somebody that you've changed or that you're sorry when they're unwilling to hear it? You can't, and—moreover—you don't have to. *I* know I'm sorry and *I* know I've changed. That's all that matters. I block him. And like magic, the bubbles disappear.

# CHAPTER TWENTY-EIGHT

I t's my last day of community service. I've been waiting for this day—
my "graduation," as it were—but now that it's here, I almost feel sad.
I'm put on the Vermont sweeping route. I take two Tylenol *before* my
shift. It's been six months of this shit. I know the drill.

"You so happy, *flaca*," Esteban, my favorite crew boss, says. "It's your
last day."

"I can't believe it. I'll miss all you bozos. Maybe I'll get arrested again
so I can come back."

"No, no . . . you come visit anytime, *guera*."

I'm sweeping this one block on Vermont and Normal—which, yes, is
actually the name of a street in L.A.—and suddenly, I'm surrounded by
three homeless dudes, all singing and dancing around me at once. It's
so bizarre and so magical that I just drop my broom and crumple onto
the sidewalk, laughing. They smile toothlessly back at me, pants stained
and drooping, hair knotted, faces dirty.

Our crew finishes early, and we're allowed to go into the Rite-Aid to
get a drink or a snack or just hang out in the air-conditioning for a bit.
Two fellow chain gang members and I slump down on the patio furniture display. A vagrant with an eye patch walks by and laughs at us.
With a fucking eye patch. That's when you know you are at the bottom
of the food chain. Even homeless pirates think you're a joke.

I get my paper signed for the last time. I feel like I might cry. Yes. I
fucking did it. I started something that felt horrible and undoable and

I finished it. I did all 240 grueling hours. It took me more than six long months. I'm proud of myself. It's easy to do things that are easy. And that's what I've been doing my whole life. But this was exhausting and humiliating and awful—and I did it. Every goddamn second of it.

I realize that I'm not ashamed that I did community labor. In fact, I'm grateful.

I take my completed signed form from community labor and trudge back to the volunteer center.

"I finished!" I beam.

The woman with severe painted-on eyebrows is unimpressed.

She copies my paper, enters something into the computer, and prints me out some official form.

"You take this to the court."

"Gotcha. Thank you."

I contact my asshole criminal attorney to ask him to meet me in court for my final appearance.

"I'll need seven hundred dollars to do that."

"It's one appearance. It's the end to what we started. I can't pay you any more money, nor should I have to."

"I can't show up without payment."

Two days later, I get an email from him asking me to post a glowing review on his website. Riiiight.

I call the court clerk and explain the situation. She tells me that it's ridiculous and says that the judge will order him to appear.

I go back to court on my own, and, of course, my lawyer doesn't show, so I am assigned a public defender. I piss off the bailiff by sitting in the wrong row. You're not supposed to sit in the front row, and I apparently can't read anymore.

They play this strange video before the judge comes in, explaining that you're in court because you've been accused of a crime and that you have certain rights. I find it surreal. It's one of those moments where you step back and think, "Umm...this wasn't on my life itinerary."

When they call my case, I'm incredibly nervous and keep interrupting the judge to explain things. Luckily, he's a kind man and sees that I'm new to the criminal life. My charges are dismissed. Holy shit...this ordeal is finally over.

When Mariana tells me that I'm going to get yet another roommate, I decide to move out. I can't stay in sober living forever. It's so easy to think you have your shit together when you're only around people who are just weeks off booze or drugs. But it's a false sense of success and security, and I know it. It's time. Time to get out of this recovery bubble, put on my big-girl panties, and go out into the real world.

I've been in some sort of "treatment" for more than three years, ever since my marriage crumbled. So the thought of going "out there" is reminiscent of how I felt at twenty-one, when I was graduating from the cozy confines of college. I guess I feel a bit..."institutionalized"; you know, like those people who spend ten years in a psych hospital or prison and then forget how to function in the free world.

What will happen when I'm on my own? Will I abuse my new freedom? Will I sink into a depression? Will I do shots of Jack Daniel's and have sex with strangers?

I give my notice to Mariana, and I burst into tears.

"You're family," she says softly to me. "You can always come home, babe."

"Thank you," I sniffle.

Still, I am terrified. And I'm terrified that I'm terrified.

As generally defiant as I am, as sure as I am that I'll love my "freedom," I also know from previous experience that I do best when I'm in a structured environment. As the kid of divorced parents, I was shuffled around a *lot*—between houses, cities, and even countries—so moving is incredibly destabilizing for me. I know that moving is generally considered one of the most stressful things any person can go through. But when you're already unstable inside, a big outside shift can feel thoroughly overwhelming.

I look unsuccessfully on Craigslist for a decent place with a roommate who might not be a serial killer or prolific drug user. I have no money for furniture, and I lost all my stuff in the divorce, so it has to come furnished. Everything in my price range (eight hundred dollars) in Los Angeles proper is a veritable shithole: small, dark rooms, shabbily decorated, dreary curtains obscuring tiny windows, shared bathrooms.

Trent, a lanky Canadian stoner and my onetime writing partner, offers me his place during the two months that he's visiting his family in Vermont. He'd rather have me than some stranger, he says. I can pay whatever I can afford. Great. Except that it's... in Inglewood, a primarily lower income black neighborhood near LAX.

"Oh," I say. "You mean, like, by the airport?"

"Kind of. Come check it out."

I drive down to his pad. From West Hollywood, it's easily a thirty to forty-five-minute trip, even without traffic.

I text him when I'm there. It's a shit-brown boxy stucco building, probably built in the fifties, with security bars on every window. He comes out and opens the locked front gate, and I follow him up to his apartment.

"Welcome. It's not much, but it's mine."

His place is pretty sparse: white tile floors, very few windows, white walls, no TV, very quiet. There's one photo of him and his daughter and a strange collection of vintage pocketknives. A meditation pillow sits on the floor by one wall. The place feels almost monastic.

"You can fuck in my bed. I've yet to. Go ahead and christen it. Just don't muck it up too much. And be easy on it. I built the frame."

My immediate thoughts are: 1) nobody—and I mean nobody—will haul their ass all the way down here to visit me, and 2) I will get super depressed in this place and die alone in Inglewood.

"I'll take it." I smile.

I call Linda, who makes a plan to come over to the sober living and help me pack up. In my closet, there are boxes I hadn't dared open in years... bail bond paperwork from my arrest, divorce lawyer files, criminal attorney files, worksheets from rehab, bills from the psych ward—all souvenirs of a life destroyed by addiction.

"We need to go to the Container Store," Linda says.

"I fucking loathe that place. It's all weirdos like you with OCD who like to put things into cool boxes. And Japanese girls...lots of Japanese girls."

Linda ignores my complaints and drags me there. I groan as we walk in. Linda is in polypropylene box heaven, stacking up different sizes in a cart she's ordered me to push.

"Isn't this fun?"

"Eat a dick," I say. I look at a price tag. "This shit is expensive! Being messy is cheaper. Why can't we just use cardboard boxes again?"

"Shut it," she says.

She drags me there two more times, and on my third and final trip within five hours, I finally get it. In a tired, robotic voice I say to the cashier, "I now have a false sense of security and control over my life and destiny. I no longer feel the laws of entropy apply to me. Is that what this store is for?"

"Umm...yeah, I guess," he says dryly.

After Linda and I pack up all the boxes, we throw them into our two cars and wagon train down to Inglewood.

After unlocking three different locks, I open the door to my new temporary home.

"Ta-da!"

Linda pokes her head in the doorway. "Wow, and I thought I didn't like a lot of shit around..."

"Yeah he's into...uh, minimalism."

Once we've dragged everything into the apartment, she heads toward the door. "Hey, call me if you're freaking out," she says.

"Thanks, mama."

The door closes behind her, and there I am. I put on music. Loudly. I've always used loud music to alter my mood. Well, truth be told, I've used just about anything to alter my mood. I say aloud to nobody, "It's going to be okay."

Trent's place has no plants. No pets. Just a few guitars and a keyboard. The sofa is a futon. The coffee table is some upcycled thing he found on the street. I drag my suitcase into the bedroom. It's hot. No central air, but there's a ceiling fan that slowly moves the stifling air around. There are bent white blinds that cover a dirty window looking out onto a tiny courtyard and into the apartments of the next depressing building.

I wander back into the living room. There is a small window above his makeshift dining table. It looks out onto the back porch of a shoddy house that is covered with assorted bits of discarded furniture. I see a huge black guy with dreads down to his waist doing flies with free weights on a plastic chair.

It hits me: I do not want to be alone. And, even worse, I want to be with Bradley. I know he's in L.A., about to start filming an independent movie. Before he came back from New York, we had an interesting/shit-tastic phone conversation.

"Look," he says, "I'm coming out to L.A. to shoot a film next week, and I want to see you, but I'm going to have twelve-hour days, and I can't have any pressure from you to hang out and I can't have any of that 'I'm not texting you back quickly enough' crap. I don't mean to be a dick, but if you start doing that shit, I will hang up on you."

"Wow. Okay. Well, I won't text or call at all. How's that? I'll just be here when you need me...like Domino's."

It's been a week since that exchange and against my better judgment, expecting nothing, I text Bradley: "1st nite in my new place!"

He miraculously texts back right away and invites himself over. "Nice! Send me the address. I'll be there by 11 tonight."

"See you later :)," I coolly text back.

Whoa! Fucker wastes no time. The refrigerator is bare so I quickly run to the nearest 7-Eleven to get some drinks and snacks. As I'm walking back to my car, a very skinny black guy with glossy eyes, sporting an unbuttoned Hawaiian shirt, asks me for money.

"Hey, excuse me, miss. Can I get sixty-five cents for a hot dog?"

I hand him a dollar and say, "I used to be a drug addict. I get it."

A huge smile comes over his face.

"Thank you for your compassion. Can I get a hug?"

"Sure."

My first night in Inglewood, and I'm hugging a crackhead. This should be an interesting two months.

When I return to the apartment, Bradley is already out front.

"Whassup?" I say, trying to sound casual.

"Not property value, I'll tell you that," he says, referring to the bars on the windows, and then flashes me that dimpled smile.

# CHAPTER TWENTY-NINE

T he neighbor to my right in this Inglewood complex is a young
muscle-bound kid from Nebraska who makes sure to tell me that
he overheard me having sex the other night.

"Thin walls," he says with a lascivious grin.

"Oh, God." I am mortified.

"It's all good. I'm friends with lots of very sexually liberated people.
When I heard you, I thought, 'get it, girl.'"

I smile awkwardly.

"Want some weed?" he asks.

"Thanks, I'm good. I've been in rehab half a dozen times."

"For...sex addiction?" he asks, in all seriousness.

"Umm...no." I can't tell if he's hitting on me or trying to bond over
twelve-step programs. These things aren't mutually exclusive, unfortunately.

The whole building smells like weed. I regularly hear a young black
couple with a newborn baby having horrendous screaming matches.
The Korean family below me is eerily quiet, and they never say a word
to me. I imagine inside their apartment it's just a lot of nodding. Jack,
my alcoholic Vietnam vet neighbor, has a daily "garage sale"—always
with the same stuff: three vacuum cleaners and one chair that he's
refinished. Bradley thinks it's a front for running numbers or drugs, but
I'm not so sure. Jack and his vacuum cleaners just seem lonely, and if I
don't rush straight to my car, I get stuck in a forty-minute conversation
about God knows what.

It's a blisteringly hot summer. Trent's place has one small wall AC unit in the living room. Sometimes I sleep in there on the futon, but usually I sweat it out in the bedroom, the overhead fan whirling. When the neighbors aren't arguing, it's peacefully quiet at night. On one of the hottest nights, I'm tossing and turning. I keep checking my phone for texts from Bradley. Nothing. Finally I turn my phone off and go to sleep.

I wake up a few hours later and look at my phone. It's 1:32. Two missed calls from Bradley and a text that reads: "Call me ASAP. Urgent."

I take out my night guard (which I have yet to introduce to Bradley for fear of killing his boner forever) and call.

"What's going on? I just woke up and saw your texts. You're scaring me."

"*I'm* scared! Tomorrow we're shooting my biggest scenes and I'm not prepared for shit."

"You got this, I'm sure."

"I'll pay you if you come read lines with me."

"What?"

"I know it's late. I really need your help. I'll pay you. That should work; you're a Jew."

"You don't need to pay me. I'll come," I say. "But I have to Skype with my boss at eight thirty a.m., so I need to work from your place tomorrow, okay?"

"Yeah, of course. See you soon."

I trudge over to the fridge and pop open a can of Yerba Mate. Why did I say yes again? He lives in a complex with a dozen other night-owl comedian-actors. Surely one them could read lines with him. Was this an excuse to see me—aside from the usual "can't sleep . . . feel like fucking?"

But Mr. Single Forever Bruh! had made himself vulnerable and expressed that he needed somebody. And not just anybody—me. Sure, it was a pain in the ass to drive up from the hood in the middle of the night, but who said love was convenient? My whole life I'd been taking. I'd been the one who needed. Here was a chance to give back and *be* needed. And maybe even prove to Bradley that people can, surprise surprise, show up for you.

We work for a couple hours. He feels better. The next day, he calls me to say thanks. "You really helped me last night. I couldn't have done it without you."

After that, something shifts in our relationship. Bradley decides to give up his West Hollywood shithole apartment and take up with me and the Crips in Inglewood for the summer. Our sudden jump into temporary domesticity speeds up the pace of our relationship quite a bit. We fuck every day and hold each other every night. We are basically in a relationship, but he won't admit it. I've yet to be introduced to his parents, who live just down in Huntington Beach. I've met maybe one of his friends. I don't know what he does all day or who he does it with, and I don't ask. He still hasn't told me he loves me. But clearly, something is keeping him here. And it ain't my luxurious digs or my cooking. What is it? The sex? Sure, I mean, I'm good. But I'm not "forty-five-minute drive if you don't love me" good.

I go to a nearby kiosk—a repurposed Fotomat—to get keys made for him. The guy manning it is an older black man wearing a huge gold chain with a diamond-encrusted crucifix. His place is stocked with everything you'd need if you were up to no good: druggie bags in every size, stun guns, pepper spray, batons, handcuffs, fake police badges.

"Quite a selection, brother," I say, impressed.

He laughs. "Variety is the spice of life."

"Wish I'd known about this place before I got on the straight and narrow," I say.


I join the local 24-Hour Fitness. It's a far cry from my swanky West Hollywood gym with its free towels and wi-fi and pretty-boy actors. The weights are left everywhere. It's 99 percent black and you check in with your fingerprint. Every time I go to work out, the black guy at the front desk fist bumps me. I've never felt so silly or white in my entire life. There is also a security guard in the cardio room. Why? Because there's the occasional brawl or stabbing on the elliptical? I'm confused and a little terrified. However, I'm white and skinny and invisible here. Nobody fucks with me.

*      *      *

I am loving house-sitting in Inglewood. After sharing a room for almost three years, this sparse one-bedroom feels like a mansion. I'm so grateful to have my own space that I keep it impeccable. I quickly realize that cleaning is weirdly therapeutic.

Linda texts me: "What are you doing?"

"Mopping."

"Dear Lord, are you okay?"

Program friends are horrified at where I'm living.

"You're in Inglewood?!" a sober friend asks me. "Isn't that a little close to the rock?"

"The rock is always close if you want to find it," I say. Ugh, I sound so program I want to slap myself.

My days are full of writing and the gym. Bradley sleeps in till twelve and works nights doing stand-up. I get into playing the good wife, a far cry from who I was when I was actually married. I religiously do his laundry, methodically folding his underwear and T-shirts, leaving them in a neat little stack by his side of the bed. I always make sure the fridge is fully stocked.

I'm driving to the market when my mom calls.

"Honey, can you please do your food shopping in the daytime? And will you call me when you get home so I know you're safe?" she asks.

"Mom, it's Inglewood, not Watts in the nineties. Calm down."

"Is it by the airport?"

"Sort of."

"Well, what are you buying at the market? Healthy stuff like yogurt and berries and organic produce, I hope," my mom says.

I reassure her that I am, but I can't help myself: "Mom, I'm forty-five, and I've been in six rehabs. I used to smoke meth and shoot cocaine. You're worried that I'm not eating my leafy greens? Really?"

One night my garage door gets tagged. Just mine.

"What the fuck?" I say to Jack.

"Yeah, that hasn't happened in years. The last time, it was across the street, and somebody got murdered," Jack tells me, beer in hand, as he's sanding some shitty chair in his driveway.

"Great..."

"Us tokens gotta stick together," he says, laughing that deep, wet smoker's laugh that ends in hacking. He lights up a cigarette and continues sanding.

While I'm examining the damage, a black kid on a scooter comes rolling by and sees it.

"Shit. That's a gang sign," the scooter kid tells me.

"What's it mean?" I ask him.

"I forget."

"Does it mean 'Kill all skinny white Jews in Inglewood'?"

"Nahh, man."

"You sure?"

Jack offers to call the graffiti-removal crew for me. "They come and repaint it for free," he tells me. "I think it's part of some court-ordered community service program."

"Uh, yeah. Unfortunately, I'm very familiar with it..."


When I was in the depths of my drug addiction, I had wild mood swings. Back then, when I considered making my bed a productive day, my dad used to say to me, "Discipline creates stability; stability does not create discipline."

It took me years to really understand what he was getting at—that having a routine helps create emotional steadiness. For years, I had been waiting for the steadiness so I could finally get into a routine. I was doing it backward.

There isn't a whole fuck of a lot to do in Inglewood, and I am desperate not to sink into my old cycle of depression and self-destruction, so I create a routine: gym, supermarket, write; or gym, write, supermarket. And, holy fuck—it works. I stay emotionally afloat, and I am unbelievably productive. More importantly, my ass looks great.

# CHAPTER THIRTY

One day, I go to pick up Bradley at the Coffee Bean in Hollywood. He gets into my car as I am blasting music, chain-vaping and drinking a five-shot latte.

It doesn't occur to me that this is out of the ordinary until Bradley says, "Oh, my God, your people need *constant* stimulation. No wonder you did coke and eight balls."

I laugh. "Eight balls are coke, dude."

"Oh."

Being around somebody who isn't a junkie really spotlights my obsessiveness and gluttony. Through his eyes I notice the vigor and speed with which I drink everything, my absolute terror if I run out of nicotine, the way I channel my compulsivity into exercise or binge-watching the newest series.

Dating a normie is strange. I can't use the well-worn AA slogans and catchphrases only known to those in the secret club. And when I say, "I've had a warrant out for my arrest!" I won't hear back those two reassuring words "Me too!" There is an innate comfort to dating another recovering addict. They aren't going to be shocked by the things you did or how many people you fucked. You don't need to feel ashamed about your past or explain why the homeless guy on the corner probably has better credit. They get how your mind works because their mind works in exactly the same fucked-up way. They aren't going to think "Okay, weirdo" when you pause during a fight to say, "Time out. I need to call my sponsor."

But I didn't get sober to live my life in the comfy confines of the recovery world or for addiction to be the epicenter of my life. I got sober to get back into the real world, to recast myself and rebuild my life. I know I'm an addict, but there's a middle ground between being ashamed of it and wearing it like some distinguished military medal on your lapel.

What probably astonishes me the most about Bradley is how non-judgmental he is about all I've done.

"I don't care about your past. I mean, if we were all judged by our past...yikes."

"Why don't you care?" I ask him. "I had a guy cancel a second date because I told him I had HPV back when I was nineteen."

"Everybody has HPV."

"I know!"

"Well, people have judged me for having a daughter from a one-night stand, for my career, for my lack of career, for never having been married. I guess I feel we all have baggage. You just gotta find someone with matching luggage."

"Umm...you've never done drugs in your life, and I shot cocaine in my neck."

"Okay, bad analogy."

Unlike people in the program, Bradley doesn't see me as some "renegade" or Olympic champion of narcotics taking. He isn't impressed that I stayed up for seventeen days on meth. He doesn't think it's romantic or cool or punk rock that I shot speedballs or had a seizure snorting coke in an airplane bathroom. He just thinks it's sad that I was in so much pain I had to do all that. He sees it all as a measure of my illness, of how far off the rails I went.

"You're just a sweet girl who had some problems and, thankfully, got over them. You're not a badass, Amy."

"I'm not?"

This makes me feel good and also makes me nervous. Let's be honest: nobody really wants the reformed bad girl. They want the party girl *or* the sweet wholesome girl. Nobody wants the girl who "doesn't do that anymore," the girl who *used* to have threesomes and do coke off strippers' asses but now meditates and drinks decaf.

Ethan (Mr. post-fuck hot, wet towel) texts me out of the blue: "I'm in town, so if u wanna get ur pussy pounded, lemme know."

"I'm seeing somebody," I text back.

"So?"

I don't text back.

"Must b luv. Whatever. If u want me 2 suck on ur clit lemme know. Staying @ usual place."

I don't text back.

"Hello?" he texts.

I finally text him: "I find this whole thing super disrespectful, but I get that I am to blame. I set up this dynamic. You might cheat on whoever you're dating, but that's not my style."

"I'm sorry. Seriously, if u wanna have coffee . . . I'm sorry."

"It's cool. No worries."

"But if u want 2 grab a cup of java . . . & my big hard dick . . ."

"Fuck off, Ethan."


Bradley headlines a lot of comedy clubs on the road. He's milling around the Inglewood apartment, looking for his favorite hoodie and his special hairbrush. He's packing up his stuff to head to Reno for seven days, and I systematically start to shut down—but without quite realizing it. My abandonment issues are kicking in big-time, making me sad, angry, withdrawn. I immediately immerse myself in my sober woman trifecta of distractions: iPhone, vape pen, and loud music. I don't want to feel what I'm feeling, and I don't want him to see that I'm feeling it.

I am lying in bed, blaring *Cage the Elephant*, arms folded, vigorously vaping, playing Ruzzle. In retrospect, I guess I can be a smidge obvious in my defensiveness.

"Are you upset that I'm going away?" he asks.

"Of course not," I snort.

I refocus on my incredibly important game of Ruzzle.

"I'm coming back, Amy . . . You get that, right?"

I drag on my vape pen like it's salvation.

"I'm leaving like all my stuff here!"

I continue to play Ruzzle with life-or-death concentration.

"Hello?"

"I heard you."

Bradley is annoyed. "Come on...turn the music down. We're trying to have a conversation. It's eleven a.m. and you're jamming out to death metal."

"*Cage the Elephant* is hardly death metal."

"Either way, turn it down. Communication is what *marriage* is all about, right?" he says, barely cloaking his contempt for the word.

"Shut up."

"I'm *coming back*."

"Are you?" I ask. And then the tears start. Goddammit. I'm losing power to him, and now I'm losing at Ruzzle, too.

He crawls into bed next to me and holds me from behind. I cling to his arms.

"You're like a wire mesh monkey, you know that?" he says.

"What the fuck are you talking about?" I sniffle.

"They did these experiments, in, like, the sixties, where they took baby monkeys from their moms and then...didn't you ever see those black-and-white photos?"

"No."

"Some of the monkeys were raised with a fake terry cloth mom. And some were raised with a fake wire mesh mom."

"What's your point?"

"The ones raised by the wire mesh moms were fucked up. They were, like...forty percent more likely to brandish a knife."

"You're an asshole."

He holds me for a bit in silence and then kisses my neck.

"I'm coming back. So don't freak out, my little wire mesh monkey."

# CHAPTER THIRTY-ONE

While Bradley's in Reno, he isn't texting as much as I want or need, and I get upset. That's another thing about addicts: we have a really hard time differentiating between wants and needs. They feel like the exact same thing. In what I decide is my final bid for a response, I text him a sexy topless photo. Four hours go by. Nothing. I finally break down and call him.

"Are you getting my texts?"

"Yeah, but it's not like all of them require a response, right?"

"Oh, my God! Just reply in some way!"

"To *all* of them?" he asks incredulously.

"Yes!"

"So if you write, 'I like cheese,' I gotta text back something like, 'Yay cheese!'?"

"First of all, I would never text 'I like cheese.' I'm lactose intolerant."

"You know what I mean."

"When I text you, I'm making a bid for connection. It's not *about* what I'm texting. Come on! You're smart..."

"Every time you text, I *have* to text back?"

"You don't have to do anything, but yeah, it would be nice to be acknowledged."

"So, you're making a rule?"

"I'm not making a fucking rule. But if you can't be bothered to text back a goddamn thumbs-up emoji or whatever, just because it's important to me, why would I even consider taking this relationship one tiny fucking step further?"

"Let me get this straight: a thumbs-up emoji would quell the savage beast?"

"Yeah, it would, actually."

"What if I text back 'message received.'"

Even over the phone, I can make out that stupid smug smile like he thinks he's teaching me a lesson.

"Oh, come on, that was funny," he continues.

"Look," I say, "I know you're stressed out about money and your career and stuff. I want to be there for you. I want to be your anchor."

"You want to be my anchor?"

"Yeah."

"I doubt anchors have meltdowns when you don't respond to their titty pic after twenty minutes."

I can't help but laugh.


While Bradley is away, I decide to do some fun and easy work on my abandonment issues. Hooray! I got wind of an ex-meth head doing "breathwork" with addicts, both privately and at various rehabs. It all seems a bit hippy dippy, but AA is a slow burn, and I need to get into that primary wound and get some goddamn spiritual enlightenment *now!* My fears and anxiety must feel like a house arrest ankle bracelet on Bradley: limiting and exhausting. I call up this breathwork guy, Nathaniel Dust, and I make an appointment.

When I walk into his cute little house, I expect it to smell like patchouli and dirty feet. I also expect Nathaniel to be some long-haired modern flower child with Birkenstocks and thumb rings. Shockingly, he is not your typical hippie weirdo. He's a completely different kind of weirdo. He's wearing a button-down shirt with a pink tie, pink socks with the words "sock whore" and kitty cats all over them, and a plaid suit jacket with a pink handkerchief peeking out of the pocket. He also has a legit Mohawk.

"Hello, Amy. Have a seat. Don't look so uncomfortable. I'm not going to have you put a fucking rose quartz on your heart chakra or offer you a yoni massage. But how about a glass of water?"

"Yeah, that'd be great. Thanks."

He brings me a glass of water and looks at me expectantly. Oh, I guess I have to say why I'm here and stuff.

"Ummm, okay. I'll cut right to it. As fucking gay as this sounds, I'm terrified to open my heart."

"I would appreciate if we wouldn't use the word 'gay' as a pejorative."

"Oh, I'm sorry." I cringe. "I actually have lots of friends who are lesbos—"

"'Lesbos'...really...Stop," he says.

He motions for me to take my shoes off.

"Okay, what I'm hearing is that you don't feel like it's safe to love or be loved," he continues.

"Exactly! I'm dating this guy and he's...um...got some intimacy issues, and I just wanna run away."

"Well...even if he does have issues, you have the opportunity to choose to love. Not because it's going to work out, or he deserves it, or some bullshit like that. But if you run away, you just reaffirm that negative core belief that you're not worthy of love. So why not give it your all? 'Cause if you don't nail it down here, you'll just carry it into the next relationship you have...which is a barrel of fun, as you know."

"Oh, I know." I sigh deeply. "Okay. So what the fuck are we doing today? I've never done this before."

"It's simple, but not easy. It's a two-stage breathing technique that will help distract the mind long enough for you to have an experience of what it's like to connect to the most intimate parts of yourself, the emotions that have been suppressed for years."

"Oh, my God, that sounds terrifying and exactly what I got high to avoid."

"You and me both, sister. Fear is a normal response, but you have a choice. You can choose to move through the fear that has been preventing you from having the relationship you want, or you can continue to let your neuroses dictate how you live your life. It's one or the other."

"Extremism. I respect that! Okay, one warning. I have epilepsy, and my other epileptic friend used to do a lot of breathwork and it gave him a seizure every time."

"I've seen one single human have a seizure doing this, but she had a traumatic brain injury, and the seizure had nothing to do with the breathing. But if you feel weird or overwhelmed, stop. I'll be here the whole time, guiding you through the process."

"Cool. Okay. Let's do it. I don't want to be an old cat lady...No offense. I saw your socks."

"No offense taken. I'm already an old cat lady."

I lay down on the table. He covers me with a blanket and hands me two stones to hold as he guides me through the breathing technique: two quick deep inhales and one slow exhale. The whole time, he's playing super-groovy but sort of melancholy music. *This is not going to work,* I think. I have a running mantra in my head that, despite Nathaniel's protestations, is basically "thisisgaythisisgaythisisgaythisisgay."

Nathaniel dabs me with some special oils and says, "Keep breathing."

Out of nowhere, I just start sobbing. Bawling like a small child. There is no conscious thought attached to it. It is just pure emotion. After I stop crying, I start trembling. I feel like I'm hooked up to a generator or holding on to a live wire with wet hands.

"That's your source. Feel that? That's what it's like to be connected to you."

"Whoa" is all I can manage.

"That's your life force," he continues. "I didn't create it. Your sponsor didn't. It's yours. And no one that's hurt you, or abandoned you, or let you down can take it away. It's yours."

"Well, I hope my life force doesn't give me a fucking seizure."

"You're okay," he says soothingly. He puts his hands on my feet.

After twenty or thirty minutes of this, he slowly guides me out of the exercise, and I open my eyes.

"Take it slow as you get up."

I stand up and almost fall over.

"Holy shit! I feel totally shit-faced. No wonder addicts like this!"

"Yeah, all those neuropeptides feel good," he says with a grin. "You're not broken, Amy. You have a lot of power, a lot of love."

I smile as I spacily try to put my shoes back on.

"Also, you should be writing a fucking book. Don't be an idiot."

"I am writing a book. How did you know that?"

He just shrugs.

"Are you like . . . a wizard?"

He laughs.

"Write your book. It will help you gain clarity around the things that are preventing you from trusting. And also there are a lot of people that need to hear your story."

"'Cause if I can get my shit together, anybody can!"

"I hope your writing is funnier than you are in person."

"You're mean. A mean healer!" I tease.

I get into my car to drive back to the hood. I do feel lighter, hopeful, more open. I look at my phone. No text back from Bradley. Seriously? How can I open my heart if this fucker never texts me back? I need cigarettes.

# CHAPTER THIRTY-TWO

A female comic friend of mine invites me to a film screening. Bradley, who's back from Reno, knows this woman, too. A lot of our mutual friends from the comedy world will be in attendance.

"We should go. It will be like our coming-out party," I tease.

"Ugh," he grunts.

"Come on, I'll buy you a ball gown, bitch! You can't keep me a secret forever, you know?"

He puts on a creepy Nazi accent and says, "There is a long history of German people keeping Jews a secret."

I laugh.

As we walk up to the tiny theatre deep in Hollywood, our comic friend greets us. "It's so cute to see you two together! I'm not putting any meaning on it, but I just wanna say it's nice to see."

"Yeah, we kicking it," Bradley says.

Kicking it? *Kicking it?!* In case I didn't mention this before, Bradley is white. Very white. Almost translucent. He doesn't "kick it." Maybe back in high school, he "kicked it" a little, but not now, as a forty-year-old man. I say nothing, but immediately go into a pouty-girl huff—which does not go unnoticed.

He pulls me aside. "What's up?"

"I'm going to say this one time, and you can do with the information what you will. We are not 'kicking it.' We are in a relationship. You are *living with me*. And it really hurts my feelings when you don't introduce me as your girlfriend. I feel like you're ashamed of me, or you worry that I'll pussy-block you."

"I was totally joking, but I'm sorry. I hear you. I've never introduced anybody as my 'girlfriend.' I hate that term. It feels so unnecessarily... possessive."

"Well, get over it," I say. "I'm fucking rad," I add lamely—trying hard not to cry. Fuck... I'm such a crybaby with this guy...

Bradley strokes my hair and kisses me.

"Come on. Let's go to the after-party, and I'll be all over you like a black guy on a chubby white chick."

"Okay," I sniffle. "And don't call me your 'lady friend' either. You did that once, and it sounded like some obscure nineteenth-century term for 'prostitute.'"

"Can I call you my 'shorty'?"

"I hate you."

The next day I call my sponsor, Jay, to complain.

"Well, honey," he says, "when you allow what somebody gives to be *enough*, it makes it safe for them to risk giving more. Does that make sense?"

"Yes."

"And—then again—they might be stingy fuckers, and that's all you get."

"Come on!"

"Just remember, sweetheart, this guy is your *choice*. He's not your enemy; he's your *choice*. So if you don't like it—"

"Choose somebody else!" we say in unison.


A few weeks later, Bradley is heading off to Las Vegas to do a few nights in a club there. He asks me to come with him.

"Vegas makes me depressed," he says, "so it would be nice to have you there."

Depressed? Vegas makes me sick. I mean, I literally get sick every time I go. The last time was in November of 2011. I was married to Clay and popping OxyContin like Pez. It was my birthday, and I decided to have some expensive red wine as a chaser. Bad, bad move. I spent the next three days in the hotel room violently puking. I never saw the light of day.

But here was a chance to have another Vegas experience—a "relapse redo," if you will—and to celebrate my three years of sobriety in, of all places, Sin City. I'd had a pretty bad cold the two weeks prior, but it had mostly cleared up, so I figured, why not? If I was going to test the strength of my sobriety, a week in Vegas would be the time and place to do it.

However, when I hit the desert with its sundry of allergens and the smoke-filled casinos with their glacial air-conditioning, I am instantly sicker than ever.

Bradley comes into the bathroom while I'm sitting in the hot bath. I am propped up on cold and allergy medicine, hair bunched on the top of my head, snot running down my face.

"Aren't you glad you brought me?" I joke feebly.

"Oh, babe...you look so cute." He leans over and kisses me. "I gotta go do my show. I might have a drink with the guys after. I'll let you know, okay?"

"Okay, baby. Go kill it."

I take some more cold medicine and fall asleep. I wake up to feel him slide into bed, wrapping his body around me.

"Ohh...my little wire mesh. You're so tiny."

"What time is it?" I mumble.

"Eleven thirty."

"I thought you were going to have a drink with the dudes."

"I told them I couldn't. My girl is sick. I need to get back."

I sleepily kiss the hand that's holding mine.

"You're the best." I smile.

He kisses my bare shoulder and holds me tighter.

"For somebody who didn't want a relationship, you're pretty domesticated," I continue.

"Don't tell the guys. I will kill every part of you to death," he whispers in my ear.

* * *

Bradley, who has a ridiculously lean and muscular body, is trying to slim down for his next role playing a famous Russian ballet dancer off-Broadway. To give himself that sinewy physique, he is on a strict diet of meat and meat with a side of meat. His caveman diet is taking a toll on him.

"I feel hollow inside all the time," he says, as we walk down the Vegas strip.

"Welcome to early sobriety, bitch!" I say, giving him a playful push.

I know the feeling. All too well. That gnawing. That sense of never being satiated. Ugh. I was about a month off nicotine, and I was having that feeling myself. It didn't help that I had recently cut out peanuts, wheat, dairy, soy, sugar, corn, and anything else derived from joy in my diet so that I might wrangle my adult cystic acne.

I had become exactly the person I'd hated—the chick who *used* to smoke meth made with Drano, but *now* staunchly refused to eat gluten. For addicts, it is ironically easier to go from one extreme to another—reckless abandon to monklike asceticism; debauchery to chastity. Moderation does not come easily to us.

It's day two, and I'm sicker than ever. But Bradley is headlining, and I want to see him dazzle on stage, so I dose myself with cold medication and, with a handful of Kleenex, drag myself out of the room.

I sidle into the VIP booth he arranged for me and order a seltzer water like an octogenarian. Most of his act is about being single or staying single. Like "don't let a girl take over your Netflix queue and suck out all your hopes and dreams" and "an anagram for 'relationship' is 'I sit on her lap.'" And "married men live longer 'cause fun shit kills you," blah, blah, blah.

Bradley says to the audience, "Why would anybody get married? It has *less* than a fifty percent chance of success. It's casino odds. Granted, we're in Vegas, but would you sit down at a blackjack table if the minimum bet was half your shit?"

The crowd laughs, and I feel my heart break a little bit.

"So, yeah, I'm single. But it doesn't mean I'm a scumbag." He points to a cute girl in the front row. "Room three oh three . . . 'sup?"

The motherfucker uses the actual room number.

My chest starts to tighten, and I will myself not to cry. I actually punch myself in the arm in an attempt to stuff the hurt back into a box.

After his set, he comes up to me. "Hey, what did you think?"

"You were great," I say coldly.

He knows right away.

"Uh-oh . . . what's wrong?"

"All your jokes are about the glories of singlehood and how much marriage sucks. Well, they hurt my feelings. Imagine if I was still doing stand-up and I was like 'who wants one dick forever when you can have a different dick every day of the week? You with me, ladies?!'"

"I can't change five years' worth of material on a dime. Also, when I said, 'I'm single,' I winked at you. I was looking right at you!"

"Well, that was stupid, because I can't see far away. I need Lasik, remember?"

Tears start rolling down my cheeks. *Goddammit.*

"Amy, *yes*, I am freaked out about marriage. I've told you that. But we could still be together forever and never get married. What's wrong with that idea?"

This quells my insecurity for a moment.

However, as the night goes on, his bits keep randomly resurfacing in my brain and pissing me off.

"Fifty percent of your shit?! You don't *have* any shit, Bradley. I'm letting you stay with me at my place for free, you mooch."

"Solid point." He smiles at me. It annoys me that he doesn't take things personally, and it really annoys me that his smile always disarms me. I punch his shoulder.

"That all you got?" he says. "Hit me as hard as you want; just don't hurt your hand."

I rear back and swing as hard as I can.

"Hey, that wasn't bad!" He laughs.

I shrug but my hand is on fire.

After the show we go to the casino bar and meet some of Bradley's pals—people he's known for as long as he's been coming to Vegas. I'd never met these people before, but two of his female friends instantly see that I am deathly ill.

"You should have a hot toddy," one of them offers innocently.

"Yeah I'm not drinking," I say.

"Why? Are you on antibiotics?"

"No. I just don't like getting arrested," I tell her.

Neither woman laughs. Two minutes later, I am introduced to their husbands, Lieutenant Whatever and Sergeant Somebody of the Las Vegas Police Department. Perfect.

There are two young male comics, Gino and Phil, in town opening for Bradley at his shows. They have never been to Vegas before, and woohoo, are they excited! I suggest we take them to Fremont Street, where the Strip used to be. The locals now call it "Old Vegas." Last time I'd gone to Fremont, it was a bit like the "Thriller" video—zombies staggering around, looking for booze, luck, and, quite possibly, Michael Jackson. This time, it still had some of that old-school apocalyptic charm, but it has become much more trendy, with a slew of cool new bars and packs of hipsters and millennials milling around.

I notice the…umm…"bunny nose" on one of our young friends and whisper to Bradley, "Phil's on coke."

"How can you tell?" he asks. What the fuck? Was this guy born in a yurt?

Moments later, Phil buoyantly offers, "We have drugs!"

"No shit," I say, laughing.

We take them to the Gold Nugget or some other shithole, and Gino and Phil are having the time of their lives—smoking, drinking for free, and loving the "character" of vintage Vegas. I, on the other hand, am distracted by the smell—years of spilled booze, stale cigarettes, and sadness. What I mostly notice are the gnarly old alcoholics staring blankly at slot machines—emaciated, chain-smoking, as if they've been there for decades.

Bradley's young friends don't notice or don't care. They have the high and the optimism of the newly indoctrinated—coked up, on a winning streak, chatting up girls on Tinder and Bumble. If there is any doubt whether or not they are picking up on the heavy stench of desperation, at one point Gino literally shouts, "Oh, my God, this is the *most* fun I've ever had!"

I am happy they're happy. But I really just want to take a hot bath and go to sleep. Is it because I am sick? Old? Sober? Yeah, probably all three. But I am a good sport. I don't complain. I feel like I need to be "on"—be the clown, the center of attention. But the truth is, I don't have the energy. It then occurs to me that I can just *be*. Be the quiet girlfriend. So that's what I do. And, incredibly, nobody seems disappointed.

At one point in our crawl, we hit a karaoke bar. Karaoke could possibly be my least favorite thing in the entire world. It's definitely up there with pearl earrings, country music, and velvet anything. I keep looking at my phone: 11:55 p.m.... 11:58. In two minutes, I'll have three years sober. Three fucking years!

Just as it becomes my sober birthday, Gino cluelessly pulls out a big Ziploc bag of blow, sticks his finger in it, and stuffs it up his nose. He crowns his subtle move with a jerky paranoid look around. Fucking rookies.

I haven't seen blow since I used to shoot it. Jesus. Maybe eight or nine years ago?

"Gino, where's your paraphernalia?" I ask.

"What do you mean?"

"Like a bullet or a straw? Unless you have a nice long Chinese wizard fingernail or a tiny spoon pendant."

"I rarely do blow."

"Well, your makeshift gear is killing me, man. Give me a pen." And with that, I fashion them a proper snorting utensil.

"You've done a lot of drugs, huh?" Gino asks.

"Yeah, I used to shoot coke."

"You can make coke into a liquid?"

"You can make anything into a liquid if you add water, dude."

\*   \*   \*

The next morning, I call my mom and thank her for never giving up on me. Then I call my dad and boast, "I'm three years sober!"

"I'll drink to that," he says.

"Cheap Chardonnay on ice, right? Go crazy."

"You know it. How's Vegas?"

"A very ironic place to celebrate sobriety."

"I bet."

"Papa, are you ashamed of me?" I ask him. "When you talk to your friends, do you ever feel ashamed?"

"My friends wish they had a kid as unbreakable as you, Ames."

"Thanks." I smile, tears forming.

"Have a great day. You deserve it," he says.

I hang up, and I climb on top of Bradley, putting my face weirdly close to his. "Baaaaaaby!"

"Oh, here it is, the yearning," he says.

That's what he calls the voracious, insatiable hole that we junkies have inside. He refers to "the yearning" like it's a living animal trapped inside me, constantly pacing in its cage, ravenous for food, sex, or attention.

"Nooo...it's not the yearning. I just want to say thank you for accepting me and allowing me the space to be somebody new. Because you've done that, I've been *able* to be somebody new with you."

As I say it, I marvel at how much I really have changed, and how I now have the love I've been looking so long and hard for. I begin to cry.

"Babe, don't cry. You're gonna make your eyelash extensions fall off."

I laugh and wipe away my tears.

"Don't worry, I'll still love you if they do," he says.

"You love me?"

"Of course, I do, silly."

# ACKNOWLEDGMENTS

"Writing is a lonely job. Having someone who believes in you makes a lot of difference. They don't have to makes speeches. Just believing is usually enough."

—*Stephen King*

Here's a list of people who believed in me, and for them I am eternally grateful. If you enjoyed this book, you should be grateful, too:

My publisher, Hachette Book Group, who thought my story was worth telling.

My former editor, Stacy Creamer, who originally fell in love with and bought this manuscript.

My current editor, Michelle Howry, who elucidated some of my biggest writing flaws and made this a much better book, as well as the rest of my dream team: Elisa Rivlin, Amanda Kain, Lauren Hummel, Melanie Gold, and Becky Maines.

My super-duper bionic agent, Peter Steinberg, who is the best agent I've ever had. (Granted, he's the only agent I've ever had, but I still know he's the best.)

My friend Amber Tozer, who changed my life by passing on some of my writing samples to her agent.

My editor at *The Fix*, William Georgiades, who always gives me the freedom to be my obnoxious, irreverent self.

My father, who told me to "shut the fuck up and write, Ames."

My mother, who told me to take my B-complex so that I would have the energy to write.

My sponsor, Jay Westbrook, who helped me become the type of sober woman I only dreamed of.

My bestie, Marni, who adopted my cat, Fatman, when I got committed and never ever got mad that I threw up in her car.

The manager of my sober living, Anouska, who loved me like a sister and idiotically trusted me with her child.

My lesbian friend, Tammy, who taught me how men and relationships work.

My breathwork guy, Nathaniel Dust, who's seen me cry more than a decade's worth of therapists and boyfriends combined.

My boss, Amy Alkon, whose dogged work ethic has inspired me and who lets me call her asshole and ho-bag and still pays me.

All my roommates in sober living and treatment who, God love 'em, put up with my inhuman snoring and constant vaping.

And finally, my friend Jeremy: because she called 911 when I slit my wrists, you just read a memoir and not a biography.

## ABOUT THE AUTHOR

AMY DRESNER lives in West Hollywood, California. She's still sober and she still writes for *The Fix*.